TEACHER, TRAINER, TUTOR

For a complete list of Global Management titles, visit our website at www.goglobalmgt.com or email us at infoGME@aol.com

TEACHER, TRAINER, TUTOR

Transforming the Learning Relationship

Liz O'Rourke

Cartoons by Douglas Racionzer

Copyright © 2011 Liz O'Rourke

**Published in 2011 by Global Management Enterprises, LLC.
Massachusetts, USA**

ISBN 978-1-61110-019-8

Contents

For Michael

Acknowledgements

There are many people to whom I am grateful. Various colleagues, both in teaching and training have helped develop my understanding of the issues discussed in this book. Betty Wackerbarth and Norman Mark have been especially influential in the passion and commitment they both bring to the learning situation. I would also like to acknowledge Brian Maunder, who took me on my first faltering steps as a tutor.

My daughters, Kathryn and Kerrie, have provided keen and enthusiastic support.

Without doubt, my biggest debt is to the many, many students I have had the joy to work with over the years. Their resilience, humor, curiosity and energy have been inspiring.

On a more personal level, I would like to thank my partner, Michael, for all his encouragement, suggestions and patience, which gave me confidence to see the project through, from initial idea to finished book.

1

Empowering Learners

Room for Improvement

Teaching, training – whatever we choose to call the process of helping people learn – is a personally challenging and demanding process. For many contemplating the role, and even those who are more practiced, there is a considerable degree of anxiety. Much of that anxiety centers around the *learning relationship*, the relationship we develop with our learners; the attitudes we have towards them, the assumptions and expectations that characterize our every exchange and the routine ways in which we negotiate with each other. And yet professionals responsible for teacher or trainer development largely ignore that very relationship. The emphasis is on methods and techniques. We somehow assume that the way we relate to our learners evolves naturally with experience. After eighteen years in education and training, I am convinced that **the quality of the learning relationship is the single most influential factor in the learning experience**. I want to encourage all those involved in helping people learn, to reflect on that relationship and to look at how it can be made a powerful vehicle for ensuring more meaningful learning.

We are too preoccupied nowadays with matters of technique and program design, learning objectives and outcomes, and we often seem to require little more from our learners than tiresomely predictable hoop jumping. We ignore the very aspect of the learning situation, which most crucially influences the confidence, and ultimately the success of most learners. What sort of role do we want them to play? Is it to be compliant, dutiful recipients of received wisdom, or is it to be proactive, critical collaborators in the learning enterprise? Most colleagues would feel obliged to identify with the latter, but the way they routinely approach learners suggests a deep-seated reluctance to relinquish their authority and control.

I am all too aware of how discouraging the learning experience can be for learners. Too many still put up with fairly indifferent learning, an experience which commonly only reinforces their view of themselves as not very able or clever. Sadly, they rarely question the competence of the teacher or trainer. How often have I witnessed in the course of my career, learners' needs regularly and systematically ignored because they did not fit in with the teacher or trainer's definition of what they believed was required in the situation.

Adult learning is still permeated by unresolved issues around power and control and until these are properly confronted, students will continue to be at risk of being patronized and even bullied. I am trying to give voice to the frustrations and vulnerability of many learners whose feelings and reactions are too easily discounted. What credibility do they have to question the teaching and training establishment? Professionals often assume an appalling arrogance, convinced they know best and are unwilling to entertain any ideas generated by those they regard as their subordinates and inferiors.

As consumers of learning, learners might be expected to exercise some influence, but they are often reluctant to express their dissatisfaction Tutors are in a powerful position to determine learner achievement, some are actually involved with the assessment process. Success as a learner is also dependent on the program of learning being seen as credible. Critical comment may not only make the individual learner unpopular, it may also undermine the perceived value of the learning program in which he or she has invested time and effort. Learners may decide they have little choice but to keep quiet. One of the most important lessons they learn is to play the game, to conform.

Action Plan

There are numerous books available on general teaching and training skills and my efforts would serve little purpose if I did not have something distinctive to say. It has still taken me a long time to come to this conclusion. My approach as both a teacher and trainer has always been somewhat intuitive. I never thought of it as especially remarkable. A more considered attitude has developed as I have become increasingly involved in trainer development programs. Observing other people in action, reflecting on learner responses and analyzing my own style has helped me to define what

I refer to as an *engaging* approach. It is one that is probably at odds with many of my fellow professionals. While there are those who try to maintain the mystique of their expertise, I am convinced the ability to help people learn is less concerned with skill and technique, and is far more dependent on a willingness to openly engage with learners in a relationship where change and growth are possible on both sides.

I have spent a great deal of the last ten years devising ways of developing trainer potential in individuals, who are decidedly ambivalent about their involvement in other people's learning. They are usually very busy managers with numerous other responsibilities, and in their view, they lack both the time and the skill to be very effective as part-time amateur trainers. And yet I have never failed to delight in the natural flair they often demonstrate. There is inevitably an enormous issue over confidence, which is generally made worse by being exposed to slick and polished professional trainers, and traditional trainer skills programs which highlight presentation skills as the main feature of the trainer's performance. However, with reassurance and a shift of emphasis away from trainer presentation, and instead toward the process of *engagement* between trainer and learners, most individuals develop a real enthusiasm and considerable ability in their efforts to develop their staff.

Although the momentum for this book has emerged from my work with such programs, it is based on the accumulated understanding from my experience of teaching and training. I explore issues that go beyond a particular learning context and are relevant to all those engaged in helping adults learn. I hesitate to include young people still in compulsory education, as very specific conditions apply in schools that are not part of the adult learning situation. I think it would be unduly arrogant for me to extend my scope when my experience is limited to the post-compulsory sector, and yet some of what I say may still strike chords even in the school classroom.

Learning is a natural activity with which we are all constantly occupied. Why does it so often become daunting and constraining when it is more formalized? It is true that much has improved with far greater emphasis now on experiential learning, but it seems we still have a way to go before people routinely enjoy learning as a truly empowering experience. I know 'empowerment' might seem just another fashionable buzzword with which people are only trying to impress one another. All such fashions should be viewed with a healthy degree of skepticism. However, despite my cynical inclinations, I rather like the idea because it does describe exactly what I think is important in helping people learn.

Engaging learners

Central to my argument is the concept of engagement, which is the process by which tutors develop a truly empowering relationship with their learners, characterized by mutual respect, where the learning is not only two way, but also is no longer entirely predictable. Innovation and challenge are cherished rather than discouraged. Learners are positively regarded in terms of their unfulfilled potential rather than their unfurnished deficit. I want to encourage a view that sees learners and trainers or teachers engaged in a reciprocal partnership, where learning is no longer just being transferred from one party to the other, but is the outcome of a positively dynamic process.

It is a radical view which fundamentally questions the traditional power relationship in the learning situation. I am not suggesting anarchy. Tutors are still ultimately responsible for the organization of the learning. However I hope to persuade tutors that by actively listening to their learners and encouraging them to become more involved as partners and collaborators, learners will be enabled to take a more responsible role in their own learning, enriching the experience for everyone.

I have set myself an ambitious goal in that I am attempting to address an audience of both teachers and trainers. This, in itself, will cause some consternation as it is a widely held view that teaching and training are so far removed from each other, there is little to be said which might usefully apply to both groups. They require their own particular specialist skills and approach. These assumptions will be questioned as we proceed through the following chapters. It is still necessary however, to clarify the question of terminology before we go any further, if only to avoid the tedious repetition of 'teachers and trainers.'

As I believe there is little fundamental difference between these roles, I had to resolve the basic dilemma of selecting a term that would be recognizable in teaching and training circles, without having too precise a definition which would unduly narrow its focus. It may well be an uneasy compromise but I have decided to use the word 'tutor,' when referring to the overall role of helping people learn. It signifies responsibility for the learning delivered and for the learners involved. Course tutors are routinely found in education and training, and in education, the role of tutor is traditionally associated with providing ongoing support to individual learners. It is not an altogether ideal compromise, and some may still resist being recast in this way. However, the device is necessary if I am to pursue my argument in a clear and coherent manner. There will be times when I will be talking about teachers and trainers quite separately, otherwise the general term of tutor will refer to both.

Experiential learning

I have always held the view that people's ideas are grounded in their experience and how they have made sense of that experience. You cannot therefore properly understand anyone's ideas unless you know something of the life context in which those ideas have developed. I do not think my own career has been in anyway exceptional, but I still believe my approach to my work has far more to do with what I have discovered from working with different learners, rather than the received wisdom from experts.

I did not start out with any real sense of a vocation. The main factors in my decision to take up teaching were entirely to do with my own personal circumstances. I was on my own with two small children and I needed to earn a living. I was a graduate and teaching appeared the obvious choice, where I could more easily combine a career with my responsibilities as a mother.

My initial experience as a part-time lecturer in further education did not convince me I had any real natural ability in my newly chosen profession. Persuading craft caterers and mechanical engineers that it might be worthwhile spending an afternoon a week doing something called general studies, challenged skill, imagination and endurance. They were there to learn a trade and saw anything not directly related to that end as a waste of time. At best, I might serve as an entertaining diversion. I had a lot of sympathy with them and severely doubted my potential to entertain.

After becoming fairly practiced in the art of crowd control and fielding truculent obscenities, I began to negotiate with the learners on how we might best approach our sessions together. I was in the fortunate position that no one was too curious about what exactly took place in my lessons, as long as I avoided any obvious disruption. I found myself enjoying the process and became very fond of even the most awkward groups. They were soon volunteering many constructive suggestions and ideas. I realized though, that the key to their rather tentative and self-conscious enthusiasm was the open and sharing relationship I had tried to establish with them. My teaching skills were still all too amateurish and woefully underdeveloped, but it was my willingness to engage with them as partners in the learning which had elicited their positive response.

My teaching career went on to include academic classes, both school-leavers and adults, as well as the euphemistically termed underachievers. My lesson planning and delivery certainly benefited from a Cert. Ed. course, but I was disappointed how little emphasis was placed on the interaction between teacher and learners. It seemed you were simply expected to present a carefully prepared lesson and all the learners had to do was duly respond in a suitably appreciative manner. It helped to explain the number of teachers I encountered who obviously relished their subject, but had little patience with learners who did not readily share their interest.

After six years in teaching, with some varied experience of social care, I moved over to staff training in a busy social services department. I was advised there was a significant distinction between teaching and training. It was held that teachers and trainers taught different sorts of things and teachers were generally more directive in their style, in other words they were rather more bossy. From my own perspective, such notions appeared to arise from a great deal of ignorance on both sides, and ultimately seemed to depend more on the type of institution in which you worked, rather than what you did. Most teachers had very little idea of what trainers actually did and most trainers drew their images of teachers from memories of the school class-room.

Having taught and trained adult learners, I have concluded that both teachers and trainers deliver across the whole range of knowledge, skills and understanding. I did not feel I was doing anything very different when I was actually working with learners, be they learners or staff. There was of course a huge difference in the organizational role I was expected to play. Identifying the learning needs and priorities was a complex process which entangled me in all manner of political agendas with different staff groups. But once the learning objectives had been agreed, the actual process of designing and delivering the program did not feel very far removed from what I had been doing in college.

In teaching, it is curious how you rarely get the opportunity to observe your colleagues in action. Professional expertise tends to be assumed and sharing of both material and ideas was, in my experience, very limited. I did try the tack of 'I'll show you mine if you'll show me yours', but it never seemed to get me anywhere. You usually had some indication from learners who they found helpful, those who were approachable, willing to listen and who gave them a feeling of confidence. There were also clearly teachers who, just from their manner in the staff room, caused you to severely doubt their ability to communicate and engage with anyone, let alone their learners. Yet I realized my experience was still very limited and narrow.

When I moved over to Social Services, I encountered a far more open culture in which trainers were quite used to having fellow professionals sitting in on their sessions. I had the opportunity at first hand to see other people in action and realized from participant feedback that many different learners shared my own instincts for what was important in the learning relationship. I began to feel I might have something useful to contribute to trainer skills programs. What perhaps I did not sufficiently appreciate is how much more I was going to learn over the years through supporting so many fledgling trainers, how they would help focus my own ideas and widen my appreciation of how learners can be engaged. And yet before we go on, perhaps I need to go even further back to look at my own experience as a learner.

When the magic happens

I have borrowed this rather cute but still curiously apposite title from a trainer skills program I once saw advertised. It does suggest an elusive process where the outcomes are not always predictable. But maybe this is precisely why helping people learn is such a continually fascinating exercise. Nevertheless, as with most things, it is possible to be rather more analytical and identify certain elements which are likely to produce the desired results.

An exercise I have often used during trainer skills programs is one which asks participants to identify their worst and best experiences of learning. Their responses have been powerfully revealing and sometimes very poignant. How often has an insensitive teacher crushed a potential enthusiasm for a subject with their inept and disinterested approach? Or worse still, convinced a student that they really are just too stupid ever to succeed. My own recollection as a student provides a useful example.

Throughout my school career, I had struggled with math. Basically I hated the subject, although that was mainly to do with my sense of complete and utter failure in the face of its seemingly incomprehensible logic. Part of me rejected its disciplined requirement to follow rules and formulae. I saw little opportunity to be creative. Given my lamentable performance, I was soon consigned to the arithmetic class. However, I was eventually faced with something of a dilemma. After making the decision to apply for a social science course at university, I discovered, to my dismay, that the entry requirements included O level mathematics. With trepidation, I signed up for a part-time course at my local further education college.

Despite my past history with the subject, I was motivated to work and to succeed. I very much wanted to go to university and this was my only serious obstacle. Unfortunately, I was about to experience one of the worst examples of apathetically cynical teaching I have ever encountered. The man had clearly not joined the profession out of any great commitment to share whatever small degree of enthusiasm he may have had for his subject. He surveyed our apprehensive group of mathematics rejects with only thinly disguised contempt. It was obvious he would rather have been anywhere, except in that room with such an uninspiring challenge before him. His attitude only reinforced our view of ourselves as not just thick, but also thoroughly foolish in assuming we might ever be able to fathom the mysteries of O level mathematics.

Week after week, we struggled with the exercises set after only the minimum of explanation and guidance. As a group, we became so cowed under his scornful tutelage that a fearful and numbing silence characterized our increasingly bewildered attempts to make sense of the endless problems and formulae. It was pointless to ask a question. Either it was regarded as so obviously banal it did not even warrant an answer, or worse, it provoked an alarming outburst of frustrated and irritable bad temper. What little confidence and ability we might have had shriveled in the face of such a remorseless regime.

After half a term, I had had enough. Unlike most of my fellow class-mates, I finally concluded that the teacher had far more of a problem than we did. In one lesson, instead of keeping my head down and pretending to pore over yet another dismal exercise, I sat and stared back as he sullenly looked out from behind his desk, at his assembled victims. My new boldness seemed to discomfort him. He no longer intimidated me. I realized he was just a very poor excuse for a teacher, and with that, I carefully and deliberately packed away my books, rose from my seat and, with an albeit rather contrived dignity, walked out of his lesson and his class, never to return again. I was subsequently told on the grapevine that he had got exceedingly drunk at the next college social, and referred to me as the only student in his experience who had ever shown any glimmer of common sense.

My gesture, although it gave me great personal satisfaction, left me with an unresolved problem. Not to be beaten, I enrolled at yet another college the following year. The contrast could not have been more dramatic. This time I found myself confronted by a man with a missionary zeal for teaching what amounted to remedial math. He was a doctor of physics and clearly had lost none of his initial, youthful enthusiasm for his subject area. He taught math as an exciting language to be discovered and deciphered. He positively relished the challenge of imparting this sense of genuine enjoyment with every one of us in the class. Instead of feeling like the college dunces, he gave us a confidence and belief in our ability to share and participate in the joyful enterprise of mathematics.

He was endlessly patient with even the most basic levels of understanding. There was no sense of embarrassment at asking the obvious and, from this reassuring position, we were all able to make steady progress. The classes became genuine opportunities to explore and work together. The atmosphere was informal, but with a busy purposefulness. He moved around the room constantly, happily available for anyone to speak to. There was a restless energy about him that invigorated all of us. While he was crucial to our success, he made us feel as though he was there simply to help us realize a potential we had never previously recognized.

Teaching math to people with no natural ability or inclination demands considerable skills on the part of the teacher. Math is perceived by many as difficult and boring, so there is usually a significant problem of confidence and motivation to overcome. My first experience only confirmed all the negative associations on both sides. We were attempting something in which we had already failed, and that failure had emphasized and underlined our sense of weary futility. When the teacher simply reinforced our own view of ourselves as hopeless and stupid, we had little chance of developing an alternative image of ourselves or mathematics. We were thick and math was only for the very clever.

The second teacher exploded all such associations. We had ability, we just needed to develop more confidence in ourselves and that was only possible with someone who continually concentrated on what we had already achieved and how that signaled the way for further progress. In addition the subject we had learned to dread was turned into a real source of fun and intrinsic pleasure. And at the end of the course I actually passed my O level exam.

A Radical Approach

Although I had very great misgivings about becoming a teacher and was skeptical about my ability and initially suffered extreme anxiety at the prospect of facing a class, there was always an ambition to do it well, to do it extra specially well, just as my math teacher had done. His success was not just a matter of skill, it was far more to do with *attitude*. We are perhaps now entering the territory of the notion that tutors are born and not made. Such assertions seem to arise from the difficulty in defining exactly what is involved in being able to effectively relate to your learners. Similar ideas used to permeate the caring professions. Caring was seen as an almost intuitive ability to recognize and respond to an individual's needs. Staff could be given the necessary technical competence but it was another matter to instill the right attitudes.

Nevertheless, that is precisely what has happened in recent years. A more systematic approach has been taken as to what is constituted by caring and how that can be developed amongst staff.

I am essentially advocating the same thorough analysis of the attitudes necessary for effective tutoring. Much attention has been given to the technical skills and very little to the process I refer to as engaging learners, establishing and maintaining the learning relationship. And yet in my experience this is absolutely crucial to ensuring that learners really do maximize their learning potential. If we ignore this aspect of the tutoring role we seriously diminish our capacity to help people learn.

In the following chapters, I want to look at how we can overcome the limitations of the traditional approach to tutoring and transform the relationship between tutors and their learners. The structure of the book is designed to explore the origin and extent of the problem in the first five chapters. Chapter 6 looks at the relationship from the perspective of both the tutor and the learner, while Chapters 7 – 11 go on to explain the principles of engagement and how to achieve it. I believe my approach is relevant to anyone helping adults learn, whether they call themselves teachers or trainers, and whether their subject area is theoretical or practical. The objective is to equip tutors with the understanding and to provide them with constructive and practical suggestions on how to work more effectively with their learners.

Much of what I say may seem contentious, and colleagues might feel I have used extreme examples to demonstrate my argument. I am aware that there are tutors who are already working conscientiously with their learners, positively developing their confidence. But I often feel that the efforts of such individuals are not sufficiently acknowledged, because the teaching and training establishments have yet to recognize the true value of an engaging approach. There is a prevalent attitude which holds that a tutor who is respectful and encouraging toward his or her learners is a desirable bonus but not absolutely essential to the business of learning. I hope to demonstrate that engagement is not just a rather agreeable experience for learners but is critical to their progress.

The Way Forward

Chapter 2 – 'The Learning Species' – examines what we mean by learning, how it is an entirely natural activity which has defined our species from our earliest ancestors. Learning is the mechanism by which we adapt to change and just as our survival as a species has depended on our ability to learn, so now in an ever more rapidly changing world, our success as individuals depends on our readiness to learn and develop.

I want to explore what we are trying to achieve with our learners. I believe a confusion remains between learning which is concerned to make us accept and fit in with the established ways of understanding and doing things, and learning which encourages us to think for ourselves, which develops our individual potential and which stimulates us to push forward the existing frontiers of what we know and are capable of. We constantly confuse these in the way we design learning and especially in the way we relate to learners.

Chapter 3 – 'A Role by Any Other Name' – investigates the presumed difference between teaching and training, demonstrating with various examples that most learning is a complex mixture of both knowledge acquisition and skill development. The 'learning continuum' analyzes learning in terms of knowledge and skill content, while the 'development continuum' analyzes learning according to the degree of tutor control and learner autonomy. Both of these concepts are set within the overall idea of the 'learning paradigm,' which provides a more effective model for understanding what we do, than sterile debates over the distinction between teaching and training.

Chapter 4 – 'The All-Singing, All-Dancing Pedagogue' – looks at the assumptions made in most tutor skills programs, which focus on an essentially one-way system of communication. Training skills are often equated with presentation skills and teaching is often still synonymous with lecturing. Where is the dialogue with learners? Such learning seems to proceed on the basis of osmosis. Even with more student-centered approaches and more emphasis on experiential learning, many learners are only partially engaged. The script is largely written, they have only to say their designated lines. The tutor is directing the performance and improvisation is decidedly unwelcome. We do not actively encourage them to challenge us, to perhaps go beyond what we are presenting? That may come at a much higher level in the learning experience, but it is certainly not the typical experience for the majority of learners today.

Chapter 5 – 'The Emperor's New Clothes' – highlights the way in which the exercise of power on the part of some tutors corrodes the learning situation and distorts the learning relationship. Fast talkers and 'precious protectionists' intimidate their learners by ensuring the learning remains inaccessible, reinforcing the idea that learners who do not readily understand are just not bright enough. What is more important, subject or tutoring expertise? But beyond this is the crucial need for honesty and openness in the learning relationship, so that learners are assured they will not lose face when admitting to confusion and uncertainty. For many adults, returning to some sort of formal learning feels very much like a return to a childlike role, one where your normal adult status is suspended. The tutor becomes the judgmental parent and meaningful dialogue is restricted. The learner/child is disadvantaged and cannot even contemplate querying what the tutor has said, even though he/she does not understand.

Chapter 6 – 'Anxiety and Empathy in the Learning Relationship' – is concerned with the considerable amount of anxiety at the heart of the learning relationship, suffered by both tutors and learners. The anxieties get in the way of either side being able to understand the other. Tutors fail to empathize with their learners and become preoccupied with maintaining control, control of themselves, their material, but mostly their learners. As a consequence, both sides constantly misread one another and retreat into more defensive positions and feel increasingly discouraged. Insights and advice are offered throughout to help tutors deal with their own anxieties and with those of their learners.

Chapter 7 – 'An Engaging Approach' – is the first of three chapters exploring the process of engagement. It concentrates on how to create and maintain a safe and secure atmosphere in the learning environment. There are many practical suggestions but the main focus is with encouraging a particular attitude amongst tutors, one that fundamentally respects and values learners, where we accept our responsibility and routinely look for opportunities to make our learners feel comfortable and confident in the learning situation.

Chapter 8 describes 'The Reciprocal Relationship.' Traditionally tutors have occupied the space reserved for experts and learners have been relegated to the space reserved for novices, waiting to be initiated. Tutors do something to learners which changes them but leaves the tutors unaffected. I am proposing that both should move into a more shared space, where the learning becomes a genuinely collaborative enterprise.

Chapter 9 discusses the idea of 'The Dynamic Dialogue' which harks back to a Socratic legacy in which tutors engaged in debate with learners, not simply as a means to an end, to establish correct knowledge, but as a process that was intrinsically valuable. Through the questioning and critical argument, minds were sharpened and analytical prowess developed. Central to this was the importance placed on challenging received wisdom and orthodoxy.

Any dialogue requires both sides to share a common language and understand one another's meanings. This is particularly difficult in the learning relationship where learners are inherently disadvantaged, and dependent on the tutor to make unfamiliar concepts accessible. Any communication is problematic and the potential for misinterpretation infinite. It is therefore essential that tutors appreciate the need for an explicit and ongoing discourse with their learners, helping them to clarify their questions and their doubts.

Chapter 10 – 'There is No Such Thing as a Bad Group' – analyzes the difficulties one can still encounter in the learning relationship. Engagement is demanding for both tutors and learners and there will be many complex individual agendas which need to be understood in order to overcome the tensions generated. Learner resistance comes in various forms, but unless we recognize how our own psychological 'buttons' may trigger the resistance in some individuals, or just make it hard to work positively with others, we will carry on resentfully blaming our learners.

The Summary Points at the end of each chapter will review the main ideas and suggestions presented, providing an accessible reference as well as enabling you to more easily negotiate your way through the book. Although it is possible to read the book in a more selective manner, its real value, nevertheless, lies in the discussion that is developed through the course of the chapters. The purpose of the exercise is not just to put forward a particular argument, but to be an encouraging guide, and as such it is more effective if taken as a whole rather than in discrete sections.

In addition, I have devised a series of Questions For Reflection to follow the summary points to help you engage more meaningfully with what is being said. The idea of the questions is to encourage you to think about how the points relate to your own experience, inviting you to consider the way in which you own attitudes and assumptions may act as obstacles in developing a more engaging relationship with your learners. The learning points of each question are then explained, although in the spirit of the book, I believe there is more value in your thinking about what I have said, than simply accepting it as another series of hoops to jump through. It is important that you find the book practically useful, but as my message is concerned with enabling learners to think more for themselves, to be critical and independent in the way they approach their learning, that is precisely the attitude I hope you will have toward this book.

Chapter 11 – ' That's All Very Well'- acknowledges that much of what I am advocating may sound reasonable in theory but rather more problematic in practice. Nowadays, when resources are being ever more restricted in education and training, the time and tutor/learner ratios necessary to properly implement an engaging approach may seem naively idealistic. However, I do believe we cannot ignore this issue if we are to ensure that the learning experience is truly empowering for people. There is a great political clamor over the importance of learning and about providing people with the opportunities to realize their potential. We are being encouraged to see learning as a lifelong commitment and yet within all this enthusiasm, there is precious little acknowledgement of how frustrating the learning process still is for so many people. And this is usually not because tutors lack the technical competence to tutor in their particular area of expertise, but it is much more to do with their inability to form the sort of relationship I am describing.

I would hope that this book helps us to think about what we are trying to achieve as tutors. We have become increasingly lost in our attempts to reduce learning to an uninspiring, rationalized process. I would hope that by encouraging a radical reappraisal of the sort of relationship we are trying to establish with our learners, we might be able not only to better empower them, but also ourselves.

2

A Learning Species

Human beings are the most highly developed species on this planet. Our behavior is almost exclusively learned. Learning is the distinguishing characteristic in deciding how far along the evolutionary tree an animal has developed. Where behavior is largely instinctive, there is only a very limited prospect of the change and adaptation, so crucial to surviving and thriving in an unpredictable world. Creatures who are capable of extending their repertoire of behavior through the process of learning are more able to exploit the opportunities provided by their environment.

For better and for worse, human beings demonstrate an infinite variety of possibilities in the way they organize themselves. That variety is the result of learning. The way we are, what we believe, how we relate to each other, develops within a social context or culture. Learning shapes and defines us. We chose to call ourselves Homo Sapiens. We are not set in a fixed mold of instincts. We are learning virtually from our birth; it is crucial in determining our successful assimilation into society. We continue to learn from our experience of just being alive, without any conscious or deliberate action on our part. The simple passage of time changes the circumstances of our lives. We grow older. Nothing stays the same. We need to be able to adapt to that inevitability. We need to be open to new possibilities, or we become stuck and find it difficult to cope with the new and different demands being made upon us. It is our readiness to learn which enables us to move on.

The idea of a learning cycle is a well established and useful approach to understanding the mechanism of learning. Experience is always our starting point. Whether it is a chance occurrence, a planned activity, new information or a physical sensation, we begin the learning with something happening, or being done to us. But we do not just passively absorb that experience like an obliging sponge, we turn the experience around and make sense of it. We stand back from it, we reflect on it, consider how we feel about it. We then try to generalize from that experience, develop theories to explain the experience and establish principles for understanding similar situations in the future. We then go on to try out those new understandings and theories in a similar situation and see how far they fit. The learning is continually building on itself, constantly throwing up questions from our experience which our own internal processing assimilates

We need to figure out how new learning relates to what we already know, so that we can integrate it into our existing knowledge. Maybe it will fit neatly and simply confirm our present understanding, or perhaps it will throw up anomalies and contradictions and suggest we need to think again. This applies as much to matters of everyday life as to more weighty intellectual musings. Sometimes we realize we have stumbled on or discovered something nobody has ever been aware of before. Or perhaps someone works out a logical connection that had never previously been recognized. Maybe they generate a completely original idea from all that has gone before.

Learning is also about acquiring some degree of control over ourselves as well as our environment. We learn to do things. That learning may require no more than the physical coordination of certain muscles, as in riding a bike. Or it may involve a complex interplay of both mental and physical agility, as in learning to play a musical instrument. This is a far more disciplined learning, which demands a degree of repeated practice in order to become competent. Nevertheless it is still part of a process which is a natural feature of being human.

Learning will invariably be judged in terms of how useful it may be in helping us to act more effectively in our world. How far does it illuminate our understanding and enhance our ability to negotiate with an objective reality which we only ever partially perceive? How much does it contribute toward helping us achieve more successful ways of existing in our problematic world? What constitutes success will obviously depend on people's competing values and priorities.

Learning is a natural adaptive activity, which enables us to exert an awesome degree of control over our environment. But learning, as the acquisition of culture, is also about shaping and defining us. Through a process of learning, we become ourselves. Without a system of language, we would have very limited means to communicate with others. It is by learning to communicate with others that we develop relationships and, through those relationships, begin to develop a sense of ourselves. We not only need others to grow into healthy, sociable adults, we need others to help us distinguish and discover who we are. Identifying similarities and differences with others is a way of establishing our identity. As children and even as adults, we thrive on being positively affirmed. It is important that others recognize, acknowledge and value the person we feel ourselves to be. Without that positive affirmation we feel undermined, possibly even threatened, or worse still, we feel negated, as though we are only pretending, desperately struggling to maintain a very precarious and fragile sense of self.

Learning to negotiate with the social world in which we find ourselves is the most fundamental and ongoing lesson we face. To be consistently successful demands a level of self-knowledge, understanding and insight as well as an empathy for others, which seems altogether too exacting for many of us. So that we may organize our social life on a reliable and predictable basis we have introduced rules to tell us how to be and what to do. Many of those rules do not even appear to us as obvious controls. They are so deeply embedded in our experience of our social world that we take them for granted. We know that the values and assumptions which shape our lives change over time and show considerable variation between cultures, and yet they have a concreteness and rightness which we find reassuring. We stubbornly try to cling on to that sense of certainty.

A confusing business

At a fundamental level, we are all engaged in helping people learn, we are ourselves continually learning. It is part of being human. It is about making sense of our experience and ourselves. And yet our need to believe in a certain, predictable and absolute world often constrains the way we learn. All through history, learning has been regarded with ambivalence. On the one hand, people need to learn where they fit in and what is expected of them, learning as socialization or social control. On the other hand, learning, in pushing forward the frontiers of our understanding of our world and ourselves, threatens and challenges the status quo. It can make us very uncomfortable. These two sides to learning might appear to have little to do with one another and yet I would argue they are constantly confused and muddled when we try to talk about what we mean by learning.

Maybe we need to be more explicit. Both types of learning try to make sense of our world, but one starts from an assumption that we all need to conform to a predetermined idea of what it is to be a responsible and reasonable member of society. Learning becomes little more than a process of molding and shaping the individual into the desired form, often justified by an unshakeable confidence that those doing the shaping and molding know not only what is best, but also what is right. Questions and challenges may be tolerated, but only so long as they provide the opportunity to assert the ultimate rightness of the system. Such a closed view cannot accommodate contradictions. Indeed contradictions are inconceivable except as evidence of wrong thinking.

We may think this applies more to totalitarian societies, dominated by political or religious dogma, but it can take hold in many far more mundane institutions and organizations, where people have been discouraged from thinking for themselves, from figuring out what their experience means to them. Instead, they are urged to see doubt and uncertainty as weakness and individual attempts to construct meaning as irrelevant. There is a need to create a world where there are clear notions of right and wrong, not only in a moral sense, but also in terms of objective truth. This is a world where it is possible to know absolutely and incontrovertibly that you are right. The subjective world is invariably regarded as subversive.

The world is smaller and changing at an ever more rapid pace. We are now exposed to many more challenging and demanding experiences, throwing up unsettling questions and insidious doubts. It is becoming more and more difficult to preserve our sense of certainty in the world as we have defined it.

A demanding world

There are various ways in which we can respond. We can become more entrenched and extreme in our existing ways of understanding the world, investing a greater sense of conviction and self-righteous zeal in what we have chosen to believe, and become increasingly intolerant of any attempt at dissent. Or we can begin to accept doubt and uncertainty as a natural part of our experience. Such an approach enables us to embrace learning as a means to push forward the boundaries of our understanding. This is learning in its dynamic sense, learning as an adventure, because we are no longer entirely sure where our questions will take us or what we will discover about our world and ourselves.

Our world is changing more rapidly than ever before. What enabled us to succeed yesterday may no longer be appropriate tomorrow. Just as learning was crucial to our species survival in evolutionary terms, so our individual capacity to learn and adapt is the single most important factor in shaping our progress in today's society. Like it or hate it, we cannot avoid the accelerating rate of change. It may feel as though we are being caught in a whirlwind, but it is one which engulfs us all, and from which there is little chance of respite. Organizations, whether private or public are aware that, unless they continue to develop, anticipating new directions and exploiting fresh opportunities, their relevance will diminish and they will go into decline. Because of this constant pressure to maintain such a driving pace, organizations large and small need people who are able to respond positively. We talk of 'learning organizations,' but all we are really acknowledging is that individuals can no longer expect to just perform a given role and remain impervious to wider considerations. Organizations require people who are not only able to carry out a specific task, but who are also willing to go on and exercise and expand their potential. Our individual learning capacity is central to everyone's future.

Most people will vaguely agree with these sentiments, albeit somewhat grudgingly, especially if they have felt themselves casualties in the whirlwind. They will accept that the pace of change is indeed so rapid today that skills and knowledge do become rapidly outdated, and so there is a real and urgent need for people to take on board the idea of lifetime learning. Politicians are urging us to rise to the challenge and are apparently willing to devote considerable resources in providing us with more opportunities. Yet it seems very few of us have considered the radical implications these new challenges pose for how we should approach learning in the future. Many learning professionals continue to maintain very muddled ideas of what sort of activity they are actually engaged in.

Jumping through hoops

We are presented with a curious dilemma. We are moving towards a future in which people will need to be able to think more creatively, and yet we are saddled with a legacy that has restricted learning to a process of social control. Whereas learning and innovation were seen by past generations as the preserve of gifted individuals who were nevertheless usually regarded with much suspicion by their contemporaries, the vast majority were discouraged from thinking for themselves. Learning was about knowing and accepting one's place. Formal learning for the majority of our citizens is a fairly recent development. It might, after all, excite dissatisfaction and unrest. People might start to actually question why things are as they are and why can they not be any different. And yet when you consider the experience people have had of formal learning, it has not really been calculated to encourage such questions. Instead formal education has been about shaping and molding people into willing and compliant citizens. Most people's encounter with the compulsory education system has been to constrain individual initiative and discourage independent thinking. Conformity and compliance are positively rewarded.

Most of us have experienced learning, particularly formal learning, as socialization or social control. Tutors have traditionally been figures of authority, concerned with ensuring learners were taught correct ways of thinking and doing things. There were lessons to be learned, i.e. a body of knowledge and specific skills which learners were expected to absorb without question. Questions were simply a means to clarify understanding, they were not meant to fundamentally challenge the assumptions upon which the learning was based. Learners were more likely to be rewarded for neatness and obedience rather than originality and initiative. Even though we believe we are now encouraging a more dynamic approach to learning, there are a great many contradictions which we choose not to recognize.

While we acknowledge that people in the future will need to be more flexible and adaptable, creative and innovative, we are putting more and more emphasis on prescribed learning outcomes and rigid assessment procedures. These have introduced a far more standardized and consistent approach, which has enabled tutors and learners to be more explicit about what they are trying to achieve. However this has inevitably led to a much greater emphasis on results. It is understandable that, with our concern to use resources efficiently and effectively, we want to ensure that a given input will produce a certain output and we need to have reliable measures for calculating those outputs. Like so many activities, it is now difficult to justify the enterprise of learning unless we can identify clear benefits in terms of grades, qualifications and levels of competence. While there have undoubtedly been many benefits in trying to establish a more objective and therefore a more open and accessible way of monitoring learners' achievements, we have made learning even more of a fixed and predictable process.

Some assessment procedures are now evaluating the process of achievement as well as the actual achievement itself, so that learners are also being required to demonstrate how they approached a particular problem, at the same time as identifying the solution. But such assessments are still based on some fairly conventional assumptions. In fact there is a real danger that learners, put under even greater scrutiny, will be subject to still further control. It is no longer enough to just deliver the right goods, you are also expected to deliver the right goods in the right way. Invariably learners are encouraged to display a methodical, planned, thorough, conscientious and organized approach to any given project. In addition, if they are working with others, they will have to show their ability to communicate, co-operate and negotiate.

These may appear very worthy attempts to develop so called transferable skills which apply in many different situations, but I am often filled with an unease that those making the judgments do so according to very personal criteria, in other words how they themselves would do it. It is extremely difficult to do otherwise. We all have our own ideas of how to organize our work and how to work effectively with others. One of the aspects of learning which has always fascinated me is how quite different strategies can all be equally successful in their own ways. I think I would rather celebrate that diversity than discourage it. We do not all have to follow the same formula. Part of working cooperatively is to recognize and value those differences.

We are supposedly trying to encourage learners to experiment, to develop new ideas, to question conventional wisdom, to generate fresh solutions. How far are we really wanting learners to explore the frontiers of their understanding, if we are designing learning and its assessment still as a series of hoops through which they are expected to dutifully jump? It may be argued that learners have to jump through the hoops in order to prepare them for less familiar territory. Nevertheless the actual process of hoop-jumping usually dulls the imagination and squashes any latent impulse for critical or independent thinking. Perhaps we consider such thinking as the preserve of the very bright and able, and only a minority will ever be able to deal with more than the hoops. The rest should content themselves with being processed. Previous generations thought it was unnecessary and even positively irresponsible to encourage the masses to learn to read, but we now regard such attitudes as condescendingly elitist. Perhaps we should employ the perspective of history and consider how we, ourselves, might be viewed by future generations.

What are we supposed to be learning?

On the one hand, we are saying people need to fulfill their potential, that they have talents and abilities which should be developed, while on the other, we are very ambivalent over how much potential we think people really have.

Maybe this is because we have some very ill-thought out ideas about what we think is constituted by talent and ability. Formal education has traditionally been almost exclusively concerned with the capacity to retain information. Learning has been little more than a memory exercise. Much of what we were required to remember has only the most marginal relevance to most people's lives. The remembering was for the purpose of passing an exam, after which most was forgotten. This may produce a more trained and disciplined mind, but it does not necessarily develop analytic skills. These are concerned with identifying the connections, contradictions, implications and consequences of information. Our ability to reason is a far more powerful indicator of our potential as learners, and yet for most of us, our experience of learning is singularly designed to frustrate that potential. Most learners are never given the opportunity to demonstrate or develop their analytic reasoning. The formal education system has already labeled them failures because they were unable or unwilling to function as encyclopedic sponges.

But maybe there is yet another angle we have yet to explore. Formal learning, throughout much of history was the preserve of the more privileged classes. For the majority of people, who depended on their physical strength or their manual skills, learning consisted of following in someone else's footsteps. Through a process of observation, imitation and practice, the necessary skills were mastered. Perhaps those who were the most adept at replicating their master's skills were not necessarily the best at figuring out the solutions to new problems. The most skilled in traditional ways are often the most determined to carry on doing things as they have always been done. Their authority and prestige is invested in continuity. Acknowledging new problems may challenge their position and provide an opportunity for someone to speculate on a different and untried approach. Again there are two distinct forms of competence. One is concerned with learning and perfecting existing knowledge and skills, while the other is concerned with being able to analyze a problem and devise a solution which extends our knowledge and expertise. The latter demands a considerable level of reasoning and creativity, and yet when it is being demonstrated within a practical or technical context, we somehow regard it as lower order learning.

Problem-solving is most certainly a higher order skill. It may well be demonstrated without any exposure to formal education. And yet there is no doubt that such exposure will inevitably develop a more systematic approach. Trial and error may eventually produce the required results, but a more efficient method would require a thorough analysis of the problem, identifying the contributory factors and weighing up the merits of a variety of strategies. A disciplined mind is one which has learned to think through puzzles in a logical and orderly fashion, organizing information and recognizing significant points. Formal education makes this more possible, but it by no means ensures it.

Academic education has traditionally consisted of learning what constituted knowledge and developing some degree of skill in manipulating that knowledge. The right sort of knowledge has been decided in a fairly arbitrary fashion, dominated for several centuries by classical language and literature. This was felt to be the proper preparation for a cultivated gentleman. There was little in this learning which had any real relevance to the experience of those gentlemen. In fact the more the knowledge was removed from experience, the more exclusively it was defined. More importantly, education determined the style and form in which an educated person was expected to express themselves. Facility with language, both verbal and written was crucial. Language enables us to deal in abstract concepts, to develop ideas such as justice and equality, even if those particular concepts did not overly enthuse past educated elites. The more complex and elaborated the language, the more it can provide a vehicle for conceptual thinking. Mathematics enables those initiated into its language, to engage in a discourse which lies completely beyond our familiar experience. It represents the ultimate expression of abstract thinking.

Constructing concepts

Conceptual thinking allows us to develop the intellectual tools with which we can construct theoretical models of both our internal and external world. Such models are expected to take account of both logic and empirical proof. These are very sophisticated constructions of meaning. With such models, we can speculate on the origins of the universe. But most of us operate at a less rarefied level. Nevertheless even the subjects which form part of the conventional school curriculum introduce us to a way of looking at our world which is more rational and more disciplined.

We learn that, to better understand our natural world, it helps to be able to describe it according to categories and classifications. We are then able to identify common and distinguishing characteristics. We may then consider why and how such characteristics developed and how they might change under certain circumstances in the future. We learn how some people have described events in the past. We should be encouraged to be cautious, aware that it is all too easy to describe events from a particular point of view. We can debate on how our understanding of the past may influence our actions in the present.

Knowledge is cumulative. We are engaged in an ongoing debate with the body of knowledge we inherit. Even the most elegant and persuasive theories can be superseded as more useful and powerful ideas emerge. Those ideas may in their turn be proved flawed, but it is in thinking through the puzzles they present that the next generation of theories are developed. This is surely a dynamic and exciting process. For most people however, their experience of school has conveyed little of this excitement. Knowledge is presented instead as unproblematic facts. The debates and dissensions are thought to be unnecessarily confusing and so the disorderly way in which knowledge is often constructed remains obscure. This certainly makes learning less demanding, but it also makes it a whole lot more boring and misleading.

Some are not deterred and will follow their natural curiosity regardless. Maybe they have more confidence than others, a healthier dose of skepticism than most, or perhaps just an insatiable need to ask why. At best, education for the majority of people equips them with the basic skills of literacy and numeracy and at least a working ability to think conceptually. It is primarily through language that we express those concepts, and it is usually our command and fluency with language which signals to other people the extent of our education. But we need to be careful about making too many assumptions. While language makes conceptual thinking possible, language proficiency in itself may signify little more than being able to follow certain socially determined conventions on how we should communicate with each other. Formal education has been dominated by the cultural ethos of the more privileged social classes.

Educated etiquette

To be educated is to be made familiar with that cultural ethos. Essentially, we are talking about the distinction between form and substance. It may be perfectly possible for an individual to be exposed to a certain environment, to become accustomed to that environment and its expectations, and to learn how to negotiate successfully within it; and because that particular cultural environment represents the dominant order and so is regarded as superior, they will be assumed to share its superior characteristics. Polite manners, refined sensibilities and an assured linguistic facility are the signs of an educated person. Education in this sense becomes the entry requirement to a privileged elite. You have to learn to be like them before you can join them. Many people from less privileged backgrounds are all too aware of how daunting it can be to move easily in that world.

A sophisticated awareness of how to function in that world, however, may not indicate anything more than successful socialization. Form and style may be apparent but it does not follow that the learning has resulted in any real substance. The learning may rely as much on imitation as the artisan slavishly copying his master and unless the learning can go beyond mere imitation, only a fraction of someone's potential is being realized. Substance is about being able to think critically and creatively. I remain convinced that we all have this capability but in some it is more tentative and needs careful and positive nurturing.

A fertile ground

Although I have severe misgivings over our readiness to be impressed by someone, who with the clever use of words, can make even the most banal of statements sound important, nevertheless language is still a critical factor in our learning. An impoverished experience of language will severely restrict our capacity to learn, simply because we will find it so difficult to think conceptually. Experience of a rich and versatile language may not in itself guarantee dynamic learning, but it does provide fertile ground, in which such learning may flourish.

Any learning that is to be effective must develop this language potential. It is recognized that young children are afforded a head start in formal education if they are already proficient linguistically. This enables them to positively engage with the formal learning process, developing in confidence, able to articulate their curiosity and their own constructions of meaning. It is vital that this process is encouraged and reinforced. Children need to be able to actively engage and experiment with language. Learning always requires a dialogue. It is by framing their ideas through language that they are able to explore and clarify their understanding. It follows then that learning can never just be a one way process. It can never just be the transmission of knowledge from the learned to the unlearned. Learners need to be able to talk back. They need to be engaged, to be given the opportunity to express their doubts, questions and confusions, to speculate and to challenge, not just in order to arrive at a given answer, but to exercise their ability to think conceptually. We recognize the cycle of learning, we recognize that people are constantly constructing their own meanings and trying to make sense of their experience, and yet we ignore the fact that formal learning provides all too few opportunities for learners to be engaged in any real dialogue.

Cabbages and kings

If we consign learners to a passive role, we are not properly enabling them to realize their potential. Learning is a natural activity, but, as we have already identified, there is an inevitable tension and contradiction between the learning which is designed to make us fit in and the learning which is designed to make us think and to question.

To an extent, we all need to learn to conform. Social life would be impossible if we did not learn through the process of socialization how we might act toward one another. But the most powerful groups in society usually ensure that socialization as social control is organized in their interests. Hierarchies benefit those at the top, while those at the bottom either have to be content with their lot, or perhaps they might be allowed to cherish a small hope, that by virtue of their efforts and ability, they too might one day rise further up the pecking order.

So learning becomes subject to the meritocratic justification for social inequality. Only those who have demonstrated real merit are able to assume positions of authority and influence. Learning becomes crucial in demonstrating that merit. It goes without saying that everyone starts out from a different position in the hierarchy and some are afforded a considerable advantaged by virtue of their background, and have merely to maintain their positions, while others have to struggle against the odds to improve theirs. Learning has long been regarded as the passport to a better future, to a more rewarding and fulfilling job and to a more comfortable style of living.

Nevertheless, we need to recognize that this is not a purely benign process. Learning as a means to success necessarily demands a degree of conformity, an acceptance of the status quo. It is only those with the most exceptional talent who may achieve success through challenging what everyone else takes for granted. That is how we have traditionally proceeded. There are the pragmatic achievers ensuring the system that provided them with success is perpetuated, and the mediocre majority who need only learn enough to service the existing system they remain incapable of challenging, while a few very rare and brilliant stars rise to prominence and cause everyone else considerable disquiet.

Many would believe this simply reflects the natural distribution of ability throughout the population, that most of us have fairly limited potential. Indeed it would upset the natural social order if you had too many dissenting voices, too many people asking why. We make it very difficult for people to think for themselves, to ask awkward questions and so it is not surprising that most of us settle for a quiet and easy life. But we are faced with a growing dilemma. We recognize we are living at a time of rapid and furious change, social and technological. Carrying on as you always have done, doing what you're told, accepting your place, are less viable options.

This poses a considerable challenge for all of us. In adapting to the demand for accelerating flexibility and innovation, we introduce far greater instability into our world. The natural world is unpredictable and increasingly so is our social world. We already accept that we need to equip people with the knowledge and skills to cope with ongoing change. We are less concerned with recipe book approaches to learning. It is no longer possible to give people all the answers, to tell them exactly how they should deal with every given situation. Such learning is too rigid and mechanical. People need instead to learn certain principles which they are then helped to apply in different situations. This requires the exercise of both judgment and initiative.

Carry on learning

The distinction between an able elite whose achievements take them to the very frontiers of our understanding and the rest of humanity who simply make up the drones, carrying out their prescribed functions is increasingly difficult to sustain. Each of us has considerably more potential than we have realized. Our traditional experience of learning has been more concerned with grading us, deciding where we were most suited, encouraging us to have realistic expectations and not question the arbitrary assessments made about us. But these assumptions are no longer in anyone's best interest. Our fast moving world needs the benefits of everyone's ability. We cannot afford to waste anyone's talents. Work in the future will be more demanding and far more complex, with specific tasks and roles becoming even more rapidly outdated. We will have to learn to keep up with this pace or we will be left behind. We cannot afford to leave anyone behind. We are already aware of the dangers a disaffected underclass would pose.

The established social order may become less stable and hierarchies less secure. organizations are already operating with flatter management structures and increasingly work is being arranged in terms of project groups rather than traditional departmental boundaries. Authority is exercised less rigidly and promotion depends on proven performance rather than time serving and how far your face fits. The modern world demands rapid responses to changing circumstances. Indeed the key to survival is to anticipate the changes and formulate proactive strategies, whether you are an individual or a large corporation. The status quo is shifting continually and those who stubbornly try to protect and further only their own narrow, sectional interests, neglecting the wider picture, will lose out.

Individuals will have to live on their wits more than they have ever done before. Our ability to use our initiative, to think, analyze, question, problem-solve and innovate will determine our success. We recognize that we should be encouraging learners to develop these skills and yet, all too often we merely pay lip service to the idea. We make sure individuals learn within the very tight boundaries we have prescribed.

Learning is more accountable and more standardized than it has ever been. More resources are being invested and there is more commitment from all sorts of organizations to developing their employees. We are moving on from the idea that people have a once and for all opportunity as learners, and if they waste it, there is no second chance. People are being encouraged to think about learning as something they will do throughout their lives. Student-centered learning and experiential learning are all positive approaches. We still need to explore more imaginative ways of involving learners in the process.

Formal learning is too preoccupied with conformity and compliance. Tutors must realize that they cannot expect to produce the sort of learners the twenty-first century requires without fundamentally reviewing the way learning is organized. It is not just about what people learn but, much more importantly, how they learn. The relationship between tutor and learners is crucial, and should engage both in a meaningful dialogue, characterized by confidence, openness, curiosity, a sense of adventure and mutual respect.

Summary Points

☐ Learning is a natural activity enabling us to adapt to change, ensuring our survival as a species. In a time of rapidly accelerating social and economic change, learning becomes crucial to individual achievement and success.

☐ Learning is an active process. The learning cycle describes how we experience something, reflect on what that experience means to us, how we feel about it, how that fits with what we already know and understand, what general principles we can then establish, and how we can practically apply those principles in the future.

☐ There are two types of learning. Learning is part of the socialization process, designed to ensure we accept the status quo and fit in with established ways of understanding and doing things.

☐ But learning can also stimulate us to challenge the status quo, encouraging us to question received wisdom, to think for ourselves, developing individual potential and driving us to push forward the frontiers of knowledge and understanding. This more dynamic learning has greater relevance in today's fast changing world.

☐ These two types of learning are frequently confused by tutors, where learning methods are not always consistent with learning objectives, and the relationship between tutor and learner encourages subordination rather than open questioning.

☐ Formal learning often reinforces the social distinctions between those who have been educated to succeed and those who have been simply schooled to serve, squandering a great deal of human talent and potential in the process.

☐ Formal learning has depended on the development of disciplined conceptual thinking, expressed through a rich and versatile use of language. Language gives us the means to think. Language provides the fertile ground which enables learning to flourish. Learning should encourage learners in a dialogue that further develops the ability to reason through language.

☐ The pace of change in the workplace is such that individuals are required to demonstrate ever greater resourcefulness, initiative and innovation. But they are being educated and trained in a system, that, in its efforts to be more explicit about what it does and what has been achieved, increasingly reduces learning to little more than hoop jumping.

QUESTIONS FOR REFLECTION

1. *How far are you willing to question your own ideas and attitudes? How much do you take your ways of looking at the world for granted? How comfortable are you with exploring quite different perspectives?*

A willingness to subject your own ideas to a process of self-critical scrutiny is crucial in maintaining a questioning mind. Recognizing and acknowledging the limitations of your own thoughts and opinions makes you less daunting and more accessible to others.

2. *How comfortable have you been to question and challenge authority and accepted wisdom? Do you believe that you might risk being identified as a troublemaker? How would you feel if you found yourself alone in holding a certain opinion?*

It is difficult if you have always preferred to accept authority rather than challenge it, to then see the wisdom in developing a more challenging attitude in others. Perhaps you have already paid the price for being seen as a troublemaker. It is understandable that you might have reservations about such a strategy. However this is more about encouraging people to question assertively rather than be subversive for the sake of it, to put forward a reasoned and persuasive argument without being perceived as aggressive and awkward.

3. *How far do you associate compliance and conformity with respect for you as the tutor? What do you think might be the consequences of developing more critical ways of thinking amongst your learners?*

If you have equated respect with dutiful acquiescence then you may find learners who do not readily accept everything you say somewhat unsettling. But how truly respectful is an attitude based on unthinking agreement. Surely it is the learners, who care enough about what they are learning to engage in a real debate, you want to encourage.

4. *How much do you evaluate someone's ability and potential according to the degree of social confidence they project? Are you inclined to associate aptitude with verbal fluency and a particular cultural familiarity? What sort of assumptions do you tend to make when you hear a certain accent or observe the way someone presents himself? Are you able to distinguish the style in which people express themselves from the actual content of what they say, their thoughts and ideas, their curiosity and independence of thought?*

It is very difficult not to be unduly influenced by the social cues which characterize someone's position in society. It is also very easy to be impressed by someone who appears confident and assured. Often a certain social position confers a level of poise and confidence. And yet we may then underestimate the truly talented and able individual who does not present in such a conventionally prescribed manner

5. How do you view your own ability to express yourself and put forward a reasoned argument? Are you suspicious of people who have an easy way with words? Or are you used to being able to use language to your advantage?

Our own experience will be influential in the importance we attach to developing our learners' confidence and use of language. If you are instinctively wary, perhaps lacking confidence in your own ability, then you may be disinclined to attach any priority to encouraging your learners in that direction. This may require a courageous step on your part where both your learners and yourself may develop together. If on the other hand you are already very confident in expressing yourself, and perhaps unwittingly, intimidate others with your fluent use of language, then you may need to consider how your learners may feel. Are you likely to encourage them if you only succeed in giving them a disabling inferiority complex.

6. How responsible do you feel for enabling your learners to develop a more confident and proactive attitude to change? How do you feel about change?

Negative experiences of change are all too common nowadays and it is easy to feel overwhelmed and drained, struggling to find any purposeful way forward. Change does place many different demands upon us, but it can also give rise to real opportunities to develop in new directions.

7. How confident do you feel about taking risks? What sort of model do you provide to your learners? Do you relish uncertainty and the chance to try something where you cannot predict the outcome, or do you remain anxious about what may go wrong, fearful of being criticized or blamed?

Maybe your experiences of taking risks have only reinforced your anxieties. Maybe you were criticized or blamed when things went wrong, but everyone should be given the opportunity to learn from their mistakes. If you are not actively encouraging learners to be more adventurous and to take risks, you will be implicitly discouraging them.

3

A Role by Any Other Name

As I have already stated, I began my career as a teacher, although my official title was lecturer. I now work as a trainer – or training consultant if I'm really trying to impress. Often I am asked to facilitate programs. I do not feel I am doing anything significantly different. Some years ago, I also helped one of my husbands learn to drive, (remarkably, this was not a contributory factor in our subsequent divorce). As such, I suppose I acted as an amateur driving instructor. It all seems rather arbitrary – teacher, lecturer, tutor, trainer, instructor, coach or even facilitator – I was helping people learn. But maybe this is being too simplistic.

Having experienced both teaching and training, I am very aware of how the most superficial criteria are often employed to distinguish the two activities, such as where and how it takes place. The same learning can be the result of teaching or training depending on whether it happens in a university seminar room or a training suite. Counseling skills courses are likely to be found in both. The Open University has produced material which I have supported, as a training officer, with in-house tutorials. Was I teaching or training? If we try to identify the differences between the two, we talk in terms of teaching being knowledge-based whereas training usually has something to do with acquiring skills. And yet I am proposing that they simply represent the extreme points of a continuum, along which you can place all learning activities, most of which combine both knowledge and skills.

Although this appears to be a futile debate, it does enable us to analyze what we are trying to achieve with learners, as well as perhaps gaining a better understanding of each role and learning from both. We often continue with our familiar routines and rarely pause to question what we are actually doing. The answer appears to be glaringly obvious and yet with further reflection we might become less certain. In some ways, we are now more explicit about what we do. We are obliged to draw up our lists of learning outcomes, but these are usually highly specific and rarely allow us the opportunity to look at what we are doing in more general terms. What *do* we mean by learning? Are we helping learners to remember, question, think, understand, analyze, investigate, evaluate, practice, imagine, create, speculate, theorize? I have included all of these with my learners as a teacher and as a trainer.

A flabby sort of learning

I would like to return again to my experience in further education. As a teacher, my task was to design and deliver lessons which would both satisfy the curriculum requirements and motivate and involve my learners. With some courses however, I was able to allow my imagination greater scope, given the absence of any meaningful curriculum or formal assessment of the learning. Indeed it was difficult to identify what the learning was really supposed to be, with subjects such as General Studies, the whole concept of which rested on some outmoded assumptions about what educated people should know. Such assumptions perpetuate the idea that there is something we can identify as general knowledge, although in fact any such knowledge may depend crucially on social and cultural experience as well as age and, dare I say it, gender. Out of all the vast range of information available to people, how do we make a judgment as to what we think properly informed people should be familiar with? Opera, jazz, rap, natural history, environmental issues, D.I.Y., computer technology, classical literature, soap opera, sports, wrestling, installation art, T.V. advertising, fashion trends, foreign travel, social history, politics, health … the list could go on and on and only serves to demonstrate how pointless it is to make such judgments.

I had relative freedom then with my learners to negotiate a program which we would all find relevant and interesting. I wanted to focus on topics which would provoke strong opinions or would provide an opportunity to introduce ideas they had not previously considered. The program varied with each group, depending on their suggestions. We followed no set textbook and were free to engage in learning as exploration. My learners were not obliged to learn anything in the sense of having to remember and regurgitate the information covered. They were not required to acquire particular skills, except in so far as they were expected to listen to one another. They were simply asked to think about the topics, to try and discuss the ideas rationally, examining their own preconceptions and prejudices. Dogmatic positions were discouraged. Instead the learners were urged to develop a skeptical approach, critically evaluating argument and evidence. At times, it all seemed a bit idealistic, and for most of the learners it was probably a fleeting experience, which may or may not have left any lasting impression.

Measuring the learning outcomes would have been counter-productive, as that would have introduced an element of performance anxiety. As it was, our lessons more closely approximated an informal debating society, where everyone had a chance to reflect on personal views and attitudes. I believe it was worthwhile to that extent, although I accept that for most of the learners it still represented an unnecessary, albeit somewhat diversionary addition to their timetable.

This early and very tentative attempt at teaching was both liberating and frustrating. I had almost complete freedom to work in the way I thought most appropriate, and yet because there was no clear purpose or goal to our efforts, it was difficult to derive any real sense of achievement. I was trying to expose my learners to a way of thinking about issues which would, hopefully, expand their horizons and imbue a more skeptical attitude. The dilemma raises a crucial issue. Learning is a process. In learning about something or learning to do something, we exercise faculties, increasing our learning capacity. Just as exercised muscles are capable of greater effort, so exercised minds become more vigorous. That exercise, if it is to be effective, has to be disciplined and focused. There needs to be a goal. Maybe it is a means to an end, perhaps to attain sporting excellence. Or maybe it is just for the satisfaction of enjoying a fit and healthy body. Whatever the motivation, there needs to be a clear strategy with some means to review progress. Similarly with intellectual endeavor. My learners learned in a flabby sort of way. Their ambivalent motivation permitted little else. I could have been more authoritarian, but to what purpose? They would then have been resentful learners, merely going through the motions. At least I mobilised some small enthusiasm, but I realized that for learning to be really worthwhile, learners had to at least raise a metaphorical sweat.

Survival skills

My role was more constrained when it came to working with under-achieving school-leavers who had been persuaded or induced by financial incentives to try again in further education. Did I teach or train those young people in social and life skills? The question is meaningless. I remember trying to work to a dull, uninspiring and embarrassingly patronizing program outline. This was hoop jumping at its most dire. There were those who had not achieved because their personalities had not conformed to the disciplined demands of the education system, and then there were those who simply struggled with even the most basic of tasks. With the former, I was trying to encourage a degree of self-discipline and application as well as self-esteem, which might enable them to demonstrate their real capabilities. At times, this felt more like social work than education. I was trying to influence beliefs and behavior. With the latter group, who were so profoundly disadvantaged in terms of their learning ability, I was trying to inspire confidence, while at the same time patiently helping them to practice quite elementary skills. My approach had to be adapted to the needs of each individual. The curriculum, such as it was, seemed totally inadequate in addressing the complex needs of these young people.

The learning objectives, as far as I was able to articulate them, were to some degree concerned with knowledge, but that knowledge would remain irrelevant unless I was able to help them change their attitude toward themselves and their future expectations. Similarly, developing skills would prove continually frustrating while their lack of motivation stunted any sense of purpose or possible pleasure in achievement. They did not see formal learning or any expenditure of effort on their part as making the slightest difference to their lives or their prospects. They had been labeled as failures and did not want to engage any further with a system which had so eroded their feeling of self-worth.

They probably represented one of the most dispiriting experiences of my career. I recognized my own limited ability, but I was also aware I was being asked to provide a very inadequate sticking plaster to the deepest wounds inflicted by a rigid educational system and an enduringly inequitable society. They were there simply for the extra money they received while on a government sponsored training scheme and, despite their limitations, had enough understanding of their situation to remain cynical about how much difference a potted and poorly thought out vocational skills program was going to make to their lives. I was employed as a teacher in an educational institution delivering something that was supposed to resemble training, and yet few had apparently paused to consider what we might realistically achieve with these young people. In the event, even if we had been able to agree more purposeful learning objectives, the actual outcomes would probably not have been very different. Bottoms on seats prevailed, and colleges were only too grateful for the extra funds.

Changing perspectives

It was something of a relief to move on to more academic teaching with a clearly defined curriculum, with specific assessment procedures, where everyone knew what was expected of them. And yet my own subject area, the social sciences, posed their own particular challenges. There was certainly a very distinct body of knowledge, and yet in addition there was a certain attitude or perspective that needed to be encouraged. It was all too easy for learners to view familiar social institutions and discuss them in common sense terms rather than try to step back and view them as a more objective spectator, attempting to figure out what is going on and what has influenced the way in which people act. It was always difficult to persuade learners to relinquish the idea that there was one particular, correct view, an ultimate right answer. They were used to absorbing knowledge in this way. Now they were being asked to compare different and opposing arguments, weighing up their relative strengths and merits, evaluating how far those arguments furthered our understanding, developed our insights or were supported by empirical evidence.

So again, in order to enable my learners to learn, I had to address their way of thinking, their way of looking at themselves and others in their world, not quite as personally focused as my previous groups, but I was still having to move beyond the simple delivery of knowledge and challenge established attitudes. Some individuals, although obviously bright and able, experienced real difficulties in moving to a less certain and absolute understanding of what they had taken for granted. They found this an uncomfortable place, where so many once reassuring aspects of social life were now open to examination. Even if they themselves accommodated to this spirit of uncompromising inquiry, their changing outlook would often cause conflict with their family and friends.

Teaching for me, had become a complex activity. It was complex because I recognized my learners were unlikely to learn, or would not learn so effectively, unless I appreciated how the activity of learning should engage them, and engage them holistically, to borrow a term more associated with healing. It was not enough to accept that you had to address the characteristics of your learners in delivering your subject, it was also necessary to see how the learning affected them, changed them as individuals. Almost in the same way as holistic medicine treats the whole individual rather than just a series of symptoms, I was uneasy with the notion that you simply taught a body of knowledge or a set of skills. It always seemed to me you were initiating a process which would have an impact beyond its stated objectives with many unpredictable consequences. I often felt I was travelling in uncharted territory, guided more by intuition and instinct as there seemed to be little shared acknowledgement of this particular dimension to the business of teaching.

Hidden agendas

I moved over to staff training in an attempt to escape the politics of the staffroom, and in the naive belief I might be able to work more autonomously. I was a lot younger then. It is invariably the ignorance of youth which deludes us. Older and wiser, our confidence and energy diminishes and we become much less audacious. I quickly realized that the most straightforward part of my role was organizing and delivering the learning. What I had completely underestimated were the competing agendas to identify the training priorities.

Senior management thought in terms of organizational developments and perceived problems in service delivery, rarely acknowledging their own responsibility for such problems. Front line staff had their own ideas about training. Many resisted any suggestion that they needed training of any sort. The standard refrain, 'I've been in this job twenty years and if I don't know how to do it now, I never will' has been heard regularly throughout my career. Never mind that everyone's job has changed out of all recognition in that time and no one is doing the same job as they were even five years ago. Of those who did accept the value of training opportunities, many defined them in terms of their own personal career advancement rather than what might be needed in order for them to perform more competently in their current job. There were middle managers who saw training as the only solution to individual performance problems. They did not appear to regard themselves as playing a significant role in addressing any deficiencies on the part of their staff. Signaling the expected standards, supporting staff in trying to achieve those standards and taking consistent measures when those standards were not met, seemed to be an altogether far too tedious or unpleasant business which many managers preferred to avoid.

The competing agendas were never explicitly articulated, for that would have brought the conflicting interests out into the open in a way none of the different parties ever really wanted. That would have left them too exposed, subject to unwelcome scrutiny, having to justify their positions, and so a covert game was played where each of the parties were convinced that they were the only ones who knew what was actually going on and who kept the show on the road, despite the way in which everyone else failed to pull their weight or threatened to undermine the whole enterprise. Nevertheless, appearances had to be maintained and a degree of cooperation ensured, and so the criticisms and reproaches would rarely be shared directly, except with the training officer, who acted as a repository for everyone's frustrations. I felt as though I was delicately picking my way through a minefield which everyone collectively pretended did not exist. And yet my effectiveness depended on trying to address many of these very issues and save everyone's face at the same time. I felt rather like a Japanese politician, albeit a somewhat reluctant one.

When people talked of the difference between training and education, I was more than willing to concede the enormous cultural difference. My role had been transformed from simply implementing learning programs, to one where every bit of tact, discretion and diplomacy was fully utilized in trying to formulate a coherent, organizational training policy and strategy. I was now responsible, in effect, for designing the curriculum. I had to analyze the learning needs from the contrary accounts I was given of people's effectiveness. On one occasion I was given to understand there was an urgent need for minute-taking training. After closer investigation of the problem, I discovered a beleaguered group of administrative staff who were expected to minute meetings where there was no proper chairperson, agenda or even any recognizable outcomes or decisions. They were skilled and experienced in minute taking and had struggled to do their best, but became demoralized when they were being criticized for problems they knew were not of their making. They were simply the most vulnerable in the hierarchy and therefore the easiest to blame. With some trepidation, I cautiously suggested 'running effective meetings' might be a more appropriate training response.

Identifying needs and outcomes

The role of training officer taught me two important lessons which helped clarify my own understanding of the learning process. The first was concerned with the difficulties involved in defining learning needs. Who was defining them? Was it the potential learner, who will certainly be able to provide the most subjective account of what they feel they know and don't know, what they can do and can't do, what they lack confidence with and where they feel they need more practice and support, depending on their own degree of insight, willingness to admit to weaknesses and appreciation of what level of performance they are expected to deliver? Was it the learner's supervisor, who may be in a position to make the most objective commentary on the learner's performance, but who may have little interest in developing staff, unable to recognize why someone is underperforming? Maybe the reasons are too complex and the supervisor simply wants a quick fix solution, which the training department is expected to produce like so many rabbits out of a hat. All too often, training is assumed to proceed on the basis of telepathy, responding to barely articulated messages. People identify a problem they are unable or unwilling to explore, but feel something needs to be done. They cannot even say how the problem would be solved, they simply want it to go away, and so the training department is supposed to duly oblige.

This leads on to the second important issue, concerned with how you define the learning outcomes. I realized when I tried to sit down with many managers and learners that few people, including myself, had a very clear idea of what we were trying to achieve. Traditionally training had been provided in a very unsystematic way. People went on training for a variety of reasons. Routinely, many were simply sent by their managers without any indication of what they were supposed to get out of it. For others it was a reward, an away-day, a chance to have a break from the normal routine. The Chinese menu approach predominated with courses being selected on the basis of an appealing venue, a prestigious speaker, even if the topic was of very marginal relevance, or simply because it was some time since they had last attended any training and it was somehow good for morale, regardless of the learning objectives. There was little attempt to match training with identified learning needs.

Much has moved on in recent years and there is a greater realization of how training should be more appropriately targeted, focusing on what sort of impact a training program should make, how will people benefit and what will they gain from it.

While training is more obviously concerned with what people are able to do, education has similarly moved on and has had to become more precise in describing what it is trying to achieve. It is part of the business of greater accountability, of being able to demonstrate the value of any activity. And so all those involved in learning, whether in training or education, are engaged in detailing not only the required inputs but the expected outputs from their labors. As I said, my own experience of both roles had led me to conclude that when it came to the actual working with learners, teaching and training did not feel so very different. Maybe the learning outputs varied, but they seemed to be part of one continuum rather than fundamentally different.

Moving along the continuum

The idea of the continuum enables us to consider more precisely what it is we mean by learning. At one end of the continuum we might place the absorbing of knowledge and information for its own sake, while at the other, the acquiring of particular skills. Teaching is conventionally seen as concerned with the former while training is supposed to concentrate on the latter. In short we presume teaching encourages people to think, while training shows people how to do something. There are very few areas of learning, however which fall neatly into these categories. Much is found somewhere near the middle of the continuum.

Where would you place the teaching of foreign languages for instance? The activity takes place in a variety of institutions and contexts, educational and business. It certainly involves a body of knowledge as well as developing the skills of being able to communicate. People do not always demonstrate those skills consistently. Some have an easy facility with written language and yet experience real difficulty with the spoken word, while others are fluent speakers but struggle with written language. Helping someone to write or speak a foreign language involves delivering a body of knowledge and encouraging them to apply that knowledge in verbal and written communication. Such communication is a skill that improves with practice, the performance of which may depend as much upon the sensitivity of someone's hearing as their ability to apply the given knowledge. But maybe we are still constrained by what exactly we mean by a skill. More often than not, we have an image of somebody doing something practical or technical.

Nurse training has traditionally taken place in hospitals and their attached schools of nursing. It was always recognized that becoming a nurse entailed both the acquiring of knowledge and the practical skills of nursing care. Nurse training now takes place mainly in colleges and people talk more of nurse education in an attempt to suitably acknowledge the professional status of nursing. Clearly the body of knowledge is more demanding, as is the level of technical competence. But the difference is really only one of degree rather than any fundamental shift in the role of nurses. It remains a combination of specific knowledge, the application of that knowledge in the performance of a range of practical and technical skills. Whether you describe the process of acquiring that knowledge and those skills as education or training would seem immaterial.

The study of medicine throws up even further anomalies. The body of knowledge is enormous. But doctors have also to learn a range of technical skills. Indeed if they subsequently work as surgeons, their competence depends crucially on their manual dexterity. Surely this demonstrates how our perception of learning is in large part shaped by notions of status and the assumed cleverness of the learners, rather than any systematic analysis of the components of learning.

A matter of status

The status issue permeates the whole area of learning. In our education system we still distinguish between academic and vocational programs as though one is somehow qualitatively different from the other. In terms of the continuum, most conventional academic courses would seem largely concerned with knowledge acquisition, although increasingly with elements of applied knowledge and certain specific skills. Science learners may be able to process a vast range of information, constantly updating themselves as research throws up new puzzles, and yet if they lack skill in the basic experimental techniques, their progress will be restricted. Many university courses incorporate a substantial element of applied learning, not just in engineering and business programs, but also in the arts and humanities. The higher education curriculum has expanded to reflect a far broader concept of learning, although there are many who believe this represents a dumbing down of academic standards.

It really is the outdated legacy from the history of education in this country that academic courses are viewed as superior because they seemingly correspond more closely to the traditional ideas of what constituted a classical education, enjoyed by gentlemen. Anything that was practical, technical or even applied knowledge was regarded as somehow less worthy and certainly not something those with the most ability would wish to aspire to. Such values subtly influence our thinking even today, with our rather arbitrary notions of success in purely academic courses somehow indicating a higher level of intelligence than success in applied programs.

We still assume that the ability to pass academic exams suggests a greater potential to learn, without distinguishing what sort of learning we mean. Is it simply the capacity to remember vast amounts of information and then regurgitate it at a fixed point, forgetting most of it within a short time? Such an approach characterizes, even today, the majority of people's experience of education. It is not until you pass further on in the system that you are expected to critically evaluate the significance of knowledge, and then usually within particular limits. We continue to make people jump through hoops, without examining the hoops or the purpose they might serve.

A creative spirit

Education in the creative arts also raises questions as to what actually is being learned. Very likely a body of knowledge in terms of learning about the cultural and historical context of the particular artistic medium. No one creates or performs in a vacuum. Ideas and particular forms of expression only have meaning within an overall context. Learning how to do something also involves understanding the theoretical framework upon which it is based. Learning to play music involves not only the practical skill of manipulating a particular instrument but also, usually, being able to read music (and write it, if sufficiently talented), although there are obviously exceptions with very gifted musicians and composers having virtually no comprehension of musical notation. Nevertheless it is an enormous advantage to be conversant with the language of music in order to fully participate in its community

So, there is clearly a body of knowledge and the development of skills, method and style. But how do you teach someone to be creative? How do you enable people to realize their potential in this highly personalized area of human endeavor? Are you simply concerned with helping them discover their own special gifts, stimulating their imagination and developing the confidence to follow their muse and give form to their inspiration. Creative writing programs usually advocate a more commercial approach, concentrating on matters of technique and ensuring conformity with established conventions, rather than urging learners to simply follow their own artistic noses. Such an approach characterizes much teaching amongst the arts. Although originality is prized, it tends to emerge *in spite of* the rigors of tuition, rather than as a consequence of it. Even the continuum does not easily accommodate this peculiar aspect of learning.

A very sophisticated learning

While there are very real problems with our assumptions as to the sort of learning which takes place in traditional educational institutions, we also confront similar difficulties in relation to vocational training. Many vocational programs increasingly include a range of learning and are no longer limited to purely practical skills. National Vocational Qualifications (NVQs) have played a vital part in this process. As an example, when they were first launched in social care, there was a widespread assumption that many experienced and valued workers would at last have the opportunity to gain an accredited qualification, without having to face the ordeal of attending college. However, it soon became apparent as the assessments got under way, that many such workers did in fact have serious gaps in their knowledge and understanding which needed to be addressed before they could be certified competent. They might have been very kindly, well-meaning individuals who were able to offer a good standard of practical care, relying on their own experience of life to understand other people's situations. However, without the objective body of knowledge which would take them beyond their personal perspective, they were not always able to appreciate the emotional and psychological complexity of others, essential in providing an understanding and empathic attitude.

It is the vocational area, in the form of NVQs, which has most systematically distinguished the nature and standard of the learning required for those involved. Many may sometimes groan under the volume of detail, but at least everyone is clear about the expectations. There may well be arguments about how consistently those expectations are interpreted and maintained by different assessment centers. But the principle has been established that learning can be identified in terms of the specific knowledge, skills and understanding demanded in different occupational areas and the various levels at which people work within those areas. It is certainly about ensuring people are able to do particular things, and if they cannot, then training can show them how. That is at one end of the continuum.

However a large part of my work is not so straightforward. It is about sharing knowledge and ideas with workers in order to establish the important values which should underpin the way they work, helping them appreciate, for instance, why it is important that clients in a care situation are enabled to be as independent as possible – perhaps the worker actually does less instead of more; why clients need to be able to exercise choice and make decisions rather than just fit into an institutional regime or care arrangement, even when that may introduce an element of risk; and why elderly residents with advanced dementia are still entitled to be treated with as much dignity as we would want for ourselves, realizing that respectful understanding is even more essential when people no longer remember where they are, or even recognize their own families anymore. All of this involves discussing fundamental value systems, challenging the boundaries of what people take for granted in the way they relate to others. This can be very powerful stuff, often demanding a profound questioning of accepted practice.

Changing attitudes is probably one of the most difficult tasks faced by any trainer and is far removed from the simple process of showing someone how to do something. It clearly requires people to think and to question as well as to apply knowledge, and as such, represents a highly sophisticated form of learning.

A more explicit approach

Academic education has attempted in recent years to take a similarly more systematic approach to the expected outcomes of any course, what should be learned and how that might be demonstrated. Whether the assessments are in the form of exams, individual or group projects or ongoing course work, teachers are trying to apply clear and consistent criteria in their evaluations.

When I first joined teaching, normative assessment was still widespread. Learners were simply compared with each other, with very little attempt to define precisely the standards applied. Marking was often on the basis of gut feeling. This was obviously more likely in some subjects than others. I can recall external moderators reviewing learners' work and being more concerned with presentation than actual content, the absence of ruled margins being a major issue one year. One also observed the marking by weight approach, which was linked with the preoccupation with presentation. If a piece of work suggested a considerable effort, that effort should be duly rewarded, even if it went beyond what was actually necessary or relevant.

Such intuitive assessments were open to obvious abuse, with conscientious, dutiful learners perceived as producing higher quality work, while more outspoken and less compliant individuals were regularly penalized. I had myself paid the penalty for arguing a more controversial line in an A level exam, initially failing and later grudgingly awarded a pass after a requested remark. Where you have no objective indicators of what constitutes poor, acceptable or good work, evaluation will inevitably be subjective, inconsistent and unreliable.

This may seem to contradict my earlier misgivings about rigid assessment procedures, which demand a hoop-jumping approach to learning. I want to now try and resolve the tension between the need for a more self-conscious and systematic approach to the business of helping people learn and one that truly empowers learners. I will return to the concept of the learning continuum and look at how it can be extended into a more helpful model, which I refer to as the learning paradigm. The learning paradigm includes the two dimensions of learning, the content and the process. I will then consider how that model can be incorporated within a more holistic approach to learning.

The learning paradigm – the learning continuum

As I have already indicated, the learning continuum distinguishes the learning content in terms of those activities which are exclusively knowledge based through to those which are exclusively skill based, and allows for all learning to be placed somewhere along that continuum, depending on the proportion of knowledge to skill. Although many academic subjects, such as the study of literature may seem to lack any element of skill, the demonstration of learning in terms of essay production or literary criticism involves the development and practice of particular skills. Similarly, learning to upholster furniture may be largely a matter of skill and technique. Nevertheless, to be properly competent, one would need to also know about and understand the various materials and their uses, as well as how certain materials and techniques are associated with different historical periods.

When analyzing the content of any learning, it is almost impossible to locate it at either extreme of the continuum. There always appears to be some mix of skill with knowledge, and it is helpful when you are responsible, as a tutor for that learning, to be as explicit as possible in identifying the various elements included in the learning. Simply defining your role in terms of the context of teaching or training seems to be a convenient way of avoiding having to consciously and deliberately identify these elements. Using the continuum also helps break down the traditional boundaries between learning which perpetuate status distinctions, attaching arbitrary values to different learning.

Some may still object, and argue that even though most learning inevitably involves a mix of knowledge and skills, they still represent fundamentally different kinds of learning rather than opposite ends of a continuum. We need to look at the learning continuum in more detail. Essentially the learning continuum is concerned with the focus or content of learning. It is less concerned with the process, which is addressed by the other dimension of the learning paradigm. The focus or content identifies what is to be learned. These are described in part by the learning objectives or outcomes.

We have become much more precise in identifying the learning objectives for any given example of learning. We can indicate the knowledge we expect someone to have gained, making it clear whether we require them to actually know in detail or simply have a general awareness. We can imply the level of understanding we consider appropriate, by suggesting how learners should be able to interpret the knowledge. This does to some extent interact with the idea of the process of learning, but essentially the concern is with the knowledge itself, what we judge someone should be familiar with. What do our learners need to know in order to demonstrate that the learning has been achieved?

Similarly with skills, it is the performance of a specified task with which the learning continuum is interested. The task may be operating a piece of equipment, communicating effectively with a colleague, designing interior decor, organizing a project, performing on stage – whatever it is, the question addressed by the learning continuum is, what do our learners need to do in order to demonstrate the learning has been achieved?

It would seem that in demonstrating knowledge you are in fact doing something, and that in doing something you are also demonstrating what you know. These two aspects are constantly working together. Let us take an example of how learning transforms from knowledge to skill as it moves along the continuum. Herbalism or the practice of herbal medicine, however its efficacy is viewed, provides a useful illustration of what I am trying to say. At the knowledge end of the continuum, one would find the study of plants and disease in their pure form. The learner would need to become familiar with plant varieties and classifications, and their various restorative properties. Learners would also have to know about human anatomy and physiology, how the body works and what happens when different parts and systems start to malfunction, deteriorate or operate less efficiently. The demonstration of the learning may entail little more than reproducing that knowledge by answering questions or providing descriptive accounts. There is no opportunity to apply the learning in a more active context.

Further along the learning continuum we might introduce the skills of recognition, distinguishing between different plants and correctly identifying them, as well as detecting the signs and symptoms of illness and disease. Moving along the continuum still further, the detection of signs and symptoms would form the basis for the skills of diagnosis, working out from the presenting evidence, the nature and cause of the problem. This would then be followed by the skill of applying the most appropriate herbal remedy, given the condition. The monitoring and review of treatment would also be included in the demonstration of these skills.

Moving on from the application of treatment, we may well consider the skill of preparing and formulating the remedies, making up compounds and perhaps introducing new combinations. This will call for specific skills in being able to work with the different substances, preparing and mixing them to recognized standards, where the beneficial properties are maximized and the administering process is acceptable to patients. Clearly the interaction of knowledge and skill is a significant feature of much of this learning.

When looking at the learning continuum, we conventionally think in terms of moving in the direction of knowledge to skill, skills usually involving the application of the knowledge. It is possible however to move in the reverse direction. Consider the example of martial arts. Although there are significant differences between the various types of martial arts, they are basically concerned with learning physical techniques, involving the use of balance, momentum and the calculated application of force or pressure in order to overcome your opponent. The emphasis is on learning to coordinate movement, to control muscles, practice specific maneuvers and develop an appreciation of tactics.

Nevertheless, the learning is also likely to include an understanding of how different parts of the body function, in order to not only protect oneself but also to disadvantage your opponent, being clear about what will cause discomfort, what will injure and what may prove lethal. The knowledge element will extend still further in becoming aware of the traditional rules, customs, rituals and established value systems which characterize the disciplines.

Pure knowledge is concerned with theoretical models and abstractions, the concepts we have constructed to describe and make sense of our world. Those models may refer to plant species, physiological functions or ethical values. They are simply devices for ordering our experience. The knowledge we have learned is the information we have been able to store. Through that learning we also acquire a certain discipline and sense of order in how we store that information. We learn to maintain a tidy mind, where knowledge is systematically organized

Knowledge has a self-contained and self-absorbing quality. It exists in itself and for itself. You may learn knowledge for no other reason than to know something. You may not use that knowledge except to demonstrate that you have learned it. That, after all, is the rationale of most academic exams. Acquiring knowledge is an internal process. It does not have to engage with an external reality. Indeed that knowledge might not actually fit the external reality. Knowledge does not have to be correct, true or logically consistent.

It is only when we move along the continuum and start applying knowledge, engaging with, and trying to make some impact on an external reality, that we are able to evaluate how far that knowledge fits. For then we are using the knowledge to do something. We are using it to some other purpose. We are moving in the direction of skills. We can then decide how far the knowledge enables us to achieve that purpose. The exercise of skills invariably concentrates our attention on how effective we are.

So far, we have been concerned with the content of learning, but as I have indicated, there is another dimension to the learning paradigm, which focuses on the process of learning, recognizing that the way in which we encourage our learners to learn is as important as what they learn. While we need to be clear and quite explicit about what we expect them to learn as minimal requirements, the way in which they learn is a more dynamic process.

The learning paradigm – the development continuum

The second dimension of the paradigm, which I will call the development continuum, switches the focus to the learner. It looks at how far the learner experiences the learning as an empowering process, how far they are engaged and involved as active participants. Again I use the idea of a continuum, suggesting there are extreme points, ranging from mechanical learning, directly and rigidly controlled by the tutor, to more engaging learning where there is a genuine spirit of active enquiry shared by both learner and tutor.

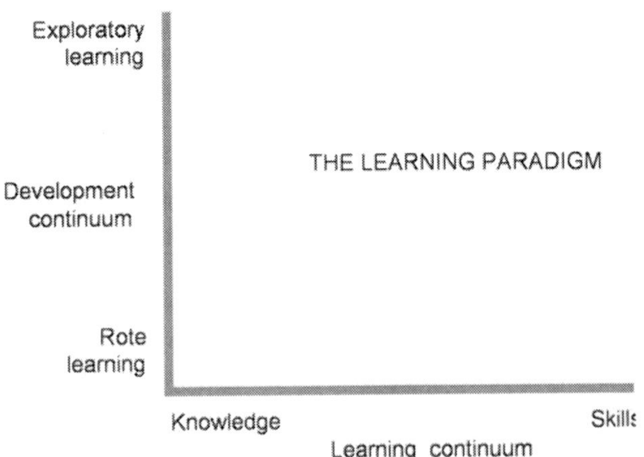

At one extreme of the development continuum, we may find rote learning, where the learner remembers information and acquires skills in a purely mechanical fashion. There is no attempt to discuss meaning or to expand understanding. It is learning by imitation, with no expectation that the learner will question or try to clarify. Learning one's times tables by repetitively reciting them would be an example in relation to knowledge, while being drilled to march in correct formation would be an example in relation to physical skill and coordination. Neither make any demands on the learner other than to do exactly as the tutor instructs them.

At the other end, there is exploratory learning, where the learners are almost directing their own learning. The tutor acts as a facilitator, enabling the learning to happen, but it is the learners who are in control of their own learning, analyzing, investigating, experimenting, speculating, evaluating and theorizing. With exploratory learning, the learners are able to extend the boundaries, to go beyond the predetermined learning objectives. It could be argued that the logical extreme of the developmental continuum is completely self-directed learning, and in one sense it is. But my concern is to employ a model which assists in better understanding the *learning relationship* between learner and tutor, and so my focus remains with that relationship, while acknowledging that extremely significant learning can occur without any intervention from a tutor.

In looking at the development continuum and trying to place a given learning activity within it, one is assessing the different learning skills employed by the learner. Learning skills are quite distinct from general skills, they are specifically concerned with exercising our learning capacity, and the more those skills are practiced, the more our learning potential can be realized. If we restrict our learners' opportunities to exercise those skills, they remain stuck, limited in their learning repertoire. Part of our role as tutors is to help in extending that repertoire and building learners' confidence to explore it, encouraging them to try out new and unfamiliar strategies. We need to think far more consciously about learning skills, identifying those we feel are most appropriate to a given activity and which at the same time stretch our learners' capacity along the development continuum.

Higher order learning skills are those which require the learner to become more independent of the tutor. They demand a facility with language and conceptual thinking, the rigorous and disciplined ability to exercise judgment and discrimination in deciding relevance, significance and causal effect, to make comparisons and identify logical connections and contradictions, to construct a rational argument or plan of action, to evaluate empirical evidence, to recognize how one's own beliefs, prejudices and emotional investments can influence and even compromise one's understanding. This is by no means an exhaustive list. My point however, is that these form a basis for more independent learning but they do not, in themselves, constitute exploratory learning, the highest point on the development continuum. That entails a more critical and challenging approach, where the learner is positively encouraged to question conventional wisdom and accepted opinion, including that of the tutor. The learning has moved into less certain territory, where it has become a matter of exploration and experiment. The tutor acts as a guide rather than someone with the all the answers, deliberately provoking doubt, skepticism and controversy, inviting innovative ideas and solutions. Such learning has moved far beyond mere hoop jumping and become truly dynamic, generating its own energy and momentum.

I am not suggesting that all learning should be delivered at this level. For many learning activities, this would not be appropriate, but I am advocating that we always try to locate the learning process at the highest point on the development continuum, compatible with the learning activity and the existing learning skills of the learners. The development continuum enables us think about how we approach the learning process as well as providing a goal, in the form of exploratory learning, toward which we can organize and direct our learning activities.

It may help to yet again use an example which moves along the continuum. Take the example of cooking. It combines both knowledge and skill and so avoids either extreme of the learning continuum, which might otherwise confuse the issue. It is possible to learn to cook simply through imitation, doing exactly what you are told. You do not ask any questions because the tutor's instruction is considered sufficient. You follow those instructions and are then expected to reproduce the finished result. This is, after all what recipe books amount to, manuals for what to do. However many people would want something more than this. They would perhaps like an explanation for why you might do something in a certain way, use one ingredient rather than another, why a technique is appropriate with one type of food and not another. In other words you are moving on to general principles. You are moving from merely copying to developing an understanding of why you use or do this, rather than that.

Armed with some general principles, you are now a little more independent. You can start to think and speculate what might happen if you did that or you tried that. Curiously, that independence is more likely to be enhanced if you had a cookery tutor to refer to, one who was prepared to engage rather than direct. Of course you can try continuing to establish general principles through trial and error, but this is not very efficient, and will result in significant and regular failures which you will find discouraging. The skill of the engaging tutor is not simply to tell you why things went wrong, but to guide you through analyzing what may have contributed to the problem and then help you to identify the cause. It is important to encourage the questions and speculations, as this indicates the learning is being more actively processed. It is not just a matter of passive acceptance, but instead generates an independent momentum to the learning. You may infer from quite separate pieces of learning that something else, which you have not actually been taught, is likely to be so. You are beginning to work things out systematically and logically.

The learning may challenge some of your assumptions about how you might approach food. Equally, where an engaging atmosphere prevails, you as the learner, should feel comfortable about challenging other people's assumptions, including those of the tutor. Why should you not question culinary orthodoxy? Your ideas might be a little eccentric but a useful debate may result, where everyone's thinking and imagination is stimulated.

Moving further along the continuum, you are beginning to use your own more creative potential and taking a more innovative approach. Your are adapting and modifying what you have been taught, exploring new possibilities, putting together your own recipes or maybe even developing your own distinctive cuisine!

I hope that by using this more familiar example I can demonstrate that the concept of a development continuum applies to all types of learning, regardless of the knowledge or skill components. Higher order learning on the development continuum may appear to be more intellectually demanding, and therefore only relevant to heavily knowledge-based learning, yet I would urge all tutors, irrespective of their subject area, to explore the potential of the development continuum and so empower their learners.

The learning paradigm is a device for helping us to clarify what we do. It avoids interminable debates about the distinction between teaching and training or academic as opposed to vocational learning. All learning can be placed within the paradigm, dependent on its knowledge relative to skill content and the degree of control and direction the tutor takes in the learning process.

A holistic approach

The learning paradigm however, is not sufficient to understand the entire picture. For that we have to consider the learner in a more holistic sense. The learners may well be exposed to the learning activity and the learning process, as organized and delivered by the tutor, but their experience of that will be something which they internalize. The impact of the learning upon them will be the result of an interaction between the objective learning and the subjective meaning and understanding they themselves construct from the experience. It could well be argued that this highly personal area lies well beyond the tutor's role to understand or take account of. But if we fail to recognize how crucially it may influence the learning and the way the learner views themselves in the process, our efforts will probably achieve little.

Learners cannot be put through a process and expected to come out at the end, like so many programmed robots. Each will be changed in a different way. They may demonstrate a shared competence in having achieved the learning objectives, but the learning will invariably have gone beyond those objectives and given rise to a range of unpredictable consequences which are peculiar to each individual learner. Some of those consequences may be profound, prompting someone to change the direction of his or her life, perhaps to go for the promotion previously felt to be beyond reach, or it may be relatively minor, equipping the individual with further skills which may give rise to a new interest.

The outcomes for different learners will vary, depending on their motivation, their circumstances, their feelings about themselves and how all those factors engage with the learning and with the tutor. Those factors may hinder or help the learning but they will certainly exert an influence. Tutors may remain unaware of the specific issues affecting each learner, but nevertheless they would be advised to be alert to how such issues may be impinging on the process and the outcomes. In this way they can help to reduce the obstacles to effective learning and better support the learners' needs.

I am not suggesting that all we have to do is be reassuringly sympathetic when learners are struggling with personal and domestic difficulties. Taking a holistic approach entails more than that. It is not just about responding to problems, it is about proactively building a relationship with your learners, actively developing an understanding where you can appreciate their perspective. You demonstrate that your focus is not exclusively concerned with the learning. You are there for them.

In addition to helping ensure the realization of the stated objectives, taking a more holistic approach provides the learner with an opportunity to more easily develop their learning potential in the fullest sense. They will move with more confidence toward the exploratory level of learning. While a holistic approach takes into consideration the negative and positive influences on the individual's learning experience, it also looks at the learners, not just in terms of their competence or otherwise in relation to the learning objectives, but also in relation to their learning capacity, their learning skills as perhaps demonstrated in a previous and maybe even unrelated learning activity. The learning skills however, may still be highly relevant and those skills should be recognized and acknowledged.

A holistic approach is central to the concept of engagement. The relationship between the tutor and the learner is crucial to the learning process and that relationship should engage the learner completely. The learning should provide a chance to grow and develop, not just in the prescribed manner but as a means to greater individual empowerment.

Summary Points

- The assumptions which underpin the distinctions between teaching and training are misleading. All those concerned with helping people learn are involved in transmitting knowledge and developing skills.

- The learning continuum enables us to conceptualize the relationship between knowledge and skill, with knowledge based learning at one end of the continuum and practical skills at the other. Most learning falls some way along the continuum, combining both knowledge and skill.

- We still retain many assumptions about knowledge being essentially theoretical and skills being practical, with knowledge learning seen as a higher order learning, requiring greater cognitive ability.

- Much academic, knowledge based learning requires learners to do little more than demonstrate their ability to remember large quantities of information. The reasoned analysis of that information may remain very limited.

- Developing skills, on the other hand, is a more active process, which may demand a complex and sophisticated application of principles in addressing particular problems and puzzles.

- The distinction between practical and theoretical learning indicates more about the relative status and value we still ascribe to scholastic discipline and technical proficiency.

☐ Because of these outmoded, but still persistent values, we routinely underestimate the ability of those involved in vocational learning and overestimate the ability of those involved in academic learning.

☐ The development continuum analyzes learning according to the degree of tutor control and learner autonomy, ranging from rote learning at one extreme to exploratory learning at the other. It helps us to consider how much we are encouraging our learners to think for themselves, to be more independent and confident to challenge conventional ideas.

☐ Tutors should be enabling learners to venture as far along the development continuum as is practically possible, providing them with the opportunity to learn in precisely the way demanded by a fast changing world, where initiative and resourcefulness are the key factors in achievement.

☐ The learning paradigm enables tutors to identify a more meaningful and useful strategy in designing learning and to be more explicit about the purpose of that activity, as well as enabling them to reflect on their relationship with their learners and explore ways in which it can be made more empowering.

☐ Just as holistic medicine assumes that you cannot treat a condition in isolation from the rest of the body, so learning should be viewed as an experience which may have many unpredictable consequences for the individual involved, causing them to reassess themselves, their lives and those with whom they share their lives.

QUESTIONS FOR REFLECTION

1. *What criteria do you use to rate the relative cleverness of people? Is it by qualifications, conventional success or by the questions they ask and the observations they make? How would you define cleverness?*

Qualifications and conventional success often indicate a knowingness in how to negotiate and play the system to one's advantage. But some undoubtedly start with a greater insight into the rules of the game by virtue of their background. Others, for their own reasons, may be unwilling to play the game. Either way, if you always expect cleverness to present itself in a certain predictable form, you may overlook those who have far more potential than even they, themselves may realize.

2. How far do you feel you are responsible for identifying unrecognized potential in learners and giving them the confidence to realize that potential?

Unless you accept a responsibility for your learners' development, beyond the narrow constraints of your program objectives, many individuals will remain oblivious to their own unfulfilled promise and valuable talent and ability will be wasted. Tutors remain in a very powerful position to influence learner aspirations for better or for worse.

3. How would you rate your own ability and cleverness? How much were you encouraged in the past? Did you experience any benefits or advantages in terms of your background? Do you feel you had to rely largely on yourself, on your own resolve and determination? In what ways do you think your personal history has influenced your attitude toward your learners?

Sometimes we take the benefits of our own background for granted and assume it was pretty much the same for others. We underestimate how much disadvantage saps confidence and dulls the spirit. Or maybe we feel we, ourselves overcame adversity, and so why can't others? But our own experience is not always a very reliable guide for understanding other people. It may make us overly judgmental, too quick to write people off because they do not measure up in our terms.

4. Where would you locate your subjects or areas of work on the learning continuum? Do you think it is more difficult to locate the skills required in a seemingly knowledge based subject, or to identify the underpinning knowledge necessary for competence in a given skills area?

Sometimes it is difficult looking at something familiar through an unfamiliar perspective. If you have always thought of your subject as essentially practical, it may take quite an effort to think of what your learners have to know in order to practice that skill. Similarly if you are engaged in largely academic teaching, you may not have ever considered the different tasks your learners undertake and the skills they require in their program of study.

5. Where would you feel comfortable as a tutor, working along the development continuum? What factors would you have to consider in deciding where it would be most appropriate to start on the development continuum with a given group of learners, and where you would expect to finish?

Your subject and the ability of your learners will obviously be influential factors. However, you may all too easily underestimate your learners and your subject may offer greater scope than you realize.

6. What would you personally find most challenging and demanding in moving along the development continuum toward more learner autonomy? What anxieties do you think your learners might have in being encouraged

to move in that direction? How far do you think your own attitude would reduce or increase learner anxieties?

Encouraging greater learner autonomy can generate some very complicated feelings amongst tutors. You may feel you risk being seen as surplus to requirements; the more they can do themselves, the less they need you, which is true in part. They do still need you but in a different way. You are no longer telling them what to do, but helping them decide what they should do. If you feel anxious about what might go wrong, you are likely to communicate that to your learners and establish a self-fulfilling prophecy. Because you had little confidence in your learners and expected them to get things wrong, they picked up on your anxiety, began to doubt their ability, saw themselves through your eyes and so got things wrong. And maybe your anxiety is such that you are not even able to give them the message that making mistakes is all right anyway as long as you can learn from them.

7. **What are your main sources of satisfaction as a tutor? Are they to do with getting learners through the course or program, or are they to do with empowering individuals, encouraging them to realize their potential and be more adventurous in their approach to their work? How far are your sources of satisfaction dependent on conventional measures of tutor performance?**

Sometimes it may seem easier to just get on with the job. Perhaps you doubt that anyone is going to reward you for developing more empowering relationships with your learners anyway. But surely this is about job satisfaction rather than just doing what is necessary. There are pressures, but if we simply succumb to them, and are not even interested in developing a more invigorating approach, then we are just simply marking time.

8. **What have been your most empowering experiences as a learner? What was it that made them empowering? How did they influence you and your life?**

It is really important to recall our own experiences as a learner and look at what we found empowering and why. They can provide an enormous incentive and inspiration for working with our own learners. Such experiences also enable us to realize the power of our own influence in our learners' lives.

4

The All-Singing, All-Dancing Pedagogue

Working as a tutor often feels like performing on a stage where you not only have to speak, but also write your own lines. Invariably, programs concerned with developing training skills are almost exclusively concerned with presentation techniques. A common practice when selecting training and teaching personnel is to require them to make a presentation. Freelance consultants are similarly put through their paces in order to evaluate their training delivery. I remain bemused by this preoccupation with what is essentially an ability to perform, and have, on occasion, been deliberately mischievous by inviting the assembled panel to become actively involved, asking them to respond to the issues I have raised. They are usually reluctant to participate and appear to regard my efforts as irritatingly provocative. My point is that helping people learn does not depend solely on simply talking at them, but also requires a dialogue between tutor and learners. How can you judge someone's potential to help people learn if you assume it is only a one way process?

Presentation skills are concerned with being able to communicate information in an accessible and interesting way. They are certainly part of the repertoire of essential skills any tutor should be able to demonstrate. The ability to organize and deliver your material in a coherent form, within given constraints such as time and resources, is undoubtedly very important. Controlling your nerves, or even panic, and speaking in a clear and confident voice, which commands people's attention are also fairly necessary. But if the spotlight remains on the tutor, the learners are reduced to no more than a passive, but hopefully attentive audience.

Teaching provides a correspondingly narrow focus. While the lecture format may no longer be the typical style of delivery in most educational institutions, it still predominates in higher education and underpins many lesson structures in other settings. There are occasions when a talk or lecture is probably the most effective means of sharing information with a given group of people. However the learning is very difficult to predict and will almost inevitably depend on how much effort the learner subsequently makes to integrate that information with their existing knowledge and understanding. In other words they will need to reflect on what they have heard, turn it around in their mind and make it meaningful and relevant to their experience. If they do not go through this more active process, the learning will be minimal. Expecting people to passively soak up information as if by osmosis, is generally a fairly ineffective way of ensuring they remember what they have been told.

There is a widespread acceptance now that people learn best by actively using the information presented to them. Much adult training, and increasingly education, relies on experiential learning, acknowledging this is generally a more successful strategy for ensuring genuine and lasting learning, which actually changes the way people think and behave. But even when learning is more active, the learners are not always encouraged to engage in the sort of dialogue I am proposing. Too often learners are left mouthing the lines, scripted by their tutors, playing their allocated parts, expected to ask the predictable questions, volunteer the routine observations, so that even the most experiential sequence becomes a comfortably, or tediously familiar exercise for the tutor.

Didactic distance

Lectures and presentations are where the tutor has exclusive control. The learners become the appreciative, or perhaps not so appreciative spectators. They may periodically be given a chance to ask questions or perhaps say if they have not understood the points made. Often this feels as if the tutor is simply looking for reassurance and approval. There can be tangible embarrassment at the end of a session when the tutor asks for questions and is greeted with echoing silence. Possibly the group is bored rigid and cannot wait to escape or perhaps they are so overwhelmed by the erudite exposition, they really cannot think of anything pertinent to ask. Maybe everything has been covered so comprehensively, there is little further to be said. Nevertheless tutors routinely expect such questions, if only as a grateful acknowledgement of their effort. But such interactions between tutor and learners may prove risky. They open up the possibility of being contradicted or put on the spot and so there is a feeling they should be carefully managed. The temptation is for the tutor to go through the motions of an almost perfunctory concluding exercise, which is designed to merely reinforce his or her role as an expert to whom the learners dutifully defer.

The pedagogues' skills are those of exposition. Their concern is with the content of the learning, ensuring their facts are correct, their information up to date, their technical skills well practiced. There may be flair in the presentation. A pedagogic approach is not synonymous with being dull. It is possible to be entertaining, to excite the curiosity and imagination of your learners in the same way as a compelling TV documentary. Considerable skill and enthusiasm is needed to organize and deliver information in an accessible, clear and coherent manner There are gifted individuals who are able to hold a group enthralled, and who may inspire their listeners to pursue the learning, investigating the topic further, following up points and ideas. This most passive of methods may still generate significant activity on the part of the learners, but there is no relationship between the tutor and learner, no *opportunity to engage*. The learning may or may not take place, dependent on the application and motivation of the learner. The role of the pedagogic tutor is not actually concerned with helping people to learn in the sense of working with learners. Their responsibility is to construct the most stimulating way of presenting the material.

Certainly, any one designing a presentation or lecture has to take some account of the listeners. It is important to be aware of their likely prior knowledge, interest and experience. How much can you assume and how much do you have to make explicit? In deciding how best to deliver the material, tutors will need to think about how they can make it relevant and meaningful to the listeners' level of understanding. Information that has been organized to emphasize the most important points, illustrated with examples the listeners can relate to, is much easier to digest. The very best exponents of this method also share something of themselves with their audience. They may impress an audience with their expertise but it will be their willingness to relate on a human level which will establish a rapport with their listeners. To this extent, even a one-way process of communication may begin to engage at both an intellectual and emotional level. But, as I have already said, the experience has to be internalized before it can be converted into learning. There is no provision for a two way dialogue apart, perhaps, from the occasional chance to ask the odd question.

A partial engagement

Most tutors would not wish to be associated with a didactic or pedagogic approach. It is regarded as overly rigid, evolving at a time when learners were regarded as so many empty vessels who needed to be filled with the prescribed learning. We appreciate the need for a more imaginative approach to learning delivery. The emphasis, however has been on the content and method of delivery rather than the learners and recognizing their needs. It is assumed that as long as the learning is well designed, the learners' needs are being met. Admittedly, much effort and attention was needed to improve standards in the organization of learning, and there is still room for further progress in this direction. Despite such efforts, we fail to appreciate how the learning relationship itself is still determined by more pedagogic influences.

We recognize that learners need to do something with their learning in order to incorporate it into their repertoire of skills or stock of knowledge. Telling, explaining and demonstrating are all very well, but unless the learner has a chance to *use* the knowledge or the skills, they are unlikely to develop any real competence. Practice is obviously crucial where skills are concerned. The application of knowledge is also a vital part of the learning process and not just as a means to demonstrate what has been learned. Learner performance is often assumed to provide a basis for assessment rather than form an inherent feature of the learning activity. It is all too easy to think of learners being exposed to a certain stimulus, and their subsequent response to that stimulus, simply used as an indicator of how much they have learned. This is an unnecessarily narrow way of looking at learner performance and one which contributes to high levels of anxiety among learners. Learner performance in the form of skills practice and knowledge application should be integral to the learning itself. This is an important distinction and shifts our perception of learning from stimulus and measured response to a participative activity, where learner input actually contributes to the ongoing learning.

Experiential learning is designed to promote learner input. It is a more learner-centered approach in that it quite consciously focuses on the learners' experience, both in terms of the experience they bring to the learning and their experience during the learning. Learners are given the opportunity to share their experiences and reflections on the learning presented. They are encouraged to participate in activities through which they will explore particular aspects of the learning and begin to discover or identify the important learning points. This is certainly a very much more time consuming method for helping people learn, but it is generally accepted that such learning will have a more lasting impact. The learners negotiate their own way toward the learning rather than being force-marched by the tutor. Experiential learning has a parallel in the discovery method which has been so influential in the education of younger children, but has made less impact on the teaching of older children, where the processing of vast amounts of knowledge demands a more intensive approach, although I would argue one where the learning is very much more short term.

Learners need to spend time working with the knowledge and the skills in order to consolidate the learning. This approach again may demonstrate significant extremes from incomprehensible exercises, seemingly designed to either humiliate or intimidate learners, to those which build real confidence and competence. The exercises and activities are derived from the knowledge and skill content, but again they cannot be selected without reference to the potential learners. There is little point in persevering with an exercise which might have appealed to the competitive urges of a more articulate and self assured group, but may only alienate less practiced learners. The appropriateness of any activity must be judged in terms of how far it meets the learning needs of particular learners. The success or otherwise of its implementation may be due to poor design, little connection between the learning objectives, content and exercise, unclear directions and inadequate or unconstructive feedback, but ultimately even though these may be expertly executed, if little attention has been paid to the learners and their specific needs, the effort will have achieved little.

Conscientious tutors will want to find out all they can about a given group of learners. In reality it is often very difficult to establish more than the most general information, perhaps some notion of educational level and occupational background, whether they are volunteers or conscripts and that is usually about it. This will obviously make planning with learners' needs in mind somewhat frustrating. Telepathy, unfortunately, is not a gift many of us are blessed with. Nevertheless we have to proceed even with this minimal insight into how our learners may present. Prior experience with similar groups normally helps, but one should always be prepared for the unexpected.

Tutors face an inevitable dilemma. They are required to thoroughly plan a given piece of learning and yet they often have only the scantest knowledge of their learners. They inevitably concentrate on designing and organizing the session in terms of the material. Even where they are working over a period of time with the same group, the curriculum still predominates and dictates their preparation. Occasionally, tutors may decide that, in the light of what they have already discovered about their learners, a revised strategy is needed. They realize that a group is not progressing at the anticipated rate, either they are struggling to maintain the pace or they are obviously treading water. The material has to be modified, exercises and activities adapted or substituted. The initiative however, remains with the tutor.

The relationship between tutor and learners is fundamentally determined by the tutor. The learners have no option but to comply with the tutor's demands. They are active in as much as they do what they are instructed to do, but they have little opportunity to influence the learning process. They are discouraged from questioning why they are being required to follow a certain procedure. Challenging the assumptions made by the tutor is likewise undesirable if they wish to preserve a favorable impression of themselves.

Even with experiential learning, the tutor is still running the show. Learners have a greater opportunity to explore their own thoughts and feelings, but only within well-defined parameters. Essentially, they are exposed to situations, or asked to reflect on previous ones and make the observations which serve the purpose of the learning objectives as defined by the tutor. In some respects, this can amount to a more deliberate manipulation than other less learner-centered methods. The relationship may appear more participative and inclusive. Learners are asked to share and discuss their experiences in order to further their understanding. Tutors may, themselves be ready to make personal disclosures and thereby prompt their learners to do the same. Valuable insights can be gained in this way and certainly there is a real exchange between tutor and learner. The method in itself does not, however guarantee the dynamic relationship in which true engagement can occur. Engagement depends on the attitude of the tutor rather than a selected learning technique. I have witnessed many tutors much practiced in the experiential approach, who nevertheless, expected little more of their learners than docile acquiescence.

It is still possible for the tutor to view the learners as so many potential converts. The learning process is then designed to induce a sort of revelatory catharsis, whereby learners suddenly see the light, like so many Sauls on the road to Damascus. In that blinding moment of understanding, they renounce unreasonable and outmoded beliefs. This is undoubtedly a powerful vehicle for change. But there is a danger that the learner succumbs and merely substitutes one set of dogma for another. If critical reflection and thinking have not been employed, the learner is simply made suggestible, easily persuaded by the latest fashionable orthodoxy.

We must move on from our pedagogic legacy where the tutor is always assumed to know best. Real power has to be shared with the learners. This calls for a very different relationship and a fundamental change in attitude. I am not suggesting that conventional tutoring methods have to be abandoned. They serve their different purposes but their limitations should be recognized. Learners need to be positively engaged and equipped to take part in a far more dynamic dialogue with their tutors. They may be wary of more demanding expectations, thinking for themselves and taking some responsibility for their own learning. The traditional relationship can be reassuring on both sides, each knows where they stand and exactly what is expected of them. Learners have to let go of the idea that tutors are still in loco parentis and be prepared to take risks and consider new possibilities.

But before we go on to examine further what we understand by engagement and how we might achieve it, I want to look at some of the most destructive ways in which tutors may relate to learners. I am highlighting extreme scenarios and while I am not suggesting these apply to any more than a minority in the profession, there is still a tendency for their influence to be very powerful and to undermine the achievements of more conscientious tutors. Their cynical attitude all too easily devalues any attempt to work more positively and constructively with learners.

Summary Points

☐ **Despite the emphasis placed on learner-centered methods in training and teaching, communication still appears to be largely in one direction.**

☐ **Training skills programs focus primarily on presentation techniques. Lectures still dominate in higher education, and form the basis of much of the teaching in further and adult education.**

☐ **Learners, who are expected to be little more than an appreciative audience, will have only the most limited involvement with their learning. Such passivity will seriously compromise the effectiveness of the learning process, as well as precluding the possibility of any engagement between learners and tutor.**

☐ **Providing the opportunity for learners to ask questions is a first step on the way to more active learning. However, that is often limited to a ritualized expression of the learners' attention and interest, rather than a genuine exchange of thoughts and ideas.**

☐ Activity-based learning certainly increases the chance of learners understanding and remembering the learning, although it often seems as though they are merely being put through their paces, required to practice and demonstrate a very precisely devised and circumscribed task.

☐ Experiential learning encourages a more reflective attitude. Learners are asked to participate in an exercise where the main objectives are to look at what happened, to reflect on how it felt and to think about what that means. It certainly does require a considerable involvement on the part of learners. Even experiential learning, however, may remain a very predictable and formalized process, where learners are expected to do little more than offer the observations and insights, which the tutor has already deemed to be appropriately significant and worthy.

☐ There is a danger that the greater involvement we expect of learners, the more vulnerable and susceptible they become to the suggestions of correct attitudes and ways of thinking espoused by the tutor.

☐ Real engagement requires a genuine dialogue, where learners are no longer required to just jump through the hoops provided, but are given the opportunity to be innovative and develop a reasoned alternative or contrary view to that of the tutor.

QUESTIONS FOR REFLECTION

1. *Which teachers or trainers stand out in your memory as most entertaining and which stand out as being most effective in helping you learn? Were they the same individuals?*

Perhaps they were, which would make them fairly remarkable individuals. All too often though, we remember the extraordinary personality and their particular eccentricities, rather than what we learned. They may have seemed larger than life, and in the process we were diminished in their shadow. Rather than encourage confidence, they are likely to make us feel ordinary and rather dull. It is the tutor who is more focused on their learners' needs, rather than themselves, who is really able to help people learn.

2. *How far is your selection of learning methods constrained by pressure on time and learner numbers? How much do you view learner-centered methods as a luxury you cannot afford given the resources available?*

Learner-centered methods are undoubtedly demanding in terms of time and do require reasonably sized groups . Nevertheless, we have most of us succumbed at times to conveniently citing pressure on resources as an excuse for resisting new and different ways of working, which we subsequently came to accept, appreciating benefits we had not expected.

3. How would you describe your own experiences of more learner-centered activities and programs? Have they been positive, or have they seemed a waste of time, or even disagreeable and intrusive?

If we have had positive experiences of learner-centered methods, then obviously we will feel more enthusiastic about adopting them. But we should be careful not simply to pick up ideas like magpies, and employ them without due consideration as to their suitability with any given group. Similarly, we should not allow ourselves to be overly swayed by negative experiences, condemning a method because it was unsuccessful on a particular occasion. There is a tendency in all of us to be too selective in how we use experience to support and reinforce our own ideas and judgments.

4. How far do you think hoop-jumping is inevitable in the learning situation? How reassuring are the hoops for both tutors and learners?

Maybe devising the hoops through which learners must jump is part of our role. Otherwise it would undoubtedly be difficult to measure what had been achieved. But the hoops may also limit our expectations in the learning situation. This may be a relief for tutors and learners alike. But each becomes locked into a purely instrumental approach to learning, where the outcomes are more important than the process. Sometimes we may feel that even though we may not be entirely in sympathy with a particular development, there is little we can do about it. If we accept the diminishing effect of hoop-jumping on the learning situation, there will be even fewer available in the future to critically evaluate its consequences, and less still confident enough to challenge it.

5. What sort of expectation do you have when you are trying to encourage learners to reconsider attitudes? Are you trying to persuade people to your point of view or are you looking to raise doubts and uncertainties which will generate their own reflections and questions?

It is very easy when you believe something is important, to seek to change someone's mind so that they agree with you. Yet changing attitudes can sometimes degenerate into crude indoctrination. Raising doubts and uncertainties may seem a very poor substitute for persuading someone by the strength of your conviction. However, perhaps helping learners to be more comfortable with doubt and uncertainty may make them more open, willing and able to weigh up the relative merits of a particular argument.

5

The Emperor's New Clothes

I have always been fascinated by this particular fairy tale. Perhaps I am just intrigued and amused by the way we routinely collude in the game of trying to make ourselves seem more important than we are. When confronted with something we do not fully comprehend, but everyone else appears to know about, we play safe and are reluctant to reveal our ignorance. Just as in the fairytale, this allows those peddling crap to profit at our expense. It also means there is less incentive for those operating on some elevated level of understanding to make their gems of wisdom more accessible to the rest of us. True popularizers are applauded, but there is often an ambivalence over the real merit of their contribution. It is generally assumed that anyone who can reduce knowledge to a more simple form is just lacking in sophistication. They are seen as lightweights.

Many of the teachers and trainers I have encountered appear to take a particular pride in refusing to dilute the integrity of their subject by bringing it down to a more basic level. They believe that if learners are not capable of operating at the level they judge appropriate, the problem is not their responsibility. Many will also be unwilling to take any active steps to motivate their learners. I accept that entry levels have to be identified in order to protect the learners as much as maintaining standards. But once someone embarks on a program of learning, it is surely the duty of whoever is running that program to present the learning in a manner which takes account of the learners' likely degree of difficulty.

Those pushing BS and the precious protectionists both pose serious problems for genuine learning. Because learners are in such a less powerful position, overawed by the apparent cleverness of the expert and painfully aware of their own limitations, they will be unlikely to ever suggest that perhaps they are simply the unwilling audience for someone else's arrogant ego-trip.

BS

I remember sitting through one year's series of seminars, when I was a university student, where there was another student who regularly dominated the proceedings. He would expound his erudite ideas at length, using language which only appeared to further obscure his impenetrable logic. I understood very little of what he said. I thought it was maybe my own limited intellect, or perhaps my impatience with academic niceties. I was not the most diligent of learners and not always properly impressed with the supposed elegance of this or that theoretical argument. But as the seminars continued, I sensed that others felt the same as I did. Maybe it was something to do with the glazed expressions and the excruciating silences in which we struggled to make some relevant response. The seminar leader seemed equally helpless in the face of this intellectual masturbation. None of us dared make a challenge. We were too intimidated, never sure whether we were really so thick or perhaps the guy was talking a lot of garbage after all. Essentially though, the dilemma was irrelevant. We were there to learn, and it was the seminar leader's responsibility to ensure we were all able to benefit from the process. The student spent the entire year parading his new clothes. Sadly, there was no little boy brave or naive enough to challenge the situation. We all meekly acquiesced and, as a result, learned very little, as well as suffering our all too fragile confidence to be eroded still further.

I have often encountered such individuals as tutors rather than learners in my career. Experience has taught me they are usually extremely ill at ease with their subject. They lack confidence in their own grasp, but cannot admit it to themselves or anyone else. So they survive by deliberately making the learning seem more difficult than it is. Tutoring in an area apparently so demanding lends them an aura of status and importance. They have a vested interest in maintaining the impression that their subject is so demanding that only the very able or clever will be able to cope with it. This serves two purposes. It enhances their own self-image. While they are actually very insecure, cultivating this perception of themselves as very smart helps divert attention from uncomfortable scrutiny. Secondly, learners are almost being set up to fail. The subject is accepted as so hard, it is taken for granted many will fall by the wayside. It is a self-fulfilling prophecy. The learners and everyone else expect that only a very select few will succeed and so the failure to provide effective learning is never acknowledged. It is in itself a neat strategy and it invariably works. Many learners have become casualties in this duplicitous game.

Fast talkers who consciously and deliberately rely on this strategy to avoid their own inadequacy are essentially bullies. They survive by playing on learners' anxieties and our natural reluctance to appear awkward and out of step with everyone else. Fast talkers intimidate their learners. We all tend to be impressed by things we believe are so clever that we are unable to understand them. There might be a nagging question as to whether this really is as clever as it is claiming to be, but our own self-doubt prevents the question ever being articulated. We feel we should understand and if we do not it must be our failing. We are clearly ignorant and without ability.

Fast talkers must continue to reinforce the self-doubt and so devise a whole series of strategies for undermining the learners. Willful obscurantism characterizes their method of presentation. Engaging with learners has to be avoided at all cost. Even where learners are invited to participate, the objective is to expose their weaknesses. Discussion will remain unrelated to their experience or conceptual capacity, exercises will be organized to make them more acutely aware of their failure to perform. Learners may, in a particularly hostile atmosphere, be subject to personal humiliation, although the fast talker has to be careful not to overplay this card, as the group may become so aggrieved they unite in protest. Far better to concentrate on one or two less popular individuals in the group, who will arouse little sympathy and whose misery will serve as a warning to the rest of the consequences of attracting undue attention. This will sound cold, cynical, calculating and cruel and it is indeed a despicable abuse of power on the part of any tutor. Yet I would suggest that most learners have either experienced or witnessed such behavior at some time.

To some extent, there is the potential to BS in all of us. I know that when

I have felt especially anxious about an unfamiliar subject area and my own credibility to deliver it, it is tempting to resort to mystifying waffle in an attempt to nonplus my learners into passive acceptance. This is not necessarily a consciously selected option, it simply emerges from one's own confusion. The words spill out in more and more complicated language and phrases, as though you are almost trying to convince yourself you are saying something worthwhile and significant. You use jargon to emphasize the distinction between those initiated individuals who should understand what you are talking about and the outsiders whose ignorance excludes them. Although I earnestly want to engage my learners, I am aware that, because I am less than certain in my role, I need to keep them at a safe distance. Engagement does require you to feel at ease with yourself, not always confident but at least comfortable.

The precious protectionists

While the BSers avoid engaging with their learners in order to conceal their own inadequacy, the precious protectionists are less preoccupied with their own anxieties. They are far more concerned with the questions, puzzles and challenges posed by their own subject. Learners who are able enough to understand those questions, puzzles and challenges will be taken seriously. Those who struggle will be viewed as tiresome hindrances, unworthy of any sustained attention. The legitimacy which we accord precious protectionists is an important means to understand why we defer to such fast talkers.

Precious protectionists are not interested in helping people learn as an end in itself. They will derive great satisfaction from working with very bright and able learners who share the same curiosity and fascination with their subject. Such enthusiasm on the part of learners stimulates the precious protectionists to pursue their own knowledge and understanding still further. It is their own development that concerns them. The learners are merely incidental. Precious protectionists believe in the notion of natural ability. Learners either have an aptitude or they do not. It is certainly not the responsibility of the tutor to help a learner discover and develop an aptitude that was not already very confidently asserting itself. Many tutoring skills would be regarded as spoon-feeding the learners, a pointless waste of time. Learners are either interested or they are not. Tutors should not be expected to concern themselves with learners' needs or motivation. They regard their subject as the only truly legitimate demand on their time, ingenuity and effort. They are dedicated people and will only engage with those who share their dedication.

Such people are usually experts in their field and resent having to trivialize, as they see it, their hard-won knowledge and understanding in order to make it more accessible to learners. They will be held in high regard by informed learners and even by those who are less informed. The latter will usually concede their unreasonableness in ever expecting to understand such elevated beings. While the fast talkers induce learners to blame themselves for their failure to succeed as a calculated strategy, the precious protectionists remain sublimely indifferent to their learners' progress or the lack of it. To put it bluntly, they are not interested. It is a tiresome distraction from their real work. Such individuals have an important contribution to make but, I would suggest, it is not concerned with helping people learn.

An exclusive club

Who is best equipped to tutor learners? Should it be someone who is an expert in his or her field, who is up to date with the latest developments, and whose reputation is both respected and acclaimed? Or should it be someone who is regarded as an excellent tutor? Ideally most learners would like both rolled into one. Practically, most learners have to make do with various diluted combinations of the two. But where should we put the emphasis? Is subject expertise more important than tutoring skills. Certainly when you look at the sort of status individuals enjoy, those regarded as subject experts achieve greater prestige than those who are simply thought of as good tutors. Scarcity value plays some part inevitably, although that perhaps depends on a fairly loose definition of what we mean by good tutors.

We have all had the experience of someone who is clearly passionate about the subject, knows everything there is to know about it and yet cannot communicate with learners. They are unable or unwilling to think themselves back to the starting point of the novice. They become impatient and irritated. There is no joy in the process of helping people learn. There is only joy in the absorbing interest of the subject. And yet our attitudes remain fairly indulgent toward such individuals. We admire their consuming enthusiasm. Perhaps we wish we felt as passionately about something. We presume that even if their learners are unable to learn very much directly, such learners are, at least exposed to a truly inspiring influence. We are prepared to overlook the sense of frustration and futility many of their learners routinely experience. Indeed we may even reproach those learners for not being sufficiently tolerant of this rare and brilliant creature in their midst.

Maybe we have some lingering and half conscious idea that certain knowledge is beyond most ordinary folk. Just as those pushing BS protect their position by creating the illusion of cleverness which most are too stupid to understand, so the genuine cleverness of the precious protectionists is similarly regarded as off limits, beyond the wit of lesser mortals. Learners are being rather presumptuous if they actually believe they might understand it. For if it could be made accessible to them, then it would not really be that clever after all. Simplifying ideas, reducing them to their essential principles, putting them in a more familiar context, renders them less powerful. The purveyors of those ideas may then seem less powerful themselves.

Maybe we need to maintain a distinction between ourselves and our learners. Maybe if we shared our knowledge too easily, our own status would be undermined. After all, if we removed the mystique and our learners discovered how much more straightforward everything could seem when taught in a lively and imaginative manner, they might be left wondering whether we were really so important after all. Formal learning is prized because it is seen as difficult – it is not something everyone can do. It differentiates between those who are able and those who are not. There is something of the exclusive club. If the membership is opened too wide, then we may appear to have devalued the exercise for everyone involved.

All of this is embedded in our notions of the distribution of cleverness among people. We justify our failure to make complex knowledge more easily understood by the complacent assumption that ability is limited. We decide that how much someone already knows is a reliable indicator for how much they might be *able* to know. How they present will determine what we expect of them. Given that most learners have been exposed to fairly indifferent tutoring which has dulled their curiosity, we conclude that the majority of learners have limited potential. We therefore regard more demanding learning as inappropriate, too difficult for them to manage. We continue to restrict access. Precious protectionists are an extreme example of something we all do. They are unwilling to compromise the integrity of their knowledge to make it meaningful for anyone not at their level of understanding. But to an extent, many of us feel that all we can be reasonably expected to do is present the learning in the standard format, and not question whether there might be alternative strategies which might more readily excite our learners' enthusiasm.

Light-weights

Is it any wonder that people have such ambivalent attitudes toward tutors. Think about the old adage, 'Those who can, do, those who can't, teach.' It may seem outmoded these days, but it still points to the way in which helping people learn remains an underrated skill. Teaching is often seen as a safe and unadventurous option, somehow less demanding. After all, your work is concerned with helping other people achieve. Essentially the only way of measuring your effectiveness is through others. And yet, when our learners do succeed or fail, it is primarily their success or failure which is identified, not ours. We are often seen to have only a very marginal, indirect involvement. Even when teachers produce consistently poor results in terms of learner failure rates, it is discouraging how automatically the learners are blamed for their failure. But we cannot have it both ways and so we are rarely credited when our learners do exceptionally well. It may seem that we never really put ourselves on the line. We can never be sure how much we have contributed and how much was due to our learners' hard work and effort.

Tutoring skills are poorly understood and consistently devalued even while we place greater and greater emphasis on the importance of learning. It is much easier to rate subject expertise. And so when tutors are recruited, there is usually much greater attention paid to how well qualified they are in their given subject specialty, rather than their ability to communicate that expertise with their learners. That is inevitable while we are so unclear about what we mean by the ability to communicate with learners. It is not just about being able to employ a range of techniques. It is the sort of relationship you are seeking to establish with learners, your willingness to engage.

Despite their adult status, learners are peculiarly vulnerable. By assuming the very role of learner, they are admitting something about themselves, that they are wanting, they are deficient and require the intervention of someone more knowledgeable and more skilled to make good that deficit. They have made themselves less powerful, focusing on those very aspects of themselves which put them at a disadvantage. Tutors can either capitalize on that disadvantage, remain oblivious to it or try to anticipate how to both support and empower learners at the same time.

The playful iconoclast

The virtue of the little boy in the fairy tale is that he was able to say what everyone else was thinking. All the other people were locked in their own little perception of reality, afraid that if they gave voice to their thoughts they would appear foolish and stupid. The role of the tutor is almost to be both emperor and little boy at the same time. You are responsible for the parade and hopefully have something more substantial to display, but you also need to be aware that not everyone will appreciate the spectacle in the way you intended and there may be many little boys who are simply left feeling bewildered and unimpressed. You need to give expression to their perception even though it appears an ungrateful response to all your hard efforts.

Taking the part of the little boy suggests another element in your approach. It is perhaps what I would describe as the playful iconoclast. This becomes essential when you, yourself, feel the beguiling urge toward self-important tendencies. They are hard to resist at times. Usually somewhere in all of us though, there is the bemused and somewhat ironic observer, ready to chuckle at all our absurd posturings. Tutors who can afford to take themselves less seriously are likely to win the trust and involvement of their learners, in contrast to those more studied individuals who never dare risk making themselves so vulnerable. I acknowledge this requires a degree of self confidence in the first place and is more difficult when one is already feeling anxious. The learning situation can readily and inadvertently erect all manner of icons. Learners may feel obliged to show dutiful deference, more so when they are unsure what it is they are supposed to be impressed with. Deference obscures genuine curiosity and inquiry. It can lead to a sycophantic collusion in reinforcing the influence of the icon. The role of the playful iconoclast is to undermine such conceits.

How many writers and other expounders of theories and ideas are themselves precious protectionists, or indeed maybe even fast talkers? Part of our role must be to help learners recognize these pretensions and develop their own critical faculties in assessing their worth. Learning is a serious business and I am not suggesting that we introduce a distracting flippancy into the exercise. However I do think learners should be encouraged to see all learning as the result of human endeavor and therefore as essentially fallible. People, even brilliant people, sometimes get things wrong or maybe they didn't quite manage the whole picture. Learners need to be given the confidence to evaluate the merit of different contributions.

Successful subterfuge

The fairytale is powerful because it demonstrates how susceptible we are to superficial frippery. We focus on presentation and assume that if it looks good, it must be good. Sadly our image-conscious modern world entices us still further in this direction. The learning situation is corrupted by it in the same way as other areas of human endeavor. It promises a dividend for those who can sell us an illusion. While ability is more often rated in terms of what people say they can do, rather than what they actually deliver, it is tempting to put the effort into maintaining appearances, to ensuring that everything appears an unequivocal success even when you know there are all manner of unresolved and messy issues which have been avoided. As a tutor, you may feel you have a vested interest in concentrating on the positive, convincing all interested parties that the learning has proceeded in an entirely predictable and creditable fashion. The learners may similarly decide that it is to their benefit to ignore their own misgivings and enjoy the reflected glow of being involved with something which is generally well regarded.

Being honest does not necessarily reap an obvious reward. And yet if we continue to perpetuate the notion that you cannot afford to admit to difficulties, differences, and all the many ways in which our labors do not always go according to plan, you miss valuable opportunities to learn, to examine why something produced unforeseen problems. We tell learners they can learn from their mistakes and then fail to demonstrate that important principle in the way we conduct our own work. I am prepared to admit that this particular idea has not always helped my own personal career. Success seems to demand a sophisticated degree of subterfuge.

The fairytale is a potent lesson about our readiness to be duped. We are all concerned to maintain an image of ourselves as competent and able. We do not like to admit to being ignorant, to not understanding, to being incompetent, especially when everyone else appears to be managing so much more successfully. And so we fabricate, we pretend, we try to convince others with our contrived assurance that everything is well. But we are rarely as confident as we appear.

The learning situation, above all others, must be one in which we feel safe to be honest with ourselves and with others. The tutor can only ensure this by being honest themselves and being alert to how their learners may be feeling. This requires empathy and courage. Both of these are more difficult when we have not yet dealt with our own anxieties.

Summary Points

☐ We often avoid revealing our ignorance when confronted with something that everyone else seems to know about. We may collude in enabling those who have a responsibility to explain and help people learn, to do the job badly and so rarely be challenged for their failing.

☐ Those pushing BS rely on making the learning seem more difficult than it need be. This enhances their own status as someone very clever and acts as an effective defense, deflecting attention away from their poor tutoring skills. Their learners' failure is easily explained in terms of the learning being demanding and the learners being rather limited. The tutor's performance is rarely scrutinized.

☐ Precious protectionists are experts in their field and do not expect to simplify their knowledge in order to make it more accessible to learners. They see their tutoring responsibility as incidental, and are only interested in those with a natural aptitude who can join them in their uncompromising enterprise.

☐ Many fast talkers and precious protectionists survive in adult learning because we are ambivalent about what we believe constitutes good tutoring. We still attach great importance to subject expertise. We harbor ideas about knowledge as currency, i.e. if it is too widely or easily shared then it becomes devalued. And so there is a tendency to maintain the mystique of learning, and we do not feel responsible for making learning more accessible.

☐ Those who are able to explain complex ideas and concepts in straightforward terms, who are able to think themselves back into the position of the novice, are often seen as lightweights. Their skills of exposition, instead of being highly regarded, may actually undermine their credibility within their field.

☐ Tutors need to be able to take on the role of the playful iconoclast, ready to take themselves less seriously, and to encourage a questioning and skeptical attitude amongst their learners. Cautious deference by learners stifles curiosity and inquiry.

☐ The modern-day preoccupation with presentation and appearances pressurizes many tutors into putting a positive spin on their efforts, even when a more analyzed review might identify particular shortcomings. Being honest and open about our performance leaves us vulnerable in today's success driven society. But the learning relationship relies fundamentally on openness and honesty, being able to admit to mistakes, to uncertainty, to ignorance. Unless learners feel safe enough to take such risks they will miss valuable opportunities to learn.

QUESTIONS FOR REFLECTION

1. *How comfortable do you feel admitting your ignorance on a subject, or your difficulty in understanding an idea? Do you feel that you risk losing credibility by acknowledging your limitations?*

While most of us will judge the overall context in which we might face this dilemma, and respond on the basis of how far we can trust people not to take advantage of our vulnerability, we still need to examine to what extent we model a defensive attitude to learners which suggests that admitting to limitations is a regrettable indication of weakness, rather than a positive attempt to learn and develop oneself.

2. *How do you feel when you have to cover a topic with which you are not as familiar as you would like to be? Do you find yourself retreating behind obscure language which disguises your struggles to say something meaningful or coherent?*

It is very easy to feel so anxious and lacking in credibility in such situations that you want to avoid at all costs any sort of exchange with your learners. Even the prospect of an observation or question can be disturbing. And so we sometimes ensure our learners' dutiful compliance by exploiting their feelings of unworthiness in the learning situation, and by elevating our own status, using unfamiliar descriptions, explanations, jargon and references with which we hope to steam-roller the session to a speedy and uninterrupted conclusion.

3. *Do you sometimes feel frustrated with your learners' lack of knowledge and understanding and the demands they make on your time and ingenuity? Do you find yourself responding more warmly to those learners who demonstrate a quick and confident grasp of what you are trying to say?*

It is often very hard to empathize with the difficulties learners experience. We are so familiar with our subject that we may become impatient with their tentative and faltering efforts. We may feel that they take the joy out of the enterprise for us, that we are forced to adopt a more self-conscious and labored approach in order to address their needs. Some level of impatience at times is only natural, but if this is a fairly routine reaction then you may need to consider whether you are really in the right job.

4. *Do you feel there might be a danger in taking the part of the 'playful iconoclast' that you may encourage learners to devalue the learning and*

lose sight of its serious elements? Perhaps you feel that such an attitude will only confuse learners, by inviting skepticism while still demanding diligent and conscientious commitment to the learning process.

It is crucial that the tutor models both the diligent and conscientious commitment to the subject and to the learners, and at the same time a constructive skepticism which leads to greater understanding rather than dismissive cynicism. This is quite a demanding combination. It is about saying there are no 'sacred cows' and I don't need them anyway to still care about what I'm doing.

5. Do you feel that the pressure to appear successful in all endeavors makes it difficult to be honest about what really takes place in the learning situation? How far do you think that such pressure contaminates the experience for learners?

You may doubt whether the learning situation can be any different from any other area in society, that it is impossible to see ourselves and our learners in splendid isolation, untouched by the dictates of the modern world. I would argue however, that we should be providing an alternative model, that too often organizations are seriously compromised by the collective collusion in pretending that everything is working more efficiently and effectively than it really is. Opportunities are missed to address problems until they become so obvious they can no longer be ignored and much damage may already have been done. We need to challenge this pressure before it becomes so taken for granted no one can imagine an alternative.

6

Anxiety and Empathy in the Learning Relationship

Part One – Tutor Anxieties

The learning relationship is often full of anxiety for both tutors and learners and, until those anxieties are properly understood, they will remain as resolute blocks to any real understanding. Until we are able to explore our own feelings and expectations and also those of our learners, we are constantly confusing what is actually happening in the learning situation. We mistake our learners' motivations as well as our own. Sometimes we negatively reproach ourselves and sometimes we just become exasperated with the seemingly impossible and unreasonable demands being made upon us. We need to clearly identify the source of our own anxieties and examine how we deal with them. Only then can we move on to work positively with our learners. By getting more in touch with our own feelings, we are also better able to empathize with theirs. Tutors tend to try and avoid this uncomfortable and even threatening issue. They wish to preserve their image as competent and confident professionals. Matters of personal anxiety are something you might admit to at the beginning of your career, but it seems less and less acceptable as time goes by. Nevertheless those anxieties remain to a greater or lesser degree and continue to influence the way we relate to our learners.

As with any other role, it feels strange to begin with, as though it is not really you, as though you are somehow pretending, just acting the part. You wonder to what extent do you really appear credible. A lot of our anxieties as tutors stem from this original self-doubt. There are feelings primarily concerned with ourselves and feelings arising from our interaction with learners. They continually influence each other but it is useful to distinguish between them so we may more clearly understand how and why we are reacting as we do. Firstly, I want to deal with how we view ourselves, the sorts of expectations we have and our fear of being vulnerable. Secondly, we will look at our preoccupation with maintaining control and, finally, I will examine our concern over challenge and rejection.

Our own worst enemies

While I have argued that subject expertise generally commands greater prestige than tutoring skills, there is an equally unhelpful assumption often made, which appears to run contrary to that attitude. When I first joined further education, it was fairly commonplace to expect teachers to deliver lessons in subjects where they may not necessarily have any particular expertise. Given pressure on staffing budgets, there are still probably many learning situations today in which tutors are called upon to deliver sessions where they are just about one page ahead of the learners. Pragmatism has always been rationalized with the belief that, if you have tutoring skills, they can be applied regardless of the area of learning. I was certainly expected to be unfailingly flexible in what I taught, which no doubt stretched me and developed my own expertise, but I am not convinced it was always in the best interest of the learners.

It is not fair on tutors or learners to have someone responsible for organizing and delivering a learning program who is not sufficiently confident and familiar with the material. That does not mean you have to be the expert, capable of answering every conceivable question. It does mean however, you should know the territory well enough to be able present the material in the most accessible and relevant way for your particular learners, identifying all the potential hooks, points on which you can deliberately exercise their enthusiasm, as well anticipating the areas where there will be the greatest confusion and difficulty. If you are still struggling to come to grips with the subject yourself, you are unlikely to act as a very competent guide. The only possible advantage you may have is your ability to at least appreciate the learners' confusion, although sympathy is probably about all you will have to offer them.

In an ideal world, learners should have the benefit of tutors who are properly competent, both in terms of their teaching or training skills and their confidence with their subject. We do not live in an ideal world and I know many individuals are still being asked to do the almost impossible. It is something that should be discouraged and recognized for the bad practice it really is. Expediency does not excuse exposing tutors and learners to a situation which all will find frustrating and of limited value.

Nevertheless, we should not confuse this quite justified concern with the often all too unrealistic expectations we make for ourselves. We may know our subject reasonably well, but still we worry that perhaps we are not enough of an expert to actually stand up there and direct other people's learning. We fear the questions and probing which might undermine our credibility and expose us as fraudulent shams. We have perhaps an idealized construction in our head of the perfect tutor. Maybe it is the flawlessly presented individual who effortlessly commands authority, exuding confidence with every word and gesture. Maybe it is the charismatic guru who inspires respect and even devotion with remarkable insights and deep wisdom. Maybe it is the technical genius who knows everything there is to know about their subject, who is familiar with every contribution and area of developing knowledge. These are obviously mythical characters, but they may powerfully influence our attempts to devise a particular style. Assuming any role, we start out with certain models in our head which we try to emulate. Depending on how we judge our performance, we may need to try a different character or perhaps just modify the existing one so as to achieve a better fit. Inevitably, we end up with a compromise between the idealized model and our own more limited selves.

The idealized models can be useful in helping us to clarify the approach we want to take. The danger is that we constantly compare ourselves against some impossible creature. We so want to get it right, we can easily become discouraged if we feel we are not performing to the standard we have set ourselves. Even if you have delivered a quite successful session, it will be the moments when you felt unsure and uncomfortable, when the right word just would not come, when you did not really understand someone's question, when you temporarily lost your logical thread, that will stay in your mind, nagging away like so many troublesome and unquiet spirits. We are invariably our own hardest task masters.

It always comes as something of a surprise on tutoring skills programs when participants have the opportunity (one they do not immediately relish) of observing themselves on video, to discover they rarely appear as nervous as they were actually feeling. The panic we were all too painfully experiencing is, usually surprisingly well disguised. We are better actors than we imagine or give ourselves credit for. And just as we are all too aware of when our carefully prepared session plan has gone somewhat adrift, and we forgot that really good example to illustrate that difficult point, our learners are probably quite oblivious to all these various hiccups. We are acutely conscious of such mishaps, because they are reminding us of the discontinuity between the perfect model and our own more humble efforts. Our learners do not require such paragons to enjoy effective and valuable learning.

The human face of tutoring

There is something about being a 'good enough' tutor. It is often our very human qualities which make for a more meaningful relationship with our learners. They prefer someone who occupies a less elevated place, who is more open and approachable. While we are anxious to convey an image of competent professionalism, which is as it should be, we should not forget our greatest strength in engaging our learners is our own personality. As tutors, we need to be authentic, to be true to ourselves. This might seem something of a contradiction when I have already said that what we do resembles a practiced performance. But just as a gifted actor or actress allows some essentially vulnerable part of themselves to be expressed through a character, so we too should be prepared to share some of our weaknesses as well as our strengths. This may leave us feeling very exposed and everyone has to judge how, and to what degree, they consider this appropriate with different groups. But I would argue that if you are not prepared to make yourself at least a little vulnerable with your learners, they are unlikely to lower their defenses with you. Until you establish such an atmosphere of trust, people will be reluctant to take risks or be receptive to new and challenging learning.

Although I have described this in terms of showing your weaker sides, I am not suggesting you subject your learners to an embarrassing display of your various neuroses! Tutors, like everyone have their fair share. It is better that you recognize them, understand how they influence your attitudes and behavior and try to come to terms with them. Only then can you feel sure enough in yourself to be comfortable meeting your learners' needs. I remain convinced that anyone working with vulnerable people should go through this process and learners are, potentially vulnerable people. They are subject to the tutor's direction and evaluation, which may enhance or damage their self-esteem, depending on the skill and insight of the tutor.

I would strongly recommend that all tutors experience some process of introspection, either through counseling or some other means to look at their own motivation, their expectations of themselves and their learners and their routine defense strategies. Understanding how we relate to ourselves and others is crucial to removing the barriers which prevent us from communicating openly and positively with others. If we are unkind to ourselves, imposing unrealistically high standards, concentrating always on what we have done badly, believing that we have to constantly justify our worth, then we are more than likely to show a similar unkindness to our learners. I am not suggesting that all tutors need to go through some period of therapy, but I do believe they have a responsibility to ensure they are not subjecting their learners to some unresolved insecurities or conflicts within themselves.

While it is important to acknowledge this more vulnerable side of ourselves, it should not then be used as a means to win sympathy or turn the learning relationship into one of mutual support. Revealing your human side is only a means to an end, and that is to open up a more meaningful channel of communication between yourself and your learners. Your primary objective is to support their learning. That must be the guiding principle in deciding the appropriateness or otherwise of any particular strategy or approach.

We should be comfortable allowing our learners to see the individual behind the role. Professionalism demands that we be efficient, but that efficiency does not have to be so obviously demonstrated that our learners find it daunting. It is possible to be efficient and also relaxed and approachable. Humor is a vital resource in all human relationships. It can be used to reduce anxiety in all manner of situations. The style of humor, so long as it is not offensive, is not the issue, it is the implicit message that this is not a situation where people are going to try and impress or intimidate one another with how important, clever or powerful they are. It is about deflating such affectations. To this end, I see actual benefits in admitting to mistakes if you can then convey the idea that mistakes provide an occasion to learn and develop. Similarly, if a learner is sometimes able to help explain a point more effectively than you, this too would seem a positive indicator of the atmosphere you had established

Our anxiety as tutors makes it very difficult to drop the professional mantle and relax sufficiently to be ourselves in the way I am advocating. It is certainly something that comes more easily with the increased confidence of experience. However, as people become more experienced, they are less inclined to jeopardize their hard-won credibility by allowing a more personal style to emerge. They remain with the safe, impersonal image they have so carefully cultivated. I am urging a different approach, one which focuses on combining professional competence with a more human presentation, one that expresses the uniquely personal qualities of the individual tutor.

Some may object and argue it is necessary to depersonalize the learning situation, so that people concentrate on the learning rather than the personality of the tutor, who they may not necessarily like anyway. But however much we may try to do that, we cannot help expressing something of ourselves. We are not automatons. The way we look, the clothes we wear, our posture, our gestures and expressions, our voice, the words we choose, our habitual responses in situations, all reveal us in a unique and characteristic manner. People will react to us as individuals no matter how much we may try to hide behind a professional mask. I am convinced from observing many tutors and groups of learners over the years, that people are more accepting of each other when there is a genuine openness, when the defenses and pretences are lowered and an altogether more honest and enduring respect may flourish. Perhaps some of your learners might not like you in the sense you would never be a chosen friend. The relationship should nevertheless be one where you do at least come across as someone they can trust and have confidence in. This is far more likely if you have established a relationship where they have a sense of who you really are and not just the front you would rather hide behind.

As both a learner and a tutor I have had the opportunity to observe all sorts of different individuals at work and come to the conclusion there is no ideal tutoring personality. We are all unique and it is that infinite diversity which makes the dynamics of the learning situation so endlessly fascinating. The only proviso I would make is that anyone contemplating a tutoring role should at least enjoy and take delight in the process of communicating with others, even if the prospect of doing so with a group is initially fairly terrifying. People might be naturally extrovert or perhaps more reflective, but they all have the potential to be effective tutors.

Learners have the option to learn in other ways than the direct face-to-face relationship with the tutor. Distance learning is one method, computer assisted learning is another. They are valuable, additional strategies in the learning repertoire. However the role of the tutor is still primary, not because they provide more attractively organized material – they very often do not. Their coverage of the subject will inevitably be less comprehensive. Learners working on their own have the additional advantage of being able to work at their own pace, so why do we still prefer the human experience? It is precisely because of our need to learn and develop through social relationships. We are social creatures. We depend on each other for approval and reassurance. We are stimulated by the exchange of thoughts and ideas. This is how we naturally grow and develop. It is the tutor's role to create the sort of atmosphere that promotes that learning. They will only be able to achieve this if they engage with their learners and this involves sharing something of themselves.

The Grand Plan

Talking to many fledgling tutors, I find their main anxiety is invariably around losing control. This may be concerned with losing control of the material, it may be about losing control of one's own nerves or it may be about losing control of the group. All of these possible scenarios generate real fear and tension. They are, in part related to the expectations we have of ourselves but they also involve how we interact with our learners.

Losing control of your material is the nightmare even many experienced tutors still dread. They may have run numerous programs, but faced with planning and delivering a new course, the anxieties start to mount. Thorough planning is essential. It is not just about the preparation on paper but the thinking preparation that goes on inside your head. I am not concerned here with the technicalities of planning. Instead I want to examine some of the ways in which our anxieties may intrude and distract us from efficient planning and delivery.

Faced with the prospect of delivering a session on a particular topic, even one we are reasonably familiar with, we may still panic and imagine there is even more material we need to access. It is entirely likely that our existing knowledge is sufficient, but we almost need to explore further so that we have the comfort of additional, if unnecessary information. It makes us feel better. We then need to work that material into some sort of logical sequence of learning, and the more we have, the more time consuming that process inevitably will be. Sometimes, we get overwhelmed with the task before us and lose sight of whose needs are we trying to meet. Are we simply trying to reassure ourselves and impress everyone with our erudite grasp of the subject, or are we instead looking at it from the learners' perspective and organizing the learning to meet their identified needs? In which case, we need to keep asking ourselves, what they really need to know, do or understand to achieve the stated learning objectives. This helps to discipline our approach and prevent our own enthusiasm, curiosity or anxiety from taking us off on so many absorbing tangents.

Our main anxiety however, will still be at the point of delivery. We have our carefully detailed plan and all our assembled material. We may even have enthusiastically decided to incorporate some audio-visual aids which adds yet another unpredictable element to worry about. Will the equipment work? What do I do if it doesn't? We need a plan to organize the learning, and ourselves. At the same time, we still need to be flexible and respond to circumstances as they arise.

Some inexperienced and highly nervous individuals, when faced with the prospect of delivering a session, are driven to write a script rather than a plan. They derive great consolation from their security blanket and cling on to it for dear life, convinced it is the only salvation between them and total, annihilating chaos. Their consuming concern to follow the script at all costs ensures the learners' involvement will be minimal. The script is used as a defensive barrier between themselves and their learners. Clearly most tutors are not reduced to such an agitated state – well not routinely, anyway. Nevertheless we all need prompts or a guide as to what comes next, the main points we want to get across, but such prompts should still be flexible and simple to follow. The object is not to become so preoccupied with your material – or indeed the equipment – you forget those who should be the real focus of your attention.

It may well happen that a valuable learning point arises you had not actually anticipated. Do you ignore it because it is not in your master scheme? Do you carry on regardless, fearing any deviation may cause you to abandon the entire plan? It will always be a matter of judgment, deciding how important a point might be to discuss. given the time available. It is not always easy making such decisions on the spot, especially when you might feel anxious over how well qualified you are to deal with the particular point anyway. Does it really matter though that you are not in a position to give an authoritative response? There might be value in just discussing the question and encouraging an exchange of views, with the added assurance you will get back to them when you have had the chance to check on the matter a little further.

Your plan should never be so rigid that you cannot respond as different issues arise. Sometimes you might spontaneously decide that the particular way you have organized a session suddenly does not make sense and is unlikely to work. Change it, alter the order, scrap something if you really feel it is unnecessary. If learners are clearly struggling to understand a difficult concept, or strenuously resisting a new idea, there is little to be gained by plowing on regardless, simply because you have set yourself specific goals in a certain period of time. Give them the time to absorb the learning and make it meaningful in their own terms. Time is something you will always be juggling with and it requires a constant process of reviewing and rescheduling. Where have I got to? What have I still to get through? Do I need to spend as much time on this as I thought? Having already answered that point earlier on, do I really need to go over it now? Is this group ready and able to cope with the next exercise or should I give them something less demanding for the moment? Have they all had enough and is it better leaving this bit until the following session? These are the sorts of judgments you are having to make most of the time. Hopefully, if your planning has been sufficiently thorough, you are well enough prepared, but this does not mean you have to slavishly follow the plan, heedless of how your group is responding. It is an indication of a confident and competent tutor, that when you recognize you are not hitting the spot, you are prepared to throw the plan out of the window and start again. You are still in control of your material, even though it might not always feel like it. The material is only a means to an end, namely the learning achieved by your group. It is for you to decide how best to use it to achieve that end.

Stage-fright

Most people, when they are first faced with the prospect of talking to a group of people, in whatever context, be it a speech, a presentation, a lesson or a training session, have had to deal with the problem of nerves. Many are overwhelmed by a sense of mounting panic. It is something we have probably had little experience of in our normal everyday lives and we feel very unprepared. Our bodies can prove all too unreliable and unhelpful in the circumstances. Most of us have had to deal with the dry mouth, the sweating hands and the shaking hands and knees. We wonder why we are putting ourselves through such an ordeal, and surely we're never going to be any good at this – who are we really kidding anyway? It doesn't help that most other people appear so much more in control. We feel we are the only ones to suffer in this way. But as I said earlier, we are all extremely good at hiding those nerves and delivering a far more poised performance than we are aware of, or give ourselves credit for.

Our anxiety is understandable. Without feedback that we did in fact look quite assured and in control, we can only imagine others see us in the same way we experience ourselves. We feel very vulnerable, as though every little last quirk and foible is open to scrutiny. We worry about our mannerisms. We worry about how we sound. Will we be able to resist the urge to jabber in an effort to get it all over and done with as soon as possible? Will we able to speak loud enough or will our throats just dry up and not permit any sound to escape? Will people understand our accents? Will they critically evaluate what we're wearing? Will they think it's too casual or too smart? I have even heard someone decide their wardrobe on the basis of what would least show their perspiration marks. All of these anxieties have been shared by different tutors and it often helps just to know we are not alone.

There are the obvious stress relieving techniques that many people use to help them in such situations. Different approaches work for different people. Some find deep breathing and other relaxation routines very calming, others depend on a concentrated mental focus on the task at hand as a preferred strategy. There are those who like to be alone and undisturbed beforehand and those who rely on the support and encouragement of friends and colleagues. Some people, in their preparations, like to imagine the impending scenario and try and anticipate how they would deal with various eventualities. In this way, they assume greater control of the unknown which is the principal factor in their fear. Many might find such a method too elaborate and instead put their mental energies into positively massaging their self-confidence. They think about all the difficult tasks they have already successfully accomplished, especially ones most similar to tutoring. These are just a selection of the approaches which can be taken.

Sometimes though, it is a matter of very simple, practical advice. If you are worried about your voice drying up, make sure you have a drink available. If you think your knees are going to knock, then sit down or if you need the advantage of height, lean against a table. If your hands are liable to sweat, have tissues or a hanky to hand. If you start to stay something and suddenly cannot remember what you wanted to say next, apologize without getting any more flustered and say you need a minute or two to collect your thoughts.

In the meantime you might suggest people discuss with their neighbor the most important issue for them to have emerged so far, or some other such distracting question. It is amazing how easily you can then recover from what seemed like near disaster. It has happened to most tutors. There is no need to reproach yourself as a total failure. The real skill lies in not letting the moment overwhelm you, quickly sorting out where you go from here and simply carrying on.

As I have already indicated, mannerisms are something we are acutely conscious of. We all have them, be they an habitual gesture or a frequently repeated word or phrase. They are not necessarily a problem. Certain mannerisms are often seen as no more than a rather endearing characteristic of a particular individual. They only become a problem in the learning situation when the mannerisms divert attention away from the actual learning. It is not very productive if you have a group so fixated on the way you constantly pace up and down, or counting the number of times you say 'you know', that they are utterly unable to concentrate on the subject at hand. These are mannerisms that need to be controlled. However, while we are very aware of other people's mannerisms, we are not always so aware of our own. We all benefit from feedback. Maybe you could arrange for a trusted and constructive colleague to sit in on one of your sessions and give their view of how you come across. Alternatively you could even mount a video camera in the room to observe yourself in action. You might not be able to get rid of the mannerism overnight. Indeed there is a tendency once you become aware of it, to get quite discouraged at how often you engage in the behavior. I became acutely and painfully aware of just how regularly I used the word 'actually' after it was pointed out to me. But it is something you can slowly gain control of, just as you learn to deal with your more general levels of anxiety.

The double act

Co-tutoring is another option that may be considered. With large groups of learners, it is almost inevitable. Perhaps the subject matter is very demanding, or requires different but complimentary expertise. Perhaps the learners need more one-to-one attention. Maybe the tutors feel they want additional support, someone with whom to share the load. Whatever the reason, the dynamics of the learning situation are altered. It is no longer just the individual tutor and the rest of the group.

For the tutors, it can feel very reassuring to have an ally. You no longer have to be center stage all the time. It is possible to take a break and have the opportunity to collect and refocus yourself, to recharge your batteries. The stress and pressure never builds to a point of becoming too overwhelming. You also have someone who can help get you out of trouble. If you feel yourself losing your thread or are at a loss as to how to answer a question or deal with an awkward situation, you have someone else to fall back on, who will, hopefully, be able to provide another perspective and maybe another solution.

Co-tutoring can be conducted on the basis of turn-taking, where you each have responsibility for separate parts of the session, or as a double act where you combine to work together throughout. Both require careful planning, so you each know what is coming next. Even with turn-taking, it will probably feel more natural if the resting partner makes occasional contributions from time to time. Any subsequent 'rescue,' which may become necessary, will then appear less obvious. One word of warning however. Do not make the mistake of setting yourself up in competition with your partner, or even attempt to compare performances in terms of who was better, provided that you both have the basic competence to deliver the learning. This will only be self-defeating and possibly jeopardize your relationship. Everyone has his or her own unique style and learners appreciate this more than anyone.

For the learners, co-training can certainly provide a more varied and stimulating experience. We all relate to people in our own way and groups may be grateful for the different sorts of inputs which different tutors will make. However, the process of engagement may become more difficult, depending on how the relationship between the tutors is experienced by the learners. Tutors who simply see themselves as facing the enemy together may reinforce each other's anxiety and negative view of the learners. They draw closer together in order to exclude the learners. They support one another by reinforcing the 'us' and 'them' perception. On their own, they may have moved closer to the learners. Just as when we attend a social gathering where we hardly know anyone, we are far more willing to make the effort and get to know people if we are on our own, than if we are with someone. Relying on someone else makes us less inclined to take the initiative and be more open.

Alternatively, you may have co-tutors who have their own shared agenda which renders the learners fairly obsolete. Maybe there is some tension and rivalry which is driving them to constantly try and score points off one another. This will obviously be very uncomfortable for the learners. More entertaining will be the tutors who turn the learning session into a comedy routine, using the opportunity to demonstrate their unfailing wit and repartee. Skillfully handled, this can be a valuable way of relaxing and engaging the learners. More often than not however, the learners are expected to be no more than an obliging audience.

Co-tutors, even more than those working on their own, must consciously and deliberately make space for learners to be engaged. They need to examine how their own relationship, as expressed during the learning process, impacts upon the learners. Are they actively encouraging the learners to be involved, or are they simply relying on one another to fill the space?

Controlling the mob

We now need to move on to one of the most complex and contentious issues tutors have to deal with. In a simple sense, the tutor's role is to help people learn, but in order to do that in a collective context, it is necessary to exert a degree of control and authority over the group. This is where inappropriate and unfortunate models from school tend to confuse our understanding. I am not always so convinced they are any more appropriate with young people, but they are certainly counter-productive in an adult learning situation.

As a tutor, you automatically feel outnumbered by your learners. With large groups of over twenty, this is accentuated, and your role may indeed seem more concerned with crowd control. The temptation is to believe that the only way you can command attention is by exercising your authority. In certain circumstances that may be true. No one will appreciate a tutor who has abdicated responsibility, unable to maintain any sort of purposeful order or offer a sense of direction. Sometimes a loud and imposing voice can be a considerable benefit. Sometimes I wish I was several inches taller. Sometimes you do need to assertively remind people there are certain ground-rules to be observed and objectives to be achieved. However, there are also many other additional strategies you can employ in working constructively with your group.

Before we go any further though, it may be useful to pause and examine some of our feelings as tutors when dealing with different groups. Anticipating any group, we wonder what they will be like. Will they be interested in what we have to say, or will they just sit there looking bored and fed up? Will they be far more on the ball than we had been led to believe and become impatient with our more limited offering? Will they start raising all sorts of awkward issues which we are not sure how to handle? Will they refuse to cooperate and not participate in the discussions and exercises we have arranged? Will they just argue with every point we try to make? It is these sorts of nightmare scenarios which every tutor dreads. It is the prospect of losing control of the situation, seemingly at the mercy of a hostile and unruly rabble.

Part of our acute anxiety in having to deal with this sort of problem arises from our expectation that we should always be in firm control, and that it is a sign of weakness to allow the learners to exercise very much initiative. They should simply be following our directions and any possible insubordinate deviation should be decisively discouraged. This attitude automatically assumes that tutor and learner are engaged in a struggle over who will dominate. Any faltering on the part of the tutor, and the learners will have the upper hand. Power and authority must always remain with the tutor, otherwise chaos and anarchy threaten. Tutors believe they have to subdue their learners to avoid any disorder and unrest. This may be done overtly by adopting an imposing and domineering attitude toward learners. This can take the form of the benevolent dictator as much as the obnoxious bully. A more subtle version might involve the uncompromising, not-to-be-contradicted expert or the patronizing mummy/daddy who knows best approach. Whatever the style, the tutor has defined the learning situation as one where they either win or lose control, depending on how determined they are in their efforts to dominate their learners.

Why is it necessary to exercise control in this way? Of course individuals who adopt such strategies justify them in terms of the disorder that would otherwise result. If you view and then treat your learners as no more than potential miscreants, they will eventually fulfill the role you have designated for them. Some learners actually prefer a more controlling tutor who defines the learning situation in familiar terms of authority figure and dutiful subjects. They do not have to think for themselves or take responsibility. But this is a very limiting option and, while it serves the anxieties of some tutors in their need to control, there is no opportunity for the learners to function as anything more than so many obedient cogs.

Yes, all tutors experience considerable anxiety about their ability to handle different groups, but encouraging a more open and democratic relationship with your learners is not a sign of weakness. They do not have to agree with your every word to show respect. Nor do they have to demonstrate a reassuring deference to affirm your authority. You can instead exert authority by signaling a clear sense of purpose to the learning. It is something that matters, that you value and care about, in which you are prepared to invest commitment and effort for the benefit of the learners. While you are open and approachable, there are certain expectations you have of your learners. This is a joint enterprise where success will depend on both sides working together. Control is most effectively won through cooperation. You undertake to provide the subject input, direct and maintain the focus, and give meaningful and constructive feedback. You are attentive to their specific needs and difficulties. It is essentially the example you set that will motivate your learners and encourage them to make the most of the opportunity you are providing.

Poorly prepared sessions, unimaginative learning methods, disorganized management of the learning situation, delayed and indifferent feedback, together with an all too relaxed attitude toward whether anything is really being achieved, all suggest a carelessness which is unlikely to inspire a diligent or enthusiastic response on the part of your learners. So, having dealt with the first hurdle of actually convincing them this is a serious exercise, where everyone is required to work to the best of their ability, you then need to promote greater participation and involvement among your learners. Encouraging them to take more responsibility is not a way of avoiding your own accountability for what happens. It is simply an acknowledgement that people are likely to use their initiative, think in a more creative way, critically evaluate the information they receive, if they are treated as collaborators and not as subordinates.

I have sometimes had the comment made that my groups appear very lively. This has been said both in an educational and training context. There has inevitably been a subtle implication that maybe they had just a little too much to say for themselves, that they posed a potentially disruptive element. Perhaps I needed to exert a little more authority. Although irritated by such remarks, I am nevertheless gratified that my learners are perceived in this way. It is so dispiriting to take over other groups, already cowed into submission, and totally unused to volunteering their ideas and opinions, let alone daring to question anything being said. Obviously, you are trying to develop considered and thoughtful observations and contributions. This may be frustrating early on, but it is possible to gently guide and steer a group to explore questions from different angles, taking them beyond their own personal experience and preconceptions, instilling a more rational and disciplined inquiry.

I may well have painted something of an idealized picture and would not wish to underestimate the problems tutors occasionally encounter. This final section will concentrate on two very potent sources of anxiety, the fear of challenge and the fear of rejection. They are inevitably connected with the previous discussion on control and in many ways represent a continuation of that theme.

Insubordination in the ranks

Challenges can arise in a number of forms and from a variety of motives. Some may be very specific and concerned with a particular point or issue we have raised. Have we got our facts right? Have we jumped to too hasty an interpretation or conclusion? We might have raised an interesting question, but how relevant is it to the learners' experience? Other challenges may feel more personally directed. There are those that seem to doubt our credibility. How much do we really know anyway? It's all very fine as a tutor to be saying what should be done, we're not working at the sharp end anymore, even if we ever did? The former are fairly straightforward to deal with. Although they may be prompted by learner anxiety, they are focused and can be dealt with as such. As I have already said, it is perfectly possible to maintain a level of amicable disagreement within the group and not lose face as a tutor. The important thing is not to confuse a specific challenge with the much more serious personalized challenge.

This second type of challenge is intensely uncomfortable for a tutor. Again, they are most likely motivated by problems emanating from the learner or learners. In these circumstances the learner's challenge will feel quite hostile, especially if it is launched in the group setting. The challenge will usually be issued after a fairly angry momentum has been generated, and the frustration will be obvious even if it is disguised by cynical sarcasm. As a tutor, you have three options to choose from in your response. You could respond to the personal attack with your own brand of aggression, perhaps by a suitably cutting remark or a very pointed put-down. This may deal with the immediate situation, although it runs the risk of inflaming things still further. Without doubt, the problem will surface again and continue as the protagonist struggles to find your weak spot even if this amounts to little more than ineffectual irritation. This is not only unpleasant, it also distracts significantly from the learning situation and other learners will resent it, possibly blaming you as much as the original source of the problem. Even if you succeed in so dominating the situation that the individual is effectively silenced, there may still be a residual discomfort at such open antagonism. The atmosphere has been fractured and everyone will be left anxious and wary.

Another option is not one which you choose, but you may just feel helpless and unable to deal with the problem any differently. The challenge may achieve its objective and make you seriously doubt your competence. You buckle under the criticism. You maybe had only a very fragile confidence to begin with, which left you all too exposed. This is where it is absolutely essential to distinguish your own anxieties from those of your learners. You accept their assessment of you, because you were so anxious anyway. It does not occur to you to reflect a little further and look at them. Where are they coming from? What is it about the present situation which is making them behave as they do? How far is their anger with you just a way of deflecting attention away from themselves? Once you have been able to make this imaginative leap you can begin to deal with the situation positively and assertively. You are possibly inexperienced and have various skills to still develop, but you are doing your other learners a disservice if you simply give way to the destructive and undermining influence of someone who is, in reality far more anxious than even yourself.

Neither an aggressive, nor an unnecessarily submissive approach is likely to resolve the situation because they are both concerned with indulging your own hurt feelings. Rather you need to recognize why someone is adopting such an attitude. As I have suggested, it is usually far more to do with them than with you. You need to regain control of the situation by asserting your role in achieving the objectives of the program. It may be necessary to remind people of the ground-rules, particularly those concerned with how everyone should show and be shown proper courtesy and respect in group interactions. You may need to discuss any issues which you sense are of more general concern, such as your capacity to understand the reality of the learners' experience and situation. It may be helpful to listen, not for them to reproach you still further, but so you may better understand their concerns and needs and arrive at a way forward with which everyone is satisfied.

You do have authority and are accountable as the tutor to ensure the learning is effectively delivered. While this does not require you to subdue your learners, you still need to exert your position in certain situations and make it clear you are ultimately in charge and responsible for directing operations. If someone threatens to negatively jeopardize the learning you are obliged to deal with them. There will be a fuller discussion of how to cope when things go wrong in Chapter 10.

The elusive warm glow

For now, I want to conclude this section with an acknowledgement of the way many tutors not only feel emotionally vulnerable to the possibility of challenge, but also to that of rejection. This may seem a rather odd idea. We do not consciously think of ourselves as setting out to win a popularity contest, but lurking not very far below the surface with many tutors is the need to be positively regarded. We do not like to suppose that a group may have spent whatever time they have with us and gone away with a poor opinion of us personally. It is always the comments on evaluation sheets which are concerned with how we came across as people that are the most powerful and memorable. They strike at a very deep level. Even very assured and confident individuals can be affected by an unresponsive group. The more conscientious you are as a tutor, the more sensitive you will probably be to your learners' reaction to you. We start to feel worried when our encouraging smiles are met with blank expressions, when our attempts at being funny seem to fall flat, when we invite participation and no one appears interested. We look for approval and our learners are in a powerful position to give or withhold that approval. It is the same for anyone performing in a public arena. You are dependent on strangers to give you that buzz or send you away to curl up in a corner. They have their own agendas and may not be on your wavelength anyway, so you may not receive the positive feedback you really want and need.

It is important to recognize again that these are all very human and understandable emotions. Being a professional does not make you immune to such insecurities, but it should help you put them in perspective. Experience usually helps you to cope with them more easily, but it can still be very tough at times. We all need reassurance that we are okay. When you deliberately submit yourself to a situation where people have the opportunity to question your ability and also your character, you can feel quite defenseless. Tutors need to remember they can never please everyone all of the time. While remaining alert to learners' needs, you still have to look after yourself. You still have to accept you can only do your best and that learners sometimes will not like you, they will not make you feel good about yourself, but that is not why you are there anyway. You are there to help them learn, to help them develop and it is a bonus if, in the process, they also give you that elusive warm glow we so much relish.

There are always difficulties in any area of work that require us to respond to other peoples' needs. All sorts of complex issues emerge as to what motivates us. Are we really engaged in some altruistic activity, where we happily and selflessly give of ourselves in order to help others develop and thrive? Or is our concern to help others a way of meeting our own needs? Invariably it will be, and there is nothing intrinsically wrong with that, as long as we understand the difference between our learners' needs and our own. Most of us like to be involved in work that gives us some feeling of satisfaction, that makes us feel good about ourselves. Tutors usually derive great pleasure from seeing their learners succeed. But the learning process is never that straightforward. Your sense of being person-ally and professionally valued can become confused. Learners may not appreciate your efforts in the way you had expected. They may be too preoccupied with their own concerns to respond as warmly as you would like. Having invested much of yourself in establishing a positive relation-ship with your learners, you may feel cheated if the giving seems to remain one way. You then have to draw on your own resources and remind yourself why you are there and what you are trying to achieve. Tutors who depend on their learners' reassuring approval will not only confuse the dynamics of the relationship, they will also leave themselves dangerously exposed.

Summary Points

- ☐ Tutors risk confusing their own anxieties with those of their learners and so misreading what is happening in the learning situation; either negatively reproaching themselves or blaming their learners, focusing on who is at fault rather trying to understand the different perspectives of tutor and learner.

- ☐ We often generate more anxiety for ourselves by believing that we have to be near perfect in order to be a credible tutor, that unless we are in complete control of ourselves, our material and our learners, we have somehow failed. We set ourselves an impossible ideal we are never able to reach.

- ☐ Effective tutors are authentic. They are comfortable with themselves. Rather than hiding behind a professional mask, they are able to use their own personalities in establishing a greater openness with learners. This may involve showing, at different times, both vulnerability and strength.

- ☐ It may be useful for tutors to experience some process of personal reflection so that they may better understand themselves, and recognize how their own feelings may influence their attitudes and behavior toward their learners, helping them to distinguish between their own 'stuff' and that of their learners.

- ☐ Planning is crucial in the organization of your material and the devising of learning strategies, but often planning becomes more concerned with relieving our own anxieties rather than effectively meeting our learners' needs. Even with our carefully prepared plan we should still be responsive and flexible in the learning situation.

- ☐ Either working on our own or with another tutor, we need to remember that our anxious preoccupation with our performance or that of our partner, can sometimes become so consuming that we lose sight of our learners and fail to involve them.

- ☐ We sometimes believe that the only way in which we can control our learners is to dominate them, that if we reveal any hint of weakness, they will take advantage and gain the upper hand. Alternatively we can adopt a more co-operative approach, encouraging a disciplined purposefulness by explicitly stating our expectations in the learning situation, and demonstrating ourselves, the behavior we wish to encourage.

- ☐ We need to distinguish between challenges which are focused on a particular issue and challenges which are personally directed. The first are straightforward and should be resolved through reasonable discussion, although you may end up having to agree to disagree. The second is more serious. It may be motivated by learner anxieties or problems which you need to consider. However, if your credibility is being challenged it is vital you respond assertively and decisively.

☐ As tutors we are vulnerable to the feeling of rejection. It is only natural to want to be positively regarded by our learners and sometimes we may feel hurt when that approval has been withheld. But our professionalism should help us keep these feelings in perspective. We need to remind ourselves whose needs we are there to meet. Essentially we are there to help people learn and to help them develop confidence and greater self- esteem. That is the measure of our success, not how much they liked us.

QUESTIONS FOR REFLECTION

1. *When you feel irritated, annoyed or upset by your learners, do you try to see the situation in their terms? Do you consider how your own attitude and behavior might have influenced them or do you just dismiss them as an unwelcome aggravation? Which is more important – giving full expression to your negative feelings, establishing who is in the right and who is in the wrong, or trying to understand why a particular situation arose?*

It is very difficult when strong feelings are involved to stand back and reflect on not just our own experience but how others involved might be feeling and how they might be interpreting the same experience very differently. Acknowledging our own responsibility makes us uncomfortable and so it is very tempting to look for someone to blame. Accepting that everyone's perspective may have some relevance makes understanding ourselves and others more complicated. We like reassuring certainties, we like to think we are right but maybe it is these attitudes which prevent us from really listening to other people in the first place.

2. *How easy do you find accepting yourself as a good enough tutor, not always able to deliver the flawless delivery, but at least able to reflect on what happened and how you might learn from that experience?*

It is crucial that we do not burden ourselves with impossible expectations that only serve to discourage us. There is a distinction between being constructively self-critical and destructively self-defeating. The first affirms our potential to develop and is concerned with identifying strategies for improvement, while the second only reinforces a feeling of helpless futility.

3. ***How comfortable are you with yourself? How do you interpret the word vulnerability? Do you see it always as a weakness that learners may take advantage of?***

Vulnerability will mean different things to different people. I am not suggesting you excuse yourself from your responsibilities as a tutor. Learners will lose confidence in a tutor they can no longer respect. However we sometimes believe that respect depends on us always being in control. But our learners will often respect us more when they see we are confident enough not to have to hide behind a mask and are comfortable in acknowledging our own limitations.

4. ***How willing are you to look at your own feelings and motivations, asking yourself why you react in certain ways, why you have different responses to different people?***

How and with whom we do this is not the issue. It is about being able to stand back and think about why we respond as we do. Some people will do this instinctively, others will find it a more self-conscious effort. At times it may feel uncomfortable, but when we better understand ourselves, we are less defensive and more willing to put ourselves in the other person's shoes, even the person who is giving us a hard time.

5. ***What is the purpose of your plan? Is it to ensure that you will so impress your learners with your great knowledge and expertise they will never suspect the enormous preparation you have undertaken to feel confident delivering the session? Is it to devise a strategy that will be proof against all eventualities?***

Sometimes our plans are more concerned with relieving our own anxieties than with designing an effective learning experience. We invest considerable effort in reassuring ourselves that we really do know what we are talking about and forget the focus should be on what our learners need. Similarly, having devised the plan we are then reluctant to deviate from it and recognize when we need to be more flexible.

6. ***How do you feel when you are co-working with a colleague? Does the potential for comparisons and competition feed into your anxieties and make you even more preoccupied with your performance?***

It is tempting when working with a colleague to become engrossed in a rivalry that undermines the relationship you have with one another and with your learners. Alternatively, you may view your colleague as an ally against the unknown threat, drawing together for comfort and marginalizing your learners in the process.

7. ***How do you assert you authority as a tutor? What sort of expectations do you have of your learners? Do you place greater reliance on sanctions or incentives?***

Sanctions and incentives are not meant to be mutually exclusive. Clearly there is always a need for sanctions to maintain minimum standards of discipline with any group of people. But incentives are usually a much more effective motivator. Sometimes models from our school days get in the way and we underestimate our own power to set a positive example and encourage an atmosphere of mutual respect

8. How do you instinctively respond to challenge? How do you feel when a learner questions or disagrees with something you have said? How do you feel when they are trying to challenge your credibility? How difficult do you find distinguishing these two types of challenge?

It is understandable that when any learner appears to be questioning what we are saying, we feel put on the spot, we feel that we, ourselves, are somehow being held up to critical scrutiny. But it is crucial to depersonalize this situation and recognize that questioning and disagreement can be conducted with a respectful attitude, and indeed should be encouraged as part of the learning process. If we are able to come to terms with this constructive challenge, then we will be able to more easily recognize and confidently deal with the more personal attack when it comes.

9. How do you evaluate your success as a tutor? Are you content with evaluations that concentrate on how much people liked you rather than what they learned?

It is all too easy when talking about the learning relationship to set the tutor up to win a popularity contest. And we are all too susceptible to the need to be liked. We should be able to look at our own needs and still distinguish the 'buzz' that we all feel when a group responds positively from our ability to analyze the effectiveness of the learning.

Part Two – Learner Anxieties

We are all learners. Everyday we are absorbing new information and new experiences which we incorporate into our understanding of our world and ourselves. Sometimes that learning leads us to modify our existing ideas, sometimes it simply reinforces what is already familiar. We are rarely conscious of this process as learning, because it is such a taken for granted aspect of our lives. We do it quite naturally without any undue effort or real anxiety. Organized or formal learning is another matter. As soon as we are in a situation where our response to the learning experience is in some way being monitored or appraised, we feel all too vulnerable.

Just as with tutor anxieties, learners experience two distinct but related sets of feelings. Firstly there are those anxieties which are primarily concerned with how learners look upon themselves and their ability to succeed in the learning situation. These usually manifest themselves in terms of poor self-image and a fear of failure. The other area of anxiety arises from apprehension over the learning situation itself. Will it be one in which the learner feels comfortable or will it just be confusing or even threatening?

A powerful legacy

For many of us, the role of learner evokes memories of our school-days. They may be happy memories, or they may be extremely painful and humiliating. Such is the power of those associations, I have heard of grown men and women unable to use an adult education center because it was housed in a former school, where those same individuals attended as children. The legacy of our school career is real. The degree of our success during that time will have had a significant bearing on the opportunities we have enjoyed as adults. Those who were judged able and bright were afforded real choices in terms of what they have done with their lives, what careers they have pursued and the style of living they have aspired to. Perhaps there is not as strict an association between academic success and subsequent financial prosperity as there used to be, but it is still a notable factor.

Our school careers have determined much in our lives, including how we see ourselves. Many of our beliefs about how clever we are, how we compare with others, what sort of ambitions we can realistically cherish, are all dependent to a very great extent on our achievements in the education system. We leave school with some fairly fundamental attitudes about how we view our own potential. If we have done well, the legacy will usually be a positive one. Although there are still individuals who, despite having gained an impressive clutch of qualifications, suffered such intense levels of stress in the process, they are reluctant to risk ever going through a similar ordeal again. In the main, those who have succeeded at school will go on and attempt further challenges, confident in their ability. The formal learning situation is one where they have already excelled and so it holds few real fears.

Many people however have very different associations. For them, school was a discouraging experience. It was a place where they felt bored and frustrated, which emphasized what they could not do rather than what they could do. Their failure to succeed was a regular feature of their everyday routine. This may have been exacerbated by brothers and sisters who were more successful and only undermined the individual's feeling of worth still further. Perhaps their background was one which did not value academic effort, and so the whole education ethos was alien and irrelevant. Whatever the reason, the formal education system was seen negatively, somewhere they did not belong, which dismissed and rejected them.

This may sound a rather gloomy account of how people are left feeling about their school days, but I am simply basing it on the number of adults I have heard describing their experiences over the years, and those adults were ones who had actually returned to the formal learning situation. So I can only but wonder at the many unskilled people who remain written off for the rest of their lives.

Anyone involved in adult education or training needs to be aware of this legacy and how it manifests itself. Even if people have decided to return to formal learning, there may still be considerable ambivalence over that decision, and the smallest echo of their prior experience will be enough to make them abandon their seemingly vain expectations. Those who have been required by their jobs to undergo training, may feel angry and extremely anxious. It is something they did not want and are there very much against their will. Conscripts pose a peculiar and demanding challenge.

While I have focused on the baggage we carry from school, there are many subsequent experiences people have had of organized learning, either as adult learners or trainees. These are also possibly powerful influences on someone's attitude toward to learning. We are often so vulnerable as learners, that even though we may have been previously quite comfortable about our ability to learn, we only need one bad experience to raise the anxious demons of self-doubt. Once those self-doubts take hold, they can be very difficult to overcome and simply act as a self-fulfilling prophecy. If we lack confidence as learners, we are more likely to become discouraged and believe we were never going to succeed anyway.

It is not always very easy as a tutor to empathize with your learners' lack of confidence, particularly in a subject you are probably so familiar with. It takes a mighty leap of the imagination to put yourself in the role of someone coming to it for the first time. We fail to appreciate how something we take for granted is able to cause so much consternation. The only way we can get in touch with how our learners may be feeling is to think back to some experience of learning we have suffered, with which we struggled, perhaps doubted our ability to ever succeed, or maybe even had to come to terms with not succeeding. We all of us have areas of skill we have just never been able to develop. I have already shared my experience of math, but this was by no means the extent of my limitations. I was also always rather hopeless at any sort of sport at school. Anything involving a ball just highlighted my total lack of hand-eye coordination. I could neither catch them, nor throw them nor hit them. My attempts caused both amusement and furious irritation among my peers. I did try with a half-hearted enthusiasm to improve my performance, but it all seemed fairly hopeless. I could never compete with those more lithe and skillful individuals who so reveled in their own natural talent, and who regarded anyone not from the same mold as something of a freak. There are many other situations in which I have felt similarly uncomfortable and lacking in confidence, and they are always extremely valuable in helping me identify with how my learners may be feeling.

Self-defeating labels

There are some individuals who perversely only feel happy when they are working against the odds, when succeeding in spite of everyone's dire predictions is precisely what they most relish, but these are in the minority. Most learners need a supportive awareness of their concerns. The problem of poor self-image among learners is something you cannot ignore as a tutor. It does not matter how well you have prepared and presented your material, you must still remain alert to this need. Learner anxiety will invariably present as fear of failure.

Learners will often stubbornly cling to the idea of themselves as not very bright. Accepting the label is one way of coming to terms with it. It becomes part of your identity so that neither you nor anyone else is likely to disturb the resigned accommodation you have already made with your lack of achievement. The label is your excuse for not pushing yourself. You do not need to make any further effort, because you already have such low expectations. Any emerging notion of self-development will only disturb the state of equilibrium you have tried to establish. And yet many individuals do experience a restlessness, an ambivalent sense of some yet unfulfilled potential. These can be very tentative dreams, easily snuffed out, by jeering comments from friends or family, or a depressingly familiar feeling of bewildered anxiety when they make their initial contact with a new learning situation.

Learning involves change. It will inevitably have some influence on the relationship you have with yourself and with others. Existing self-images have their own momentum. They are at least familiar, even if sometimes constraining. Challenging these images involves moving into unknown areas, investing effort with an unpredictable return, exposing yourself to the risk of failure. It can often feel safer staying where you are. If you do dare set out on the venture you need all the encouragement available.

It is important to recognize that learners have an investment in the status quo as well as a desire to move on. As a tutor you need to realize there will be times when learners are quite unsure where they really want to be, and as a consequence will be sending out very confusing signals. At one moment, they will be suggesting they really don't think they are able to put in the necessary work and commitment to succeed, apparently ready to give up, but still almost wanting to be dissuaded, to be reassured they have what it takes and that everyone goes through equally frustrating periods from time to time. You are in a powerful position with your learners, you can reinforce the doubts just by ignoring them, or you can help someone get through the pain barrier of self-doubt and start to believe in themselves. Sometimes you may seriously doubt the likelihood of their succeeding yourself. But experience has taught me never to be surprised, and often the most unpromising learners are the ones who subsequently excel. Yet they might have all too easily given up. I am not suggesting you bully people who have clearly made a considered decision about their own limitations, but I am advocating spending some time to explore with learners why they are lacking in confidence and how you can best help them.

Fear of failure and avoidance strategies

Fear of failure is real. Failure can be a devastating experience. It reinforces all the self-doubts that have haunted you along the way and makes it less likely you will expose yourself in such a way again. It may have lasting consequences for your future, frustrating new opportunities or extinguishing cherished dreams.

Learners are nothing if not innovative in the many ways in which they may present their fear of failure. Some may develop a whole series of diversionary tactics which shift attention away from the quality of their work and performance. Broken and sprained fingers and wrists are commonplace before examination time among learners. Some learners develop all manner of domestic and health problems during a course. Anticipating they will fail, they construct circumstances to justify the inevitable, and so invalidate any objective assessment of their performance.

It can be difficult sustaining learners who resort to this particular strategy, as they will often seem totally overwhelmed by all the different pressures in their lives.. You need to distinguish between those who are experiencing very genuine problems and those who are simply trying to deal with their anxiety. The former need support and perhaps some recognition they are going through a temporary period, when it would be helpful to reduce the demands of the learning situation. However the second group need a very much more directive and purposeful approach. Your focus is their learning, and your responsibility is to help them achieve that. If they are so anxious about that learning, they are using issues in their personal lives as an escape strategy, then you need to concentrate on giving them very positive and reassuring feedback. Even if they are not making startling progress, you still need to reinforce that progress, and emphasize their strengths, concentrating on what they have already achieved. You hope their confidence will gradually increase and their dependence on various personal crises, as a way of dealing with their anxiety, will diminish.

Certainly the whole experience of being tested, evaluated or assessed may seem quite overwhelming to many learners. While they might enjoy the stimulus of absorbing new information and insights, any demand to demonstrate what they have learned can be met with panic. You may then encounter the frightened rabbit syndrome, where an apparently very bright individual is unable to perform accordingly. They are so convinced they cannot deliver they will not even try. All of us are subject to performance stress, we all get nervous, we all wonder why we are putting ourselves through such an ordeal, but with most of us there is an underlying confidence, based on successfully managing such stress in the past, which enables us to cope.

Acknowledging how they feel and then accepting it as understandable are vital steps in how you deal with such individuals. It may be useful employing some other sympathetic members from the rest of the group in offering reassurance. Frightened rabbits feel very self-conscious and worry painfully over what other people think of them. It will be important for them to hear that they have not lost respect from the other learners simply because of the difficulties they are having. This is when you reap the rewards of establishing a supportive group, where members are prepared to help one another You may need to negotiate with the individual what they feel they can reasonably cope with, in an attempt to build towards the actual level at which they should be performing. It may take time and some patience, but such individuals are usually enabled to overcome their fears.

Some learners may not present in such an emotionally charged manner as the frightened rabbit, but they will nevertheless routinely avoid having to perform. It is sometimes difficult to always identify such performance avoiders. They are adept at maintaining a low profile and submerge themselves into the group. They are undemanding learners and will give the impression of quietly getting on with things. However, it will come as a surprise to tutors to discover that such individuals have been silently struggling and quite unable to communicate their difficulties. They can devise a whole range of various ploys to avoid being put in a situation where they are required to perform. This may include carefully timed absences as well as diversionary tactics, focusing on any issues other than those directly related to their performance. Certainly where the emphasis is on group work, there are ample opportunities to escape being noticed.

They are reluctant to make contributions and rely on others to take the initiative and do the work. As a result such learners may be ignored for sometime, and only identified when it is very much more difficult for them to make up the lost progress. It is important, therefore, not to assume that just because learners are undemanding, they are necessarily coping. Having discovered a learner in this situation, you need to enable them admit to the trouble they are having. Again it is about giving a positive message, that you understand their anxiety, that you still respect them, that you do not judge them adversely because of their difficulties, and that it is part of your role to offer individualized help where it is needed.

In contrast to the learners who try to disappear into the woodwork, there are others who openly confront you with their anxious demands. The tutor-dependent individuals invariably prefer the hand-holding type of relationship with the tutor. They look for constant approval and will often be unable to do anything without the tutor's involvement. Tutors may find themselves virtually doing the work for such learners. Over-dependence can also take the form of the learners feeling compelled to check every last detail first with the tutor before they undertake anything. The learners want the tutor to tell them exactly what they must do and actively seek to put themselves in a child role with the tutor playing parent. Here there may be a distinct danger in being overly supportive. The important thing is to give the learners the confidence that they are doing well, and encourage them to undertake tasks that require them to use their own initiative. Very often such individuals have been severely criticized in the past for their efforts, and are now reluctant to put themselves in such an exposed position again. They need to hear that they are capable and often will respond to being asked to give support to another learner. In this way they move beyond their own anxiety.

Fear of failure is often at the root of many learners' antagonism and hostility in the learning situation, particularly if they are angry conscripts. They may reiterate the time honored refrain about being in the job twenty years and if they don't know what they need to by now, they never will. While obviously pointing out that few jobs have remained the same over such a period, and that changing circumstances and expectations have posed new demands, the tutor also needs to remember that attack is often seen as the best form of defense. Such learners, are in reality desperately worried they will be found wanting and so they divert attention away from themselves by going on the offensive, attacking the value of the learning program and sometimes even the credibility of the tutor themselves. This can feel quite personal and may provide many tutors with their worst professional experiences. But it should always be remembered that such a reaction has far more to do with the learner's fears rather than with any meaningful criticism of the learning situation itself. It obviously depends on how aggressively the learner's anxiety is being expressed.

Learners may need publicly reminding that there are appropriate and inappropriate ways to indicate their dissatisfaction. Certainly no tutor should have to suffer abusive behavior from a learner. However, it will probably be constructive to try and discuss discreetly with learners their feelings about the learning. You will need to identify where the anger is coming from. Is it unrelated to the learning and more to do with their relationship with their managers or their attitude toward their jobs? In which case you need to point out that this is not a scenario in which to address such matters. However, if you conclude that there is an element of anxiety in their manner, then you could perhaps negotiate a way forward, where, despite their reservations, they are persuaded to take a more open approach toward the learning, while you meanwhile acknowledge their concerns, stated and unstated. You could try to diffuse the tension with humor, not directed at them but at the situation, although you need to be careful since this can all too easily backfire. You might try being more overtly sympathetic without compromising your own authority and position. Your objective is to demonstrate that you are able to deal with their hostility constructively. You are not worried by it, because you have realized it is more to do with their feelings about themselves rather than you. From that more confident position, you can work with the learners rather than against them.

Just as hostility may be difficult to recognize as an indication of anxiety, so too may humor and so you may encounter the distracting comedian. This reaction can range from the individuals who compulsively play the fool, a strategy that probably first emerged in the school classroom, to the learners who will neither take the learning situation nor their own efforts seriously enough to invest the necessary effort. Their failure to progress can then be safely explained in terms of their lack of application rather than lack of actual ability. It is quite a complicated strategy in that they are clearly quite prepared to be thought of us as idle and even cynical. But this is preferable to being seen as incapable. They avoid submitting themselves to the judgment of someone else, where their more vulnerable weaknesses might be exposed. Again you need to deal with the underlying anxiety, encouraging learners to focus specifically on those aspects of the work they can more readily relate to and derive some satisfaction from. When they have become more involved, they are often more willing to discard their amused or cynical detachment and begin to properly apply themselves.

Fear of failure can present in many varied forms. I have by no means exhausted all the ways in which you may encounter it. Some are obvious and some involve ingenious and often unconscious devices for evading the issue altogether. To this extent you do have to be something of an amateur psychologist in determining your learners' real motivation from their apparent behavior. Performance anxieties can also impinge on the second main area of learner anxiety and that is the learning situation itself. It is important to distinguish between the two to enable the tutor to identify the relative dynamics of the situation. Fear of failure needs to be understood in terms of how individual past experiences have shaped and defined the learners' views of themselves. It is inevitably highly personal and will require an individualized response. Fear of the learning situation may also arise from prior damaging experience although not necessarily, but this particular anxiety can be dealt with more generally.

What will they do to me?

Fear of the learning situation may be prompted by the simple fear of the unknown. Yes, perhaps there are vague recollections of school, but with some awareness that an adult situation is likely to be different. Where learners have access to some sort of grapevine or network of information about other learners' experience, there may be powerfully influential messages about what to expect. You probably have little control over such informal systems, but never underestimate their effect. The messages may accurately reflect other learners' unfortunate encounters with less sympathetic tutors, but they can be misleading, even downright mischievous. People are quite capable of playing games with each other. Enormous satisfaction may be derived from describing a learning situation in daunting terms. This not only enhances the prestige of those relating the event as survivors able to tell the tale, but also serves to intimidate those not similarly initiated. Such are the preoccupations with power and one-upmanship we all engage in. So even though you may have relative novices for learners, there may still be all sorts of preconceptions which you have to overcome.

Learners who are less familiar with more contemporary adult learning situations will normally be at a real disadvantage. They are visitors in an alien territory, and will possibly find many of the taken-for-granted activities strange and even uncomfortable. Imagine how it may feel as an individual sent on a course for the first time, introduced to one of the more novel ice-breaking exercises. Even if it only involves throwing bean bags to one another as you desperately try to remember people's names, it can be enough to send anxiety levels through the roof. Your discomfort will be further intensified by the obvious ease of others clearly more relaxed and at home in the learning situation. If you don't know the rules of the game and others obviously do, you are going to be far more nervous about playing.

As a tutor, I always make the assumption that every learner will bring with them baggage which includes negative and destructive experiences of learning. These will include all manner of insensitive, overbearing and arrogant behaviors on the part of tutors. Hopefully, learners will have had other more positive experiences which will help to balance their view and restore an optimistic view of learning. However they are sensitized and alert to any indications of past horrors and will react accordingly.

Learner anxiety will be concerned to some extent with how relevant the learning will be. How far will it meet my needs? How much will the tutor understand my situation? Will the level be right, not too basic and not too advanced? Will it be organized in a style that suits my own approach to learning? What will the other learners be like and how well will I get on with them? Will we be very similar or will there be such a range of experience and ability the tutor will find it difficult to establish the right pitch? These are quite natural and understandable questions which any learner is likely to have in their minds. That is why you will generate greater confidence among your learners if you adopt a more attentive style from the start, and actively show you are prepared to listen and if necessary, adjust the learning to meet their needs.

Ritual humiliation

The single biggest area of anxiety is however, concerned with the relationship between the learner and the tutor. This relationship does not exist in isolation. Every learner will have his or her own particular relationship with the tutor and indeed learners will have relationships with each other. The peculiarity of this situation is that these relationships, and especially those the tutor has with the learners, exist in a public domain. In other words, there is an audience for the interactions. The audience is usually sympathetic, but that makes little difference, they are still spectators to what may prove ritual humiliation. So many learners cite being put on the spot or openly criticized as their single greatest fear. While they might find this unpleasant with their supervisor, it at least takes place in a one-to-one situation – or should do. Within a group learning context, there is little escape. If a tutor insists on putting learners through such an ordeal, the spectators are as constrained as the victim. Some unusually confident learners might be able to offer a robust challenge, but this is made more difficult in view of the tutor's position of authority and power.

Essentially, tutors who engage in this sort of behavior are abusing their position in the most despicable terms. Learners who have been casualties in this process will have understandable reservations about putting themselves in a similar situation again. Even if the experiences are more awkward than actually distressing, they still leave their mark and make learners more cautious in the future. The sarcastic response to a poorly thought out question or observation, sends a message to everyone that this is not a safe situation. The insistence that the tutor's view is the only one with merit is another very effective putdown. The exercise of petty authority by publicly chastising learners for arriving late when they are clearly already flustered, reduces them to the level of wayward children in need of correction. The possibly astute question, which nevertheless feels more like an interrogation, is only likely to make the learner more defensive and less likely to consider the difficult issues being discussed. The reproof for not performing as expected maybe justified if delivered in private and with some sensitivity to the adult status of the learner, but not otherwise. The expectation that learners should engage in any wacky learning activity dreamt up by the tutor, regardless of their dignity and likely reserve, is fairly counterproductive in encouraging participation and involvement.

Learner anxiety is not just uncomfortable and even upsetting for the learner, it actively interferes in the learning process. I am not advocating greater sensitivity and awareness on the part of tutors simply to make them nicer people as far as their learners are concerned. I do happen to personally prefer a more courteous and thoughtful approach in dealing with other people, because that is how I would like other people to behave towards me. Nevertheless, my experience in education and training has convinced me that if you ignore this issue, learning becomes far less effective. People do not learn by being routinely undermined and implicitly criticized, they learn rather by being positively valued and encouraged.

Summary Points

- [ ] **Learner anxieties stem from feelings about themselves, poor self-image and fear of failure. They also arise from learners' fear of the learning situation itself, will it be too demanding or threatening and how will they cope with it?**

- [ ] **Many learners may carry a powerful legacy from previous learning, especially school, which either confirmed them as able and clever or as limited and dull. Such legacies will have an enormous impact on how they view any future learning.**

- [ ] **It may be difficult to empathize with your learners' lack of confidence and sense of trepidation. It takes a great leap of the imagination to think of the subject, with which you are so familiar, from the perspective of your anxious learner. It may be helpful to reflect on how you have felt when you lacked confidence and competence in a new and different area of learning.**

- [ ] **Learners may have very ambivalent feelings around their commitment to the learning process. They may well have come to a resigned acceptance of their limitations and lack of** achievement. Further effort may well only result in more disappointment. They need considerable encouragement to help them overcome these self doubts and crises of confidence.

☐ Fear of failure may lead to a variety of behaviors by which learners avoid submitting themselves or their work to any process of assessment or evaluation. It is important that tutors recognize the anxiety, interpret the particular avoidance strategy and respond accordingly.

☐ Learners may have different levels of familiarity and confidence with the adult learning situation. Some will know the rules of the game, others will not. Those who have only limited or negative experiences will need a more careful and reassuring approach.

☐ The most dreaded experience for learners is the public put-down by the tutor. It will invariably leave them feeling humiliated and probably very resentful. Tutors who engage in this sort activity may justify it in terms of maintaining control, but they are abusing their authority as well as seriously undermining their learners' confidence and potential to learn.

QUESTIONS FOR REFLECTION

10. *What are your own experiences as a learner? Are there situations where you have felt anxious because you feared failing or did not know what to expect? What are your own legacies from your school days?*

Being able to identify with those feelings will be very important in being able to empathize with your learners. Sometimes it will be our experience of failure that will be the most valuable for us to examine and reflect on as tutors.

11. *How did you deal with those anxious feelings? Did you feel obliged to deny them or cover them up and just get on with it, or did they act as obstacles which you struggled to overcome? How far do you feel that your learners should try and cope as you did?*

Our own coping strategies may have worked for us but they may not work for everyone. It is all too human to use our own experience as a basis to judge others. Indeed our own strategies may have set up their own problems, making it more difficult to acknowledge our own feelings and those of others.

12. *Do you find it difficult to accept that people may hold very contradictory attitudes at the same time, that they may want to develop themselves and yet also be frightened of trying and risking disappointment?*

Again it can be difficult for more single-minded and successful people to understand how self-doubt can undermine even the most apparently enthusiastic learner. We may feel we are getting mixed messages from our learners about their commitment to the learning process and yet all they are really looking for is reassurance.

13. How far are you able to recognize learners' avoidance strategies? Are they only obvious with hindsight. Are you inclined to just accept people's behavior without considering what it may signify?

It is very hard to try and see behind someone's behavior and recognize how they might be deflecting attention from the real issue, especially when they may be doing this unconsciously. We are not psycho-analysts, yet I think there are very typical ways in which learners do respond when they are not coping, and by just by being a little more alert, we may be able to intervene more effectively.

14. How far do you assume that the adult learning situation is, or should be familiar and unproblematic territory for most learners?

Again there is the danger that we take for granted the world of adult learning which for us is a routine and an everyday part of our lives. We need to try to imagine what it might be like for learners who may have all sorts of preconceptions about us and one another.

15. How do you feel about your own experiences as a learner of being humiliated by tutors or witnessing the humiliation of others? Is it something that you shrugged off and feel people can get overly sensitive about?

But we need to remind ourselves that people do react differently and if your basic self-confidence and self-esteem are already very fragile, you will find it that much more difficult to cope with being made to look stupid or foolish. The 'toughening up' approach may sometimes develop great fortitude, it often blunts sensibilities and can occasionally seriously damage someone.

7

An Engaging Approach

Having dealt with both our own anxieties and those of our learners, and how they can conspire to obstruct meaningful communication and understanding between the two, it is now possible to go on and examine in more detail what I mean by engagement. This chapter is the first of three exploring what is involved in engaging with learners, and will look at how we establish a secure atmosphere. Chapter 8 will point to how we build the 'reciprocal relationship' and Chapter 9 will cover how we conduct the 'dynamic dialogue'.

Essentially, engagement is about creating a certain sort of relationship between tutor and learners in order to promote learning. As such it is more concerned with attitudes and approach rather than a matter of technique. However, practical suggestions are also included to illustrate how those attitudes might translate into actual behavior. Some points may appear to be rather mundane or merely stating the obvious. Nevertheless, it is often at a very basic level that the relationship between tutor and learners is jeopardized.

Secure Foundations

Engagement is a concept that has grown out of my own experience as both a learner and an organizer of learning. I have never felt it was a particularly startling idea. It seemed quite natural to look at the learning situation from my learners' perspective. I realized though that this was not something everyone did. As I have already described, for many of us, our own shoes get in the way of us being able to stand in those belonging to anyone else. But once we are able to do that as a quite routine way of interacting with others, it becomes much easier to understand their needs and frame our own approach to meet those needs.

If tutors are to really engage with their learners they need to enter into a particular sort of relationship. Openness is probably its most overriding characteristic. Tutor and learners should be able to approach each other with confidence. I remember one group of learners saying to me that what they valued most in a tutor was feeling safe, feeling they could trust that individual. That feeling of security is only possible when you feel someone really cares about you and is concerned that the way he or she acts toward you makes you feel good about yourself. Curiously this sort of concern does not have to depend on personal liking, although there may be few learners you would select as friends, nevertheless you develop a sympathetic regard for them. You try to make their relationship with you a positive experience for them. This does not have to degenerate into a mutual admiration society. The relationship should still encourage frank and assertive exchanges. The feedback should be two way, with the learner also expressing an opinion on the tutor's performance, in a spirit of joint and reciprocal responsibility.

Ensuring that your learners feel secure involves striking a fine balance between protecting and empowering. Learners will not thrive if they are exposed to learning experiences which are too demanding for their present stage of competence. They will merely become discouraged by their sense of inadequacy. On the other hand they do sometimes need to take risks and experiment, but also need to be assured that any failure will not be used against them and that any success will be properly credited. Providing learners with such security is not just about your own relationship with an individual learner, but with the group as a whole and the interactions between learners.

Tuning in

We have to develop a much greater sensitivity to our learners and what they may be thinking and feeling. We need to move from merely accepting what they say and what they do at face value. It helps to try and imagine what might be going through their minds when we first meet them. Letting them know you are able and willing to do this is immensely reassuring. Just making them aware that you are able to anticipate some of their concerns, encourages them to have more confidence and trust that this is a place where they will be safe and accepted. Encountering any group for the first time, you can speculate on their likely thoughts. What is going to happen? Will I get on with the tutor? Will I be asked to do things I don't really want to? All learners will experience these questions in their own way, some with a high level of anxiety, some much less so, but it is still useful to acknowledge these questions and uncertainties, not in a deadly earnest and serious manner, but with a light touch that signals it is perfectly normal to approach any unfamiliar situation with such feelings. Sometimes you have an almost tangible sense of the obvious relief people experience when their very thoughts are being voiced by someone else, who isn't judging them but instead saying it's all right and you're not the only one feeling that way. People need a considerable degree of reassurance that any sign of uncertainty, hesitation or anxiety on their part will not be seized on as an indication of personal weakness or individual inadequacy.

I believe it is also important to make some statement about your particular style and approach. Everyone owns a unique style as a tutor, but essentially you are trying to demonstrate that you want your learners to become active and enthusiastic participants in the learning. Right at the beginning of your relationship with your learners, you have the opportunity to show them how you intend to conduct the proceedings. Yet I have watched many tutors so concerned to impress learners with their professional authority, that they monopolize this initial critical period with imposing descriptions of their own history and experience, accompanied by seemingly self-evident accounts of the value and significance of the learning they are about to impart to the uninitiated. Exhaustive lists of learning objectives will be examined to lend an often spurious technical legitimacy to what is essentially an arbitrary and far from precise science.

At a more banal level, you may have the interminably tedious descriptions of the domestic arrangements and health and safety procedures. These preliminaries may go on for some considerable time. The more concerned with control the tutor is, the longer this introductory period will last, and the longer learners will have to wait before there is any indication their role is to be anything other than a dutiful audience.

While tutors need to set the scene, they should always keep in mind that the object of this early exercise is to orientate learners to the learning situation, to ease them in and indicate they are involved in a shared endeavor. I not only describe my style as informal, I hopefully demonstrate it at the same time. I try to convey the message that the only point of my presence is to be of some value to the learners, and if I am not connecting with them, then I am not delivering the service they are entitled to receive.

I need to keep reminding myself that I am not there for the benefit of my own ego, although it is difficult to subdue that rather unbecoming motivation completely. We all like to feel admired and respected. But we need to make sure we do not get in the way of our learners realizing their own potential. I quite deliberately emphasize the value I place on learner contributions, and how I do not believe the learning is simply about bestowing my pearls of wisdom. The learners themselves can add to one another's learning. I genuinely invite them to contradict and challenge me if they don't agree with what I'm saying, or they don't see its relevance to their own experience. You need to give the message that it is your responsibility to organize the learning to meet their needs, and if that is not happening, it is you, and not they, who are being ineffective. In that way they are encouraged to admit when they are having difficulties or it is just not making sense, without worrying about being seen as slow, stupid or awkward.

I have never been totally convinced about the value of identifying a set of ground rules. This always seems to run the risk of becoming rather an overly self-conscious, formal and even patronizing process. However, I think it is useful to establish a set of principles for how you will all work together, and while you might talk about them, your learners will only take them seriously when they observe you putting them into practice yourself. Nothing is more quickly devalued than the message which does not seem to apply to the messenger. So you may say that listening to and respecting one another is important, but if you routinely talk over and ignore contributions from your learners, they are unlikely to be convinced. It is no use expecting promptness on their part if you fail to start sessions on time. You have to actively demonstrate yourself the very principles you want them to follow. Ground rules are an explicit way of stating what your expectations are of both yourself and your learners. For my part, I believe they should always be negotiated rather than imposed. And learners should always have the opportunity to make their own suggestions as to what is included.

Essentially, you are trying to establish an atmosphere of mutual respect, where everyone will feel they have something valuable to contribute, and appreciate the contributions made by others. Mutual respect does not preclude tackling difficult or troublesome issues, but it does mean that during any discussions, where even quite contrary ideas are being propounded, there is still an underlying understanding that everyone should abide by a commonly agreed set of principles which preserve the dignity and sense of self-esteem of each individual learner. To that extent, I would argue that it is necessary to clarify with your learners what your expectations are of yourself and them, and likewise what their expectations are of you and of themselves. It then depends on what you all feel most comfortable with, whether that process is then formalized into a set of ground rules, or simply left as an informally agreed way of working together.

As you proceed through the program, there will be times when you sense your learners may be struggling, either because they are giving you fairly obvious indications, e.g. you are being met with puzzled and frustrated expressions or perhaps you will have to deduce from more subtle clues, e.g. a previously relaxed and chatty group becomes unusually quiet and thoughtful, or restless and distracted.

Perhaps you are aware you have come to a particularly difficult bit, which you anticipate, or have discovered from past experience, is likely to cause problems. Again it is well worth giving voice to what you sense they may be thinking, letting them know you quite understand if they are somewhat unsure or confused at that moment. By so doing you are actively acknowledging the issue, rather than assuming everything is all right merely because no one is saying anything. Simply asking everyone if they are all right and have they understood is a woefully ineffective way of finding out what your learners are actually feeling. They need to feel secure enough to let down their defenses and admit what is really going through their minds. It is not enough to ask if everyone is all right, without also implying you will not think any the less of someone for admitting they are not.

Inevitably, your sixth sense or practiced antennae will not always get it right. Sometimes you may imagine difficulties which are not there, and sometimes you will miss your learners' concerns altogether. None of us is perfect. While you do not want to make a labor of repeatedly checking your learners are still comfortable with what they are experiencing, which may perversely result in them feeling obliged to constantly reassure you, nevertheless you will have a profound effect on their confidence to speak up if they are confused or unsure, by the way you reply to the first individual who is prepared to say something. It is absolutely vital that you respond positively and respectfully to this initial contribution. Every other learner in the room will be closely observing what happens. This is your opportunity to demonstrate that you meant what you said when discussing the ground rules.

Perhaps you have inadvertently blundered on, oblivious to a mounting unease or frustration on the part of one, some, or all of your learners. Hopefully your attention will eventually be drawn to the problem, and at that point, I believe it is essential to quite sincerely apologize to your learners, without indulging in any embarrassing self-flagellation, for not picking up on the problem any earlier. You will not lose any face by again demonstrating that your primary concern is to meet their needs.

The learning space

There are also some very practical matters when organizing any learning situation. How you arrange the furniture may not seem a very profound consideration, and yet I would argue it has a significant bearing on the type of interaction possible between tutor and learners. Clearly, some venues do not permit many different options, and the need to make room for various items of audio-visual paraphernalia may inhibit your scope to create the ideal space. However, judging by the design of many so-called designated training rooms, I am not at all convinced we have a very clear idea about what the ideal space really should look like.

The nature of the task will obviously dictate the most appropriate arrangement, and as any given program may involve learners functioning as a whole group or in separate smaller groups at different points, concerned with varying activities, some reflective, some practical and some physical, it is valuable to have the flexibility to move furniture around accordingly. This should be so apparent, it might seem pointless to even mention such considerations. Nevertheless, how often do we associate high-tech props and sophisticated surroundings with a desirable learning environment? How many training rooms seem more designed to resemble executive board rooms? Tutors and learners will no doubt derive a sense of importance and status from such prestigious settings. A degree of comfort will go a long way to put learners in a receptive mood. None of us can readily concentrate if we are too cold, too hot, distracted by noise, harsh lighting or the lack of it, squeezed into an overly cramped area or forced to sit on chairs that leave us feeling as though we have been in the saddle for several days, as one learner graphically complained to me on one occasion. But assuming certain reasonable conditions are met, how desirable is it to have such elaborate trappings in the training space?

Maybe it is a somewhat puritanical streak in my nature, but I remain uneasy with all such attempts to gratuitously impress. The more imposing the layout and furnishings, the more likely it is that everyone will merely perform, trying to look important, maintaining a dignity which they feel is in keeping with their surroundings. Oneupmanship characterizes interactions with little likelihood of people really being prepared to be open, honest or spontaneous. Environments can greatly influence behavior, and the more grand the setting the less people will relax and be accessible to be truly engaged.

Much of the very advanced training equipment available today, while it may be capable of some fairly clever tricks, is often unnecessary and positively hinders effective communication between the tutor and the learners. Everyone becomes focused on the means to convey the message rather than the message itself. I have witnessed tutors so intent on demonstrating the technology at their disposal, they lose sight of their learners. The technology is allowed to dominate the proceedings to such an extent that the sort of relationship I am advocating becomes almost impossible.

The more tutors can hide behind their equipment and learners can retreat behind oversized desks and tables, the more difficult it is for anyone to display the informal openness necessary for a genuine dialogue. I know there are learners who feel uncomfortably exposed when required to dispense with the security blanket afforded by a piece of furniture. However, I believe this can be easily and speedily overcome when learners discover, through the tutor's reassurance, that they no longer need such defenses. Clearly a desk may serve the very practical purpose of providing a surface to write on if this becomes necessary. Yet I would still argue that the physical barriers need to be minimized as far as possible. Tables or desks should be kept small and lightweight, easily moved out of the way when appropriate. Better still are the chairs incorporating an optional writing surface which can be slotted in accordingly.

When I used to teach college evening classes, every week I would arrive to find the furniture lined up in disciplined rows, and every week I would spend ten minutes or more laboriously dragging tables and chairs into a three sided open square. Only then could I address everyone while at the same time, they could also focus on each other without having to turn round or listen to some disembodied voice from the back of the room. The channels of communication were immediately altered. I no longer monopolized attention. I was still able to direct what was happening, but my learners could engage directly with one another, sharing in a genuine discussion and exchange of ideas.

I have always favored an arrangement where the lines of communication were not solely directed toward the tutor. Three sided squares or open horse shoes have featured with virtually every group I have ever worked with as a tutor. Admittedly sometimes room size, shape and dimensions can make this difficult to achieve, but it has a fundamental impact on how your learners relate to you and to each other. Theatre style may well enable you to pack more bums on seats, but you have quite deliberately constrained your learners into behaving as an audience. The physical lines of communication must emphasize the importance and value of interaction between everyone involved. A formal space makes this more difficult to achieve. However, informality alone does not guarantee the sort of dynamic I am suggesting.

On one rather novel occasion, I experienced just how powerfully seating, or should I say lying arrangements can affect a group. I arrived at a venue, organized by a very efficient but somewhat idiosyncratic administrator, to find mattresses available. Chairs, I was informed, would present a problem. General consensus favored the mattresses. However, the training space took on an increasingly disorganized character as people adopted all manner of postures, facing in various directions, depending on how they were feeling. Far from being relaxed, they became more restless as the day wore on and they seemed curiously isolated from each other. The absence of a secure physical structure and focus to the group interaction fundamentally undermined the establishing of any purposeful group identity.

Comfort, flexibility and practical requirements are the main considerations, but in addition the physical environment should encourage a positive atmosphere, where everyone can engage with each other honestly and authentically. The training space should support a sense of shared purpose between the learners where they will feel confident exchanging contributions, participating in a process from which they will all learn and develop.

It goes without saying that, if you want to create a situation where learners will be truly engaged, there are certain limits to group size. Working with groups of over twenty-five may well degenerate into mere crowd control. The interaction can become unruly as people vie with each other to have their say. On the other hand, people can feel lost and outnumbered, reluctant to speak up or put themselves forward in front of so many people. It is also less likely that any real group cohesion will develop and the learning will become dissipated. People will instead splinter off into more comfortably sized units. Numbers below ten may pose different problems, in that people feel too much under the spotlight. The advantages are that people have the opportunity for greater individual attention and they may well feel more confident discussing certain issues within a smaller, intimate group. However, they no longer have the option of just being able to merge with the crowd.

There is little point in being too prescriptive about the ideal group size. Different learning tasks will influence the appropriate number of learners, and the individual personalities within a group may well mean that a certain group size works brilliantly on one occasion and proves disastrous on another. The sort of interaction I am advocating between tutor and learners, and between the learners themselves, depends on a group size where everyone feels able and confident to participate.

Anything you can do

Group dynamics are crucial in creating a positive learning atmosphere. It is not just about how you are engaging with your learners, but how they are engaging with one another. We are naturally wary of others, especially in a potentially competitive situation. It has not been my experience that people's learning, or even the performance of that learning, is significantly enhanced by being pitted against other group members. The small gratification enjoyed by those who succeed has to be weighed against the frustration of those whose efforts compared less favorably. Competition, in any learning situation is a vexed question. At one time, it was taken for granted as the only way to motivate people. Much of this arose from the emphasis on individual achievement. It was assumed that people needed to compare their performance with one another in order to spur them on to their very best effort. The virtues of cooperation were then extolled and learners were encouraged to see the advantages of working together rather against each other. We now seem less clear about the relative merits of the two strategies and it does appear to be the case that males, whether as a consequence of nature or nurture, respond more positively to competition. Meanwhile the advantages of cooperation within the workplace are more clearly recognized, resulting in less time-wasting antagonism and damaging loss of goodwill.

In the learning situation, we face something of a dilemma in how we resolve this question. My own natural inclination is a deep unease with the more negative aspects of competition, while accepting that without it, learning can become directionless, with learners experiencing little real sense of purpose. Tutors have traditionally relied on competition as a fairly easy and simple device to motivate their learners. The wish to be best and to be seen to be best is a powerful incentive. We all relish the approval and admiration such achievement commands. Even a boring task can be approached with more enthusiasm if it provides an opportunity to prove your superior ability. Witness the way children, particularly boys, will become absorbed in endlessly, pointless competitive games and exercises simply in order to demonstrate their oneupmanship. The activities often seem limited, repetitive, with little intrinsic interest. Their sole purpose is to prove you are better than someone else. It is perhaps not surprising that this attitude has been harnessed in the business of learning. On the same basis, tutors can deliver the learning in a tedious and boring format and trust to the spirit of competition to motivate their learners, compensating for their own lack of imagination and ingenuity.

Competition almost gives permission to be lazy as a tutor, to not think about how you might make the learning intrinsically interesting and enjoyable. There is no doubt that if you reduce the competitive element, you need to invest greater effort in engaging your learners and encouraging them to become involved with the learning for its own sake and not just for some extrinsic reward. It is a much harder task you make for yourself. While many tutors have abandoned the competitive incentive, concerned over its destructive effect on social relations, they have not given sufficient thought to how they need to then reinvigorate their learning, to make it more appealing. Some learners have certainly floundered as a consequence. But I do not believe this means we should simply return to the quick fix offered by competition. Surely we can be more inventive than that and consider a whole range of strategies which not only motivate our learners, but also give them a sense of achievement.

Learners undoubtedly need feedback, they need to know how they are progressing, how their efforts are being received. We have to redirect the focus. Competition centers the focus on comparisons between the learners with each other. The energy is dissipated in trying to beat their fellow learners. The learning almost becomes incidental, as a means to an end, with the end being to come out on top. I am suggesting that we need to turn the attention back to the learning and to the learning process, and look at how we can create ongoing opportunities for the learners to see the learning itself as the pleasurable challenge, and engaging with that challenge as the real satisfaction.

Implicit in the idea of competition is the notion of winners and losers and while many might argue this is a fact of life, which people are better off coming to terms with, rather than being protected from, consigning a considerable number to the fate of loser is not only destructive but wasteful. Individuals are very vulnerable in the learning situation, since their self image and self esteem are on the line. There may be many reasons why people are not actually performing to the best of their potential at any moment, and to use that measure to reproach, devalue or reject them, ignores the complexity of the process and the individual learner. Learners need to feel safe. They need to feel sufficiently secure so that when they are uncertain, anxious, unsure of themselves, afraid to perform, worried when their performance falters, they know their weakness will not be exploited or used as an indictment of them. Failure in one area at one time does not mean the individual is a failure.

Competition quite deliberately sets learners against each other as rivals. It is possible to enjoy a healthy rivalry, provided this does not come to dominate the social interaction of the learning group. But there is usually far more value in the group seeing each other as further resources to draw upon, rather than jealously comparing progress. Admittedly, there is an uneasy tension between the pursuit of individual excellence and the cohesion and solidarity necessary for group achievement. I think they should be seen as different but complementary strategies, neither one being superior to the other. Even when the frontiers of knowledge are being pushed forward by some brilliant and inspired individual, the foundation upon which that achievement is based and the consolidation of that work will usually depend upon a more cooperative effort. We should be encouraging our learners to recognize the value of each group member's contribution.

Having observed a great many learners in my career, I am quite certain that learners have much to learn from each other, and that we restrict that process if we merely cast them as rivals. Clearly this applies more to learning where people are exploring and reflecting on their experience. But even where knowledge and skills are being acquired, group members can still be a powerful and significant source of support to one another. An important objective with any group of learners therefore, is to encourage them to develop positive relationships with each other as much as with myself.

Getting to know you

How do you actively promote a supportive group? Their first encounter with one another will be crucial, serving either to whittle away the barriers between them, or to reinforce their suspicion and unease. The manner in which they are introduced to each other will have a significant bearing on subsequent relations, which is why so much effort and imagination is lavished on devising endlessly novel introduction exercises. I regard many ice-breaker activities however, with extreme caution. The intention is supposedly to help learners feel more relaxed and focused on the learning at hand. Why, then, do so many ice-breakers seem devised only to thoroughly disconcert learners? I understand that they are used to break down inhibitions and so are often deliberately playful. Nevertheless, what one learner may regard as playful, another learner may regard as humiliating or inane, and not because the latter is uptight and finds it difficult to get in touch with their inner child, but simply because they have very different expectations and taken for granted assumptions about what they regard as customary in a given situation.

By relying on a repertoire of wacky icebreakers, tutors risk alienating many of their learners. Icebreakers, by their nature, are usually undertaken before any group norms have been properly established. Any learners who are uncomfortable will feel they have little opportunity to express their disinclination to participate. They will be concerned not to appear uncooperative and resistant and will often go along with the activity, albeit reluctantly. Tutors could well make the situation somewhat easier by acknowledging that some individuals may feel a little foolish, but nevertheless they will hopefully find the activity more fun than they had imagined. But few tutors even make this concession. They forge ahead, oblivious to learners' misgivings, determined to ensure an unquestioning group conformity.

The unpleasant suspicion has occurred to me that, for some tutors, bizarre icebreakers are consciously or unconsciously used to assert the dominant position of the tutor. Such activities so disorientate learners that they become suitably pliant material in the hands of the tutor. Having relinquished control, they will then do whatever they are bid. If an ice-breaker is simply to help people to get to know other members of their group and feel comfortable, why do the exercises have to be so embarrassing? There may be excitable laughter but it maybe only hiding a great deal of anxiety. One particularly questionable game which is not untypical involves asking everyone to write down on a piece of paper something about themselves they have never told anyone before. All the pieces of paper are then dropped into a hat and pulled out one at a time and the group asked to identify the writer on the basis of their first impressions of one another. Just think how personally vulnerable people are going to feel taking part in such an exercise.

I believe icebreakers need to be very carefully selected and should be appropriate for the group. Undoubtedly, there are some learners who are almost professional course goers and remain quite unfazed by whatever strange activity they are asked to participate in. Indeed there are learners who will be disappointed if they do not have the chance to play. But there will be others who are less familiar with such whimsy. One-upmanship can rear its ugly head when some learners clearly have been there, done that and got the tee-shirt, while others just look on bewildered and confused. I have always preferred a more gentle if somewhat measured approach. Maybe my nonexistent hand-eye coordination has just made me rather less enthusiastic about throwing bean bags.

For almost every learning situation, I use a deceptively simple but enormously effective exercise. I partner an individual with someone they do not already know, allow them five minutes or so to find out a little about each other and then ask them in turn, to introduce their partners to the rest of group. It is possible to introduce variations on a theme and also ask them to include something specific to the course topic, e.g. their most admired leader for a leadership program. The exercise serves several purposes. It ensures the isolated person on his or her own has talked to at least one other course member before the coffee break. It helps to disrupt established pairs or small groups, who might otherwise remain as detached subgroups. It enables everyone to learn something about everyone else, not only their names but also what they do in work and in their spare time. Such information may link some otherwise unlikely individuals. It also ensures that everyone has spoken to the assembled group without having to endure the ordeal of actually talking publicly about themselves, worrying about how much or how little to say. It never seems to matter so much when you are describing someone else. I am able to observe how people have responded to the exercise. How much interest did they appear to show in their partner? How confident were they in speaking to the group? Will they need some hand-holding or perhaps some respectful restraint? I am also able to glean something of their varied experience which will help me to ensure the learning is relevant for them as a group.

At the same time I have the chance to make a note of people's names, together with some identifying feature, e.g. clothes, hair color and so on, which enables me to remember them individually. I can then routinely use their name as I respond to them, which incidentally helps everyone else become more familiar with each other. Admittedly, name badges may make this process even easier, but name badges are often difficult to read from any distance and name cards require tables and invariably add to the formality of the situation. People always react very appreciatively to the effort made to learn their names. They have a very concrete sense of being recognized and valued in their own right. It may seem a fairly trivial point but it is enormously important in generating a warmer and more relaxed atmosphere.

A friendly face

Even more basic than remembering people's names is being aware of just how much all our non-verbal cues are affecting our learners. I never cease to be fascinated at how significantly the lack of something so commonplace as a smile can influence the way in which people view each other. It is an immensely potent gesture and its absence leaves us unsure how we are actually being received. I sometimes feel the most valuable feedback I have given on training skills programs is to remind people how vital this simple signal can be in establishing a positive rapport with their learners. So many times, I have witnessed groups remain reserved and wary, believing the tutor was cold and disinterested just because he or she did not extend a friendly smile. At the same time, I know the reason why many tutors feel inhibited is because they are too apprehensive and anxious in the situation. Yet another example of how the communications become confused and misunderstood.

A dilemma for most tutors is that the most vital point in any program is the very time they are most nervous and self-conscious – right at the beginning. It is tempting to remain rather formal through the preliminary introductions. However it is precisely at this stage that you need to indicate the more distinctive characteristics of an engaging approach. Invest the effort now, and you will find your group gels far more quickly than you may have thought possible. You will also discover they more readily involve themselves in the learning and are prepared to contribute and participate much earlier on.

It will be at this early stage when you most need to come out from behind the role and show something of yourself. humor is vital at this point. I am not suggesting we all have to become stand up comics. In fact the telling of jokes is a peculiarly skillful business, and if you are less than confident, and your joke doesn't quite conclude with the flourish you had intended, your learners may feel obliged to provide a polite acknowledgement of your effort, but a general awkwardness will have descended upon the proceedings. Jokes tend to emphasize your role as performer, which engagement is trying to actively avoid. Far better to draw your learners into a warm and light-hearted exchange, where your humorous asides and observations encourage them to relax and respond and share what they find funny and amusing.

To return to the issue of non-verbal cues. Eye contact is another thorny issue in the learning situation. Confronted with a sea of expectant faces, there is a temptation to avoid their gaze and concentrate on some absorbing point at the back of the room, or to become thoroughly engrossed in one's material, props and equipment, and so avoid the troublesome business of having to negotiate eye contact with possibly twenty-something individuals. Indeed, I have encountered tutors being advised to fix their attention over and behind the heads of the learners. Undoubtedly, eye contact can be difficult to manage successfully. There is the danger that you gravitate towards the friendly reassuring face, ignoring those who seem less responsive. You may even find you have a natural tendency to direct your attention to the left or the right of your group. I am aware that those learners to my right are often in danger of feeling neglected because of my inclination to look to my left. Furthermore, individual learners may feel uncomfortable if you routinely and for prolonged interludes focus in their direction. The trick is to maintain eye contact with your group as a whole rather than individuals. That may seem a contradiction in terms, but it is a relatively straightforward skill, once practiced. You are looking at your learners and making eye contact but maintaining a roving eye. Your gaze is constantly moving on; you are essentially scanning your group. There is the risk of feeling rather sea sick if your eyes are shifting too quickly or erratically. The objective is to achieve a smooth, steady and equable movement across your group, where you remain constantly alert to the non-verbal cues they may be signaling to you.

Your learners will also react to your posture and how you move around the room. All of this is very basic communication skills, but again I feel it is worth saying explicitly, if only because I have observed so many people who should be familiar with these ideas, and who still approach learners with all too limited awareness of the impact of their own behavior. Tutors, who can appear relaxed and open, able to occupy the training space comfortably, will immediately put their learners at ease. Whether you stand or sit will depend on the activity at hand and the size of your group, but it also conveys something of the interaction you are trying to establish with your learners. Standing gives you the advantage of height which may be crucial with a large group if they are to properly hear and see you. Standing also reinforces your role as conductor of the proceedings. It enhances your authority.

You are still endeavoring to engage with your learners but you are more clearly in charge. Sitting signifies a far more participative role where you are temporarily one of the group, although still nevertheless ultimately responsible for ensuring constructive learning takes place. Both are appropriate at different times and being able to move from one to the other quite naturally, without any undue sense of contrivance, will add to the spontaneity of the proceedings. Learners will soon adapt to the varying dynamics and understand how their own roles subtly shift in these changing circumstances. They will probably require a little coaxing initially and look to you to provide some reassuring guidance.

While we are considering the impact of non-verbal behavior, we cannot overlook the significance of our voice. Unfortunately, nature plays a rather sneaky trick and never allows us to hear our voice as everyone else hears it. The only opportunity we are ever afforded to hear how we really sound is through a recording. As a consequence people often become far more preoccupied with their voice when watching a video than with how they actually looked. Allowing for this handicap, we need to be especially aware that the manner in which we say something is usually far more significant for the listener than the actual words we have used. For a tutor, the voice is one of the most important assets. There is no doubt that an unappealing voice can seriously disadvantage us. Some voices are too high, some too soft, some too strident, and learners respond accordingly, as if to a distracting mannerism, unable to concentrate on anything except the jarring or sonorous tone of voice.

We need to try and consciously extend the range of our voice and I am not simply talking about volume. If that is all you rely on to command attention, you may find yourself having to cope with a chronic medical problem eventually. You will also have probably caused a great deal of discomfort to your learners over the years. It is through the voice that we are able to convey a whole variety of emotions to our learners – enthusiasm, warmth, concern, interest, fun. Through the voice we can inject energy into the learning situation.

Tone and pace need to be constantly varied to maintain our learners' interest. But over and above making our voices more lively and agreeable to listen to, we should be using them to further the process of engagement. Too often, tutors are characterized by an imposing and domineering voice. Their voices have become their principal instrument of control. We should take care that our voice, while sufficiently authoritative to focus our learners' attention, is still signaling a readiness to listen to their contributions. So at the very least we should avoid the too adamant tone and adjust our pace to give our learners the opportunity to interject.

As a tutor, never underestimate how a look, gesture or tone of voice – never mind what you actually say – may be interpreted by learners and how that may then influence their behavior in the learning group. You will be constantly judged in terms of how approachable you seem to your learners, although an irritable reaction may be perfectly reasonable given certain circumstances, nevertheless it is not particularly professional; neither will it help your learners establish the necessary confidence to work with you effectively.

Feeding back

Receiving feedback on performance is when learners feel most vulnerable. This is the point at which they really discover how much they can trust their tutor. A previously charming individual may be viewed very differently after learners have experienced their first feedback. No matter how much positive capital has been accumulated in the early encounters, any indication that the tutor's appraisal may not be fair, consistent and constructive will leave them feeling insecure. Tutors may be uncomfortable with the prospect, or they may just not appreciate how what they say and, more importantly, the way they say it, can affect learners confidence and motivation. Crucial to the whole process is to distinguish very clearly in your mind, and then in the way you communicate with your learner, between the performance and the person. Learners can improve their performance, but they cannot change who they are. So often the feedback is perfunctory, poorly thought out, unclear and learners are forced to draw their own conclusions. One implicit message is that the learner did not merit any further time or trouble.

Let me first deal with perhaps an even more frustrating aspect of the feedback issue, and that is the absence of any feedback at all. Many learners may feel this is a frustration they can readily live with. However the absence of feedback leaves learners in an aimless limbo. With no guidance on how their performance is comparing to expected standards, learners may perhaps enjoy a false sense of security. On the other hand and much more likely, they may become more anxious about their progress, worried that they are not able enough, not working hard enough or just not applying their efforts appropriately. They may feel as though they are floundering and find it difficult to maintain any real motivation. There is no sense of achievement to encourage further endeavor. Learners are usually reluctant to share their anxiety with one another in these circumstances. They risk losing face and appearing inadequate. Consequently they will be convinced that they alone are struggling in the face of the tutor's seeming indifference.

Providing prompt and effective feedback is a vital part of any tutor's responsibility toward their learners. That feedback, however, must address issues of performance and not appear to infer something about the person.

This can become a minefield of unintended meanings. So often I have observed someone giving feedback, clear in their own minds that they are concentrating on performance, but the choice of words and especially the tone of voice and facial expression conveys something far more personal, i.e. that you are rather an incompetent and inconsequential individual to require that sort of correction in the first place. In essence, the manner is disrespectful, maybe not intentionally so, but that is how the learner perceives it. The tutor may judge that the learner is being over sensitive and should be able to take such criticism, but no one is going to be able to respond favorably to criticism that diminishes them. Their own defense mechanisms will automatically come into play to protect against perceived attack. This will make them much less likely to listen to what is actually being said. Instead, they will continue to nurture a sense of wounded grievance. Even if the learner goes away determined to succeed in spite of you, you have still failed to establish any effective understanding which might enable you to reflect with the learner on their performance, depriving them of a vital opportunity in the learning process.

Giving constructive feedback is every bit as demanding as delivering the learning. Feedback needs to be planned, focused and specific. You need to think very carefully about what you want to say or write, and how you want to put it. All too often the message becomes muddled because tutors appear to be trying to say different things at the same time. Maybe their own thinking is confused, maybe they are hesitant about what needs to be said. Being positive does not always mean saying nice things. Sometimes more difficult issues have to be tackled, but if they can be approached respectfully, then it is still possible for the learner to listen, inwardly digest, discuss and move forward. Bad feedback simply leaves the learner stuck, possibly backed into a corner, unable to see or negotiate a way forward.

Learners appreciate clarity. You need to ensure that any particular feedback has several definite points which have an overall coherence. Maybe you don't tackle all the areas which need to be addressed, at the same time. This might leave learners too demoralized and overwhelm them with a sense of what they still have to do. So you make a judgment about what are the areas which are more urgent. and what can wait a little longer. The focus must be with the performance, but nevertheless there will still need to be an awareness of the individual learner, so that the way in which the feedback is delivered demonstrates a degree of empathy with how the learner is likely to respond. It is crucial in any feedback process that the learner has a chance to comment on his or her own performance and on the feedback, so that there is a genuine exchange of ideas, opinions and feelings.

One aspect frequently overlooked in the learning situation, especially where adult learners are concerned, is the need to reinforce progress and achievement with positive feedback. We tend to think feedback is really concerned with identifying the areas for improvement, rather than wasting time talking about what people are already doing perfectly competently. We are all comfortable with the idea of praising children when they have done well, but somehow we often feel more awkward with adults. We fear it might sound patronizing and indeed sometimes, ineptly done, it may well come across as just that. However we all need the encouragement of hearing that our efforts are being recognized. We are not always very good at receiving praise, often mumbling an inaudible or incoherent response. Nevertheless we still thrive on positive feedback and become disheartened without it. Learners who are constantly reminded of what they are doing wrong and what they have not yet mastered, start to doubt their ability to succeed.

Positive feedback should be a regular feature of any learner's experience. That is not to say tutors merely invent nice things to say. The feedback should still be authentic and focused. Even where you have learners who are able, but have not far so applied themselves with any real commitment, you need to focus on the potential ability as the basis to build on, exploring why there is a problem over commitment. On the other hand, you may have a learner who is intensely keen and committed, but is still finding the work very challenging. The positive focus will obviously concentrate on effort and enthusiasm, identifying any small success and breaking down the challenging learning into more easily digested chunks. I find tutors paying lip service to this in principle, and regularly ignoring it in practice, especially if they feel their initial attempts are not bearing fruit, impatiently giving up when the learner does not immediately respond to the wave of their magic wand.

Constructive feedback is not just about telling learners what they have done well. It is also about analyzing how and why a certain approach was successful. It requires the tutor to identify those elements which contributed to the achievement. From such an analysis it is possible for the learner to generalize from those points and apply them in a further task. So the learning is constantly building on itself. Not only does the learner feel more confident, but also better understands what is required. The bald grade with some fairly inconsequential comment in no way enables the learner to distinguish why one particular effort is rated more highly than another. As tutors, we are always far more willing to analyze people's failures than their successes. We expect to spend time pointing out where they have gone wrong, what they missed out. We assume that, if someone has done well, there is no need to tell them why they succeeded. And yet learners can remain just as mystified over their achievements as their failures and miss out on a valuable opportunity. We can learn from our attainments as well as our mistakes.

Where we have to draw learners' attention to areas of their work in which they need to improve, that should be precisely the purpose of the feedback. It is not to criticize or make someone more conscious of their failings. It is to suggest why something did not work and how that problem may be overcome in the future. Whenever we have to focus on a less than satisfactory area of someone's performance, we need to leave the person a way forward rather than back him or her into a corner. The individual must have some other option than to become stubbornly defensive. It may well be that someone needs to reach a certain level of assurance with the subject before being ready to receive more demanding feedback. Such feedback, given too early on or at a stage when the learner may only become discouraged, will be counter productive. You need to judge how best to deliver the feedback so as to enable the learner to use it positively. This may involve playing down deficiencies until the learner feels more comfortable with what he is doing. It goes without saying, that any feedback on an individual learner's performance should be given discreetly, and not attract the attention of spectators.

The vital point is to emphasize how valuable mistakes can be in providing learning opportunities. As a tutor, you can give a powerful message to your learners. If they observe you becoming flustered, impatient and irritable when you yourself make mistakes or things do not always go according to plan, then they may conclude from you that mistakes are a reflection of personal failing. If on the other hand you can handle those occasions calmly, accepting that not everyone gets things right all the time, and actively demonstrate your own reflective process for trying to understand why things happened as they did, then your learners will feel reassured that they can make mistakes without losing face and without losing your good opinion of them. Rather than making them smug and complacent, this greater sense of confidence is likely to make them more constructively self-critical. Learners who are anxious about making mistakes will be more defensive. Those who feel more secure are more willing to really look at what they have done, reflect on it and identify where they might have improved. You, as the tutor, are in a critical position to give your learners a real belief in themselves. Without that belief they will struggle to maintain their own motivation and to develop the potential which they constantly question and doubt. But when a group is truly engaged the learners can also do this for one another.

Safe in your hands

While much of this discussion has examined the ways in which interactions between the trainer and learners can be used to promote engagement, the learning itself must be designed to further this process. Certain activities may have great appeal in terms of both learning and entertainment value. As tutors, we may feel terribly enthusiastic about a really novel idea we have discovered or dreamt up ourselves, but if it is not matched appropriately with different learners, it will not only fail to achieve its objective, it may also generate resistance amongst your group. Too often, we design learning activities without really imagining what it might be like for our learners attempting them. This is where a naively optimistic view of our learners' confidence and ability may actually prove counter-productive. We may say it is all right to make mistakes, but no one wants to be set up to appear incompetent. Learners require a safety net if they are going to take risks, but finding yourself thrown into that net on a regular basis does little for anyone's self respect.

Whatever activities you choose, they should be calculated to develop your learners without stretching them so far that they are almost being set up to fail. And if you are contemplating something quite exacting, you must acknowledge the level of challenge, offer sufficient support and reassurance, and be very explicit that the process is of greater significance than the objective outcome. In other words, the point of the exercise is not about who can deliver the best and most accomplished performance, rather it is the learning value of the collective experience of attempting a task, reflecting on what happened, why some things worked better than others, and how you might do things differently the next time.

Learning activities need to be very carefully distinguished from evaluation. Clearly there are going to be occasions when learners do have to perform and their performance is being measured. But if this sort of evaluation is an ongoing feature of the learning process, it will undermine the sort of relationship I have been advocating. Learners will feel too tense and anxious, constantly concerned about their progress or the lack of it. They will see their fellow learners only as rivals, comparing performance and only working collaboratively when it is clear that individual achievement would be better served by collective effort. So learners may quite deliberately share a task or given work load which they can more effectively accomplish by working together. This is not the same as the collective experience of learning which characterizes engagement.

This collective experience is concerned more with the process than the outcome. Learners are encouraged to undertake an activity, not just to demonstrate their skill and ability, but as a genuine development opportunity. So the activity is not a means to an end, but an end in itself. Its value lies in the learning it stimulates. This needs to be communicated very clearly to learners, otherwise they may become so preoccupied with their own performance anxiety, that they miss the actual point of the exercise.

This is essentially what experiential learning is all about, asking learners to participate in a particular experience, which will further their understanding and awareness. As a consequence, their proficiency and effectiveness will be developed, but the actual immediate objective of the exercise is to stimulate learners' thinking and feeling responses. Learners need to concentrate on what is happening both to themselves and to others they may be working with, rather than exclusively focus on a successful outcome. Their experience becomes a collective resource from which they can all learn. There is more value in understanding why something did not work and what alternative strategies you could try in the future, than simply achieving a successful, competent outcome which does not provoke any such speculation.

Anyone who has already been initiated into the tutoring role, or who may be contemplating it, will perhaps appreciate the level of panic many of my learners have suffered when asked to deliver a videoed simulated learning activity as part of a training skills program. It is a demanding exercise which leaves individuals very personally exposed. I always state why it is so important and how it will provide them with crucial feedback. However, I make it very clear that the value lies in the experience as a whole, including the preparation and the discussions with me and one another about possible ideas and how best to implement them, the actual delivery and how that felt, the observation of others in action and what sort of response they provoked, the reflection and analysis on what happened, both planned and unplanned, why things went well and some things went less well and on occasions, why an approach that appears to break every rule in the book can still be effective.

Although still very nervous, they can approach the exercise with the reassurance that they have permission to get things wrong, to give a less than polished performance, because that is usually when the real learning occurs. They need to know this is a safe and supportive environment where no one will think any the less of them simply because they were not an unqualified success. And no one, not even the most experienced tutors, ever gives a flawless performance, so if you think you have, then maybe that is the time to worry. Complacency is a considerable liability as a tutor. What I am trying to encourage is the confidence to be reflective, to be able to objectively stand back and think about their role as tutors, how what they do impacts on their learners and how and why their learners respond as they do.

It is still important to acknowledge the likely feelings such an exercise will generate and allow people to express those feelings, rather than their trying to maintain some sort of contrived professional facade. It is understood that people will be anxious, which is perfectly natural in the circumstances. I always try to give learners some degree of control over what is happening. People are allowed to work in pairs if they find that less stressful. They can be as creative as they wish in designing their learning activity and it can be on any topic in which they have an interest. The preparation time is organized as an informal workshop where people are free to spend it as they want, talking to one another, sharing feelings, exchanging ideas, organizing materials. I remain available for consultation but am no longer directing anyone. My role is often to maintain a light-heartedness to the proceedings, reassuring and reminding people this a safe situation in which to try out their skills and ideas. It is an opportunity for everyone to reinforce the sense of being part of a collective enterprise, where they are all looking out for each other, rather than trying to compete to give the best performance.

In all the years I have been running these programs, I have only ever had one individual refuse to be videoed. Despite my reassurances, she was clearly so distressed at the idea of being filmed, little would have been gained by insisting she go through the ordeal. She delivered her activity. The group were immensely supportive. They took great pains to participate in her session and provide very constructive feedback afterwards. The whole experience was so positive, she admitted she might not have minded being videoed after all. Perhaps I should have taken a firmer line, but I do not believe it would have been productive. She had to arrive at that conclusion herself. Similarly another learner was quite prepared to be filmed, but would not watch the play-back of her sequence. Again the rest of the group took it upon themselves to give her detailed feedback on how well they judged her. Such experiences testify for me the value of engagement. When I observe a group completely at ease with one another, encouraging and sustaining each other through such an arduous ordeal, sharing and learning together and growing in confidence, I am convinced this is the sort of learning experience which can truly empower people, generating its own energy and dynamic quite independent of the tutor's input.

Summary Points

☐ Engaging with learners depends on being able to understand the learning situation from their perspective, imagining how they might be feeling and establishing a sense of trust and security.

☐ Anticipating and openly acknowledging your learners' concerns signals your commitment to them. Preliminary introductions should include a clear invitation for learners to be actively involved. However you approach the setting of ground rules, you are trying to clarify expectations on both sides and generate an atmosphere of mutual respect.

☐ The learning space should be flexible, comfortable, and suitably equipped, without the technology taking center stage. Seating should be arranged to enable the learners to communicate directly with one another as well as with the tutor. The physical environment and group size should support open, informal and authentic exchanges between all those involved.

☐ Promoting competition between learners may simply dissipate energy and waste a valuable opportunity to learn from each other as well as reinforcing individual feelings of inadequacy. Competition also serves as a compensatory motivation where the learning has been rendered dull and uninspiring by the tutor.

☐ Ice-breakers should be concerned with making learners feel more comfortable with one another. Activities which are likely to cause embarrassment, confusion or encourage one-upmanship, and leave individuals feeling at a disadvantage should be avoided.

☐ Non-verbal signals, expression, eye contact, sitting or standing and how you use your voice will all act as powerful tools in the process of engagement, either encouraging or discouraging your learners.

☐ While constructive feedback is vital to learner progress, it is the occasion when they feel most vulnerable and so should be delivered respectfully. Tutors need to remember that the feedback should focus on performance not on the person. It should be clear, specific and provide an opportunity to explore and understand how performance can be improved. Analyzed positive feedback is also crucial in furthering learning and developing learner confidence.

☐ While learning activities should promote a sense of achievement and accomplishment amongst learners, the emphasis needs to be more on process than outcome, with development rather than evaluation. The exercise itself becomes a collective learning resource.

QUESTIONS FOR REFLECTION

1. *How readily do you empathize with others? Do you imagine how you would feel in a similar situation or do you try to remove your own shoes before moving into theirs? Do you try to imagine how it would feel to be them with their own quite different experiences, attitudes and expectations?*

Sometimes it is very tempting to think we have understood how someone else might be feeling by simply imagining ourselves in their situation. But while that might be a useful way to start empathizing with others, it can lead us to miss the point that our reactions and responses are our own and may be very different from someone else's. We need to understand other people in their own terms.

2. *What are your feelings when you first meet a group? Is there a tendency toward a 'me and them' attitude, characterized by a wariness on your part until you have established that the natives are friendly?*

While it is quite reasonable to weigh up any group, it is all too easy to reinforce a feeling of distance by waiting for your group to reassure your anxieties before you attempt to move closer to them. Learners usually respond to you in the way you have behave toward them.

3. *How do you feel about encouraging your learners to talk to one another? Do you prefer the idea of controlling the channels of communication in the learning space?*

Clearly tutors need to maintain some control of the discussion between their learners and ensure that it is appropriately focused. Nevertheless it is important that learners are encouraged to be active participants in the learning space and value the sharing of different experiences and ideas.

4. *What have been your own experiences of competition and how have they affected your view of competition within the learning situation? Were you motivated to achieve and succeed through competition? Did you anticipate competition with confidence or with self-questioning doubt?*

The issue of competition will inevitably touch on some very powerful experiences for people which have shaped their own views, but again it is important not to look at the world entirely from our own perspective. Competition from a position of confidence and strength may be stimulating and positive, whereas from a position of vulnerability it is often only intimidating. But the very sensitivity which undermines our confidence may yet increase our empathy with others.

5. *How do you rate icebreakers? Is it in terms of their originality, their novelty which you somehow believe will reflect on how interesting and entertaining you are perceived by your learners?*

Sometimes one senses that tutors almost try to outdo one another in their pursuit of the most bizarre icebreaker. The icebreaker becomes a means to express something about ourselves, a style statement. We do not want to appear dull and predictable and may then overlook the purpose of the exercise, which is concerned with how our learners feel rather than how we feel.

6. *How comfortable do you feel reflecting on the impact of your body language and non-verbal communication? Does it induce an awkward self-consciousness which inhibits your ability to interact with others?*

It is understandable that when we are asked to focus on our behavior, it can leave us so preoccupied with our own performance we become ever more self-absorbed. Our non-verbal behavior is the area where we feel we have least insight and over which we have least control. We can end up feeling very exposed. And yet we need to remember that as with any communication it is about how we interact with others and how we read their signals. The more we develop an awareness of our learners' signals, the more effective our signals will be to them.

7. *How do you feel about giving feedback? How do you view your learners when you have to give them negative feedback? Do you resent them for necessitating such a disagreeable task? What about the idea of positive feedback. Do you feel embarrassed about praising your learners?*

Sometimes when we have to deliver a negative message our own discomfort can lead us to either confuse the message, or deliver it in such a detached manner that our learners feel personally humiliated. Our unwillingness to deal with our own uncomfortable feelings constructively, makes it impossible for us to acknowledge or deal with those of our learners. Similarly we need to reflect on our attitudes towards being praised and how they influence our willingness to praise others.

8. *How far do you feel you have a responsibility to ensure that learners have a positive experience of any given learning activity, so that whatever the outcome in terms of their own performance, they will have felt supported and valued?*

While learners will obviously engage in activities where their performance may not rise to either their or your expectations, it is important that they do not see that experience as a failure, and instead are encouraged to view it as an opportunity to better understand their own strengths and weaknesses and how to develop in the future.

8

A Reciprocal Relationship

In this chapter I want to examine what is involved in a truly reciprocal relationship between tutor and learners. We will look at how such a relationship requires tutors to develop a new and different understanding of their role, one which respects learners as partners, where power and authority are recognized as problematic issues, and tutors and learners move from their more conventional positions into a shared space which they can explore and define together.

Facilitators and catalysts

I dislike the word, 'facilitator' – it has a clumsiness that is very unappealing. However, to use the description 'learning facilitator' is nevertheless quite helpful. As facilitators we are responsible for the process of learning. It is not enough to direct operations, organize a series of inputs, evaluate the outputs and believe that is the extent of our involvement. Engagement demands a far more active and participative role on the part of tutors. They are being asked to form a dynamic relationship with their learners, where the learning arises from their interaction, rather than simply being passed from one to the other.

I have toyed with the idea of tutors acting as catalysts in the learning process. In some ways this is a useful analogy. Tutors are there to ensure that the right conditions are created for the learning to take place. They are concerned with exposing their learners to a carefully calculated experience. It is not so much what tutors do which is important, it is what they cause to happen. Catalysts are change agents. Their presence brings about a transforming reaction. However, there are still several problems with this view.

Implicit in the idea of transformation is the notion that it is inevitable, that it happens independently of the actions of those being transformed. While learners will always react to the learning in some way, the precise form of their reaction is rarely that predictable. We have to accept that learners play an active part in the process. They are all different, and their responses will vary accordingly. But the more fundamental problem with thinking of ourselves as catalysts is that catalysts in chemistry remain unaffected by the reaction. They bring about the change, but do not change themselves. Many tutors would fail to see any problem with this. After all, it is the learners we are trying to change. However, if we are not open to the prospect of change ourselves, we not only miss an exciting opportunity, we remain detached and isolated from our learners. The whole point of such an idea is that both sides are engaged in an interaction which will affect everyone involved. If we are unwilling to entertain this possibility, the relationship will never be reciprocal.

Obviously, the main thrust of the change will be in the direction of the learners. But if we are unwilling to enter into the sort of relationship I am proposing, it will be difficult to consider new and challenging suggestions from your learners or to question your own comfortable assumptions. We need to move on from the reassuring position we have enjoyed. This obviously entails risks. Once you are open to the possibility of change, you feel less certain, maybe less credible. Exposing yourself to what might seem unnecessary risk may make you feel vulnerable. You wonder whether people will lose respect, or your authority be undermined? But these anxieties are associated with rigid and traditional ideas of what constitutes authority. We can afford to be more flexible, indeed we need to be more flexible. We need to be confident with change and to provide a powerful example to our learners. If we are expecting them to embrace this process, then I think we have to show that this a joint endeavor.

An outdated recipe

It is never easy redefining relationships we have taken for granted; this applies to both learners and tutors. People like to know where they stand, and learners may be quite content to slip into a more customary role. After all, it's the tutor's job to tutor them, isn't it? Very often this sort of attitude is accompanied by expectations of being told how to do things, assuming there is always a correct and incorrect method. Such simplistic notions generate a recipe book approach to learning. Learners may not be used to exercising their own initiative and judgment. They prefer to wait and be told, as they were in school, and find it difficult adjusting to a more responsible role in the learning situation, often feeling aggrieved and somewhat short-changed if they have not been given a specific set of instructions.

While some learning undoubtedly fits this model, increasingly people are having to adjust to learning which requires them to reflect on a situation or problem, generalize certain principles with which to understand that situation, usually dependent upon previous learning, and then construct various options and consider their relative effectiveness in responding to the situation or problem. Although this is initially quite demanding and may be met with some resistance, most people begin to discover that it is ultimately a far more rewarding way of both working and learning.

The traditional pedagogic role of the teacher is no longer appropriate to this style of learning. It is too constraining. We need to be aware that the process is as important as the outcome. It is not just about arriving at a certain result by mechanically following a set procedure. Learners need to appreciate the underlying rationale of that procedure. They need to make sense of it and incorporate it into their own understanding. This more dynamic way of learning has inevitable implications for the sort of relationships we develop with our learners.

Improvising and collaborating

Engagement ensures that the relationship is redefined and that learners are truly empowered. It follows that tutors are no longer in a controlling role. They direct the organized program in line with specified learning objectives. They set the scene, organize the props, outline the basic story, provide some of the script, but the assembled cast should still have ample opportunity to improvise. They should still be able to take the story and make it meaningful in terms of their own experience. This takes us back to some of the issues we examined when looking at tutor anxieties. Tutors find it hard to relinquish control. Some still feel it is part of their professional responsibility, and that sharing with learners may compromise not only their own position but also the quality of the learning itself.

There may be a reluctance to allow the learners to improvise, fearing that they do not know enough about either the learning expectations or the process of achieving them. Tutors may feel that, as they carry the responsibility, they should also be able to exercise the authority in the learning situation. Clearly we, as tutors, are far more informed and are much better placed to identify the most effective learning strategies. But just as we recognize that people usually learn better by figuring out a problem, within certain guidelines, and arriving at the solution for themselves, rather than just being told what to do, so I think we can afford to give learners the opportunity to be more actively involved in shaping their own learning.

I am not suggesting the sort of situation where a tutor looks benignly upon the assembled learners for the first time and simply asks them what they want to do. I have witnessed this sort of laissez-faire approach, where tutors seem content to hand over complete control and responsibility to their learners and inevitably anarchy follows. Learners become discouraged, because they perceive that the tutor is not sufficiently bothered to even make the effort to organize events, and the outcome usually depends on what the dominant members of the group decide. The learning agenda is supposed to evolve from the interaction between the group members, with the tutor's role far from clear to anyone else, except possibly themselves. This is an extreme attempt to avoid any sort of exercise of authority or control by the tutor and to hand power over to the learners. But the consequence is usually frustrated confusion.

Tutors have a clear responsibility to ensure that learners have the opportunity to experience effective learning, which entails appropriate preparation and organization. There should be an explicit agenda, something to start with. Learners should have a clear sense of what is on offer, but there should also be room for them to formulate their own response to that agenda and to make their own suggestions and contributions. Their knowledge and understanding will be more limited, but they can still be encouraged to share their experience of the learning, what works for them, what doesn't work so well, ideas for how the learning might be made more meaningful. The initiative does not have to come solely from the tutor. The learners themselves may prove a richly creative resource, and by actively harnessing that resource and involving them as collaborators in the enterprise, they are able to shape and influence the learning process and maybe even the outcome.

Tutors will have to review how they look upon their learners. Rather than focusing on the learner simply in terms of the skill or knowledge they lack, the gap which has to be filled, there needs to be a genuinely holistic perception. We should be developing a more respectful attitude towards our learners, acknowledging their strengths and abilities in a general sense.

There may be all manner of ways in which learners have demonstrated their various talents and it helps to be aware of these so that we may see learners more positively. How many times have you discounted an individual's ability to succeed, only to find, to your considerable surprise, that they have excelled in other subjects? You may believe there is no necessary link between one type of ability and another, that it is perfectly possible to be a high flyer in one area of learning and struggle painfully in something else.

Even though ability in one area does not indicate ability in another, it helps to think of our learners in terms of what they have already achieved, in order to foster this positive image. We need to remember that our learners are very dependent on the image of themselves we reflect back to them. If that image suggests only deficiency – that you are not as clever as me, you are not as clever as others, you are not as clever as I think you should be – the learner has an uphill task indeed. If instead, we suggest that even though the learner may not at the moment know very much about our particular subject, we acknowledge that they may be far more able in other areas, including ones *where we might learn something from them*, we are reflecting a far more empowering self-image, one where confidence may flourish and potential be realized. So many tutors regard their learners with a superior, if weary disdain, undeserving of any favorable perception until the learners have somehow proved their worth. Approval is withheld and only grudgingly conceded as the learner strives to dispel that negative view. Mistakes and performance problems can be used to reinforce that negative view, or they can be accepted as perfectly natural steps along the way to further learning.

Learners need to be engaged as partners rather than subordinates in the learning process. Too many tutors still try to exercise some very traditional ideas of what they understand by authority. Tutors expect to control both the learners and the learning. But as I have already argued, control may ensure an orderly process and predictable outcome, but it may also stifle initiative, confidence and independent thinking. Clearly, tutors need to exert some authority in order to ensure the learning task is addressed, and a structure is provided in which the learners can work to achieve that task. But a fine balance has to be struck – and it helps if tutors see their input as primarily one of facilitation rather than leadership, providing situations and experiences from which people can learn. It can be argued that the most effective leaders are often those whose efforts are more subtle and less apparent to their followers, and yet who still ensure the task is achieved, encouraging independence and autonomy when it is appropriate, and providing guidance and support when it is still needed.

If tutors insist on so controlling the learning situation, there is little room for learners to really explore their own potential or that of the subject. Surely it is far more exciting as a tutor to encourage such enthusiasm among your learners, so that they want to contribute their ideas and thoughts in response to the learning. Possibly you discover an individual learner with greater knowledge or experience than yourself in a given area. If you can get over your own anxiety about acknowledging that a learner may know more than you, there is a real chance to enhance everyone's learning by collaborating together. This is not about abrogating your own responsibility or giving someone carte blanche to simply indulge their own ego. You may also have to weigh up to what extent someone is able to express him- or herself clearly. This individual might have something very interesting to contribute, but you may still need to paraphrase so that everyone else is neither bored nor confused, while at the same time judging how relevant the additional input might be. However, the value of that sort of interaction is enormous. You have allowed the learning to be extended. You have acknowledged that the learning is not a one-way process. You have actively invited someone else's participation and shown that you are sufficiently confident and comfortable in your role – you do not need to monopolize control. You have demonstrated that learning is more important than your own vanity. You have sent a powerful message to the rest of the group that *you are willing to engage.*

Sometimes, it is rather unnerving to find yourself confronted with highly knowledgeable and informed learners. You are inevitably more wary. If they are unlikely to gain anything from your input, you accept that the learning needs have not been properly identified, and agree there is little point in their remaining. But there are many people who have very specific areas of expertise. Within any group you will find a range of knowledge and experience. Individuals will have their various strengths and weaknesses. Part of a tutor's role is to be alert to these potential contributors. There may be points in the program when you are covering something that directly relates to a particular learner. They might be rather hesitant, unsure of the situation, and need you to positively indicate you would welcome their comments.

Setting the agenda

Part of the problem of engaging learners in a real partnership is that tutors are powerfully placed to define and control the learning situation. Their position as subject expert, director of operations and group leader lends a legitimacy to their own definition of the learning situation. This may be at odds with various learners, who will often feel their definition is less valid, even though it may still be very meaningful for them. Tutors are able to impose their perception and way of understanding the learning situation. Usually they have identified or agreed the learning objectives and the learning content. They will have devised the learning methods and may play a significant role in any evaluation and assessment. More importantly, they will be communicating, by every word they utter and every action they take, a far more fundamental insight into how they think and feel about the world, what and who they think is significant, irrelevant, worthwhile, useless, intriguing, tedious, ethical, unfair, courageous, timid, amusing, dull, caring, mean and so on. They will be putting forward a set of views, values and principles, if not explicitly, then implicitly in the way they respond to their material and their learners. As tutors, we cannot avoid doing this, we are simply expressing who we are, but there is a danger that our perspective will predominate and define the prevailing reality. What we take for granted as valid becomes what is taken for granted in the learning situation. Our learners may not necessarily agree with us, but they may well feel constrained in seriously expressing any alternative view.

We set the agenda not just in terms of the learning, but in the way in which the whole learning process is conducted. We communicate something about how we expect learners to behave to us and to each other. Every interaction is to some extent a consequence of that agenda. The atmosphere that characterizes a particular learning group is largely dependent on the tutor. We may remain oblivious to how far our own perspective is at odds with that of our learners. We may assume that most people see the world in much the same way as ourselves and if they do not, we do not feel especially inclined to try and accommodate their view. We usually find it very difficult to consider the possibility that opposing positions may have something valid to offer. Indeed many of our learners will probably share a similar reluctance. We seem to need a sense of certainty, that our own view is essentially right. It is too disruptive to contemplate different views as so many options, perhaps each offering some useful insight or understanding.

I would argue that the learning process should bring people together in a more self-conscious and systematic attempt to develop understanding. That group activity may simply reinforce the most dominant view, normally that of the tutor, or it can accustom us to a more open and less certain experience where we are all, including the tutor, required to engage with different possibilities and no one's contribution is rejected. That is not to say everyone's contribution will be judged equally right or valuable, but it is important to listen and try to understand the learners from their own perspective, helping them, if necessary to express themselves, and then, rather than merely correct them, examine their argument together and contrast it with other ideas.

A truly reciprocal relationship allows for differences to be expressed. Learners will not want to challenge if they feel the tutor will only become anxious or hostile. Some tutors remain oblivious to how their manner implicitly deters learners from any sort of questioning or alternate points of view. There are tutors who appear so timid and nervous, no one feels comfortable making any sort of interjection. More typically there are those individuals who have such an adamant view of their own rightness, they regard it as inconceivable that any learner could say anything to make them pause and consider what they have stated. They do not usually regard themselves as overtly controlling. However, such individuals present as so sure of themselves, that few learners are likely to risk the all too predictable, assured and determined demolition of their only very tentative argument. Learners will avoid engaging in any sort of debate if they feel their point of view is going to be ignored, trivialized, dismissed or summarily demolished.

There are other ways in which tutors routinely and often inadvertently put learners at a disadvantage. Many take it for granted that learners will automatically have a given store of general knowledge and understanding, and will react incredulously when someone is obviously unaware of something they assumed everyone knew about. Just because many people might be familiar with a particular body of knowledge or have certain experiences, it is quite arrogant to believe everyone is the same, or should be the same. People's store of cultural knowledge will vary enormously and is greatly dependent on their background. Why should we have such a rigid idea of what we think constitutes general knowledge? Knowledge is now so diverse, it is impossible to be too judgmental about what we think people ought to know. We are all ignorant of things others seem to know all too well. No learner should ever be made to feel uncomfortable or marginalized because of what they do not know.

This problem is not necessarily confined to the actual learning, it is far more often something that arises in the informal interactions that occur during the breaks and ongoing asides between participants. These are occasions when people can feel awkward, foolish or even excluded because they are not familiar with the topics of conversation. It is all too easy in such situations to imagine how other people might be thinking of you, as perhaps rather dull, unsophisticated or just plain ignorant. I am sure we can all identify with such experiences. However I am again suggesting that, because learners have already placed themselves in a vulnerable position, their discomfort may be more acute. Sometimes it is not just about different cultural assumptions. Sometimes it is about the different opportunities available to people with very different levels of disposable income. No tutor can or should feel obliged to protect learners from such situations. Any attempts would quite rightly be seen as patronizing. Nevertheless, they can still send a powerful message through their own attitude and behavior, that everyone, regardless of their circumstances, is entitled to be positively and respectfully valued.

Empowering learners

Empowerment is about releasing energy and potential. It recognizes that people are able to contribute far more when they are positively encouraged. It is also about enabling people to move beyond the boundaries which have been imposed on them, or that they have imposed on themselves. Empowering people involves affirming them as they are, while at the same time helping them believe in the potential they have still to realize. The two objectives may seem contradictory. They may appear to parallel the not untypical scenario between lovers, where the woman falls in love with the man, whom she then sets about improving, leaving him wondering who it was she fell in love with in the first place. We need to be careful. Most learners will respond positively when they feel that their talents, abilities and individual worth are being recognized. We like to feel good about ourselves. We like to feel valued. We like to feel affirmed. There is a danger that in suggesting to someone that they should be developing their potential, we are somehow implying that they still have to prove themselves, that they are not really deserving of our good opinion until they have achieved, until they have been successful. I have certainly encountered many staff in my career in training who have felt very ambivalent about the expectation to develop themselves. They assume this suggests some lack, some inadequacy on their part.

It is vital when working with learners to give them a very firm sense of their individual worth, irrespective of their performance. We should be starting out with the assumption that every learner is deserving of respect and unconditional positive regard (to borrow a phrase). We only modify that assumption if experience suggests the learner is quite deliberately abusing that respect. Otherwise we should be trying to maintain our affirming attitude even though their performance may falter.

Working with learners is in many ways an act of faith. It is about believing in their ability to learn and to use that learning to push their individual limits still further. Many of us find it difficult to imagine ourselves doing things and taking responsibilities way beyond our current routines. We are not bold enough. True, it is that sort of self-confidence which usually distinguishes the high flyers from the rest of us. But most of us are to some extent dependent upon the encouragement of other people. I was certainly far more motivated to write this book after others had reassured me it was a worthwhile project to consider and not simply prompted by some idle and vain fancy.

In organizations, it has always amazed me how we make so many judgments about someone's ability simply by the position they occupy. I recall, as a training officer, the general consternation caused when a member of staff employed as a driver within social services wanted to pursue a qualification in personnel. She had worked all the time her children were growing up, although she had never seriously entertained a career. When she reached the point where it was possible to put in the required time and effort, she was determined to achieve something more fulfilling in her working life. She later went on to become a senior personnel manager. There are many very able and competent heads of residential homes who have started out as care assistants and even domestics. Such stories are commonplace nowadays and yet we still pigeon-hole people far too readily. We assume their present position somehow defines them and their future. But traditional career paths are disappearing. People are moving in many different directions as they try to survive the turmoil of the modern world of work. They are also espousing new and different aspirations, which may no longer be just concerned with success in conventional terms, but have much more to do with personal development.

We need to be both alert and perceptive in recognizing the potential people have to offer. There may be all sorts of reasons which have contributed to their taking the particular direction they have. Circumstances conspire in many people's lives to push them along certain paths which do not always reflect their actual ability or the ambitions they may secretly cherish. Empowerment acknowledges that people often have a lot more to offer than might seem obvious. There are perhaps opportunities within their existing jobs to develop further.

When I ran my own training team, the administrative staff had long been used to playing a very subordinate role to the training officers in terms of the setting up and organization of courses. This led to many problems, usually around poor communication on the part of the trainers. I decided it made greater sense for the administrative staff to take a far more active role in the whole process, coordinating dates and venues, organizing publicity and processing applications. This involved increased liaison with staff at all levels. They no longer had to wait to check every action with the trainers but were encouraged to exercise their own initiative. Having worked as mostly routine clerical officers, it was somewhat alarming at first to be expected to work so independently. I offered support when needed, but they quickly relished the extra responsibility and were soon making many worthwhile suggestions for improving systems and procedures. Their motivation and self-confidence developed in leaps and bounds. They were able to fully participate in the team as a whole, making valuable contributions in team meetings. The traditional distinctions had been broken down. My trainers were no longer afforded some privileged status because of their professional background. Everyone was expected to respect and value the part played by everyone else. I was determined to demonstrate in my management role the principles I had advocated as a trainer. My administrative staff were given the opportunity to derive more fulfillment and satisfaction from their work as well as enhancing their self-esteem and pointing to further possibilities for development. At the same time, the organization benefited from having a more efficient and effective service. Even the training officers welcomed the changes, relieved of the tedious administrative involvement they had little real enthusiasm for anyway. Although initially perhaps somewhat unsure of the consequences for their own position within the team, they came to appreciate the value of a more open and collaborative way of working.

Empowerment is crucial to any real understanding of how ongoing learning and development may enable organizations to maximize the potential of their staff. However people may initially present, in terms of their existing qualifications or the lack of them, their experience or their level of confidence, we need to remember that the process of learning can literally transform them, revealing strengths we might have only vaguely guessed at. If you do not have this conviction as a tutor you will never be able to help give your learners the positive belief in themselves they so much depend on to sustain them.

Empowerment has become fashionable simply because today's world is expecting people to actively contribute in the workplace. They will have to think for themselves and exercise much greater initiative. In addition the rapid rate of change makes lifelong learning inevitable. It follows that tutors cannot continue to approach learners with traditionally limited expectations. They will need to incorporate these ideas into the way they relate to their learners and how they view their own role. Their task is no longer to control and channel people's talents along conventional pathways. Instead it is about drawing out people's potential, sharing with them the responsibility for the learning and forging together a way forward through new and constantly changing territory.

For the duration

So far, I have made no differentiation between the varying periods of time the learning relationship may last. In the training scenario, the relationship is often short-term, perhaps only one day, usually no more than several days. While trainers are sometimes involved in longer-term programs, these are more typically the preserve of teachers. The duration of the relationship obviously has an impact on how that relationship is managed. Where one has only a relatively brief encounter with one's learners, the experience is very concentrated. Longer-term affairs can be conducted on a more leisurely basis.

If you are running a one-day program, there are definite constraints on the extent to which you are able to get to know your learners. There will be a considerable pressure to establish the engaging approach immediately; to signal very explicitly the sort of interaction you want to encourage. You should be proactively demonstrating the principles of engagement rather than simply waiting for opportunities to present themselves. Learners need to be positively involved at the earliest possible stage. One effective strategy is to organize, almost as soon as the introductions are out of the way, activities in which your learners can share their different experiences, views and ideas relevant to the learning at hand. The concern is not with performance, but rather with helping to establish a clearer understanding between all parties involved in the learning relationship. It goes without saying that your response at this point will crucially influence the level of participation to follow.

Learners who are exposed to engagement over this short time scale may feel it has been a very intensive experience, which hopefully leaves them feeling excited, stimulated and perhaps not a little exhausted. I think there should always be some acknowledgement of the effort they have made in the learning situation, and some time given to looking at how they will take the experience forward after the learning program has finished. This enables learners to adjust from the rather unfamiliar and demanding atmosphere of the learning situation to their more normal routine. I am not advocating contrived and ritualized course closures and have never really relished the group hug, but I am suggesting learners will appreciate some opportunity to consolidate and meaningfully conclude their learning experience. At the very least, they will value the chance to say how they have felt through the process and what difference, if any, they think it has made to them individually.

For learners involved in a longer-term program, the pace can obviously be more relaxed. Indeed, both tutor and learners would find it difficult to sustain the hectic pace of the short program over any longer period. The relationship will be ongoing, established more gradually, developing and evolving over time. Everyone will have the chance to reveal more of themselves and explore many different aspects of one another. Nevertheless the principles of engagement will still need to be activated fairly quickly, otherwise you may find your learners assuming a more traditional relationship which then generates its own momentum and is difficult to turn around. Course closure may require greater consideration, acknowledging the commitment learners have made to the process and more especially to each other. They will need time to say good bye and move on from an experience which has required a considerable personal investment from everyone involved.

Respecting professional boundaries

Establishing a reciprocal relationship with your learners involves engaging them at various levels, emotionally and intellectually. We need to appeal to their curiosity, imagination, sense of fun, empathy, skepticism, logical reasoning – their humanity. Although we are playing the role of tutor and they are occupying the role of learners, we still need to try and define those roles so we may continue to explore the relationship and move beyond conventional and traditional models. It is nevertheless important not to confuse personal and professional boundaries. Tutors who wander into a more personal domain risk numerous problems that will invariably jeopardize their ability to function effectively. Engagement does not entail developing personal relationships with your learners. You need to remember your relationship is a professional one. Some trainers and learners may try to meet more personal needs through the learning relationship. This is inappropriate and will inevitably divert attention away from the learning. It is possible to be warm, understanding, accessible and responsive to your learners and remain professional.

Perhaps this may seem a tall order, to engage with our learners on a more human level and still be professional. It is about demonstrating that we care and that we appreciate our learners as individuals with varying needs in relation to their learning. But it is also about recognizing our role as tutors has a cutoff point. Otherwise, we become too involved and lose the capacity to exercise any objective judgment. That is the ultimate guiding principle. If we feel we are getting to the point when our judgment is becoming compromised by our own personal needs to be approved, to be liked, we are no longer operating in a professional capacity. We have crossed over into uncharted territory, where the terrain is unpredictable and potentially hazardous.

The reassuring aspect of professionalism is that you provide as good a service to your least preferred learner as to those you like best. You cannot help having different feelings towards different individuals. That is only natural. But it should never be a justification for discriminating between those individuals. Every learner is entitled to a professional level of tuition. There is nothing less edifying than a tutor who is deliberately encouraging a fan-club mentality among their learners. They relish being showered with presents at the end of the program. Inevitably learners who have not elected to participate in so massaging their tutor's ego run the risk of being left out in the cold. In this sort of situation, there will be an inner clique who enjoy the tutor's special attention while those more independently spirited souls have to make do as best they can.

As I said earlier tutors need to be responsive to the individual needs of their learners and this may well necessitate spending more time with some than with others, but this should be on the basis of the learning needs, and not some more dubious personal agenda. If you have allowed yourself to stray across the professional boundary, you are open to accusations you may not even be guilty of. But that is the risk you have inevitably invited. If learners see you courting favorites, they will lose confidence in your integrity and distrust your motivation in more general ways. You will no longer have their respect and an essential part of the relationship has been damaged.

This can happen in relation to individuals and to whole groups. Tutors can court favorites and they can also go native. They are so concerned to identify with the group culture they lose all sense of objective judgment. They become so tuned in to the group, they are no longer capable of maintaining their essential distance. This again raises difficult issues about the delicate balance which tutors need to maintain. They are trying to develop a warm and empathic relationship with their learners and yet they have to remain apart and somewhat removed if they are to be effective. They have to retain an overview of the dynamics of the whole group and not become identified with sectional interests. The group may well be working through various issues and it is vital the tutor is able to look at this impartially. Tutors who go native lose their ability to recognize and respond when a group is becoming self indulgent, complacent, in denial or just avoiding difficult areas. They may begin to sense their position has been compromised but it then becomes increasingly difficult to extricate themselves. This obviously leaves tutors in a somewhat lonely position. They may enjoy a temporary sense of honorary membership with a group, but they are not one of the group and should never expect to be. Their support must come from other colleagues within or outside their organization, but I shall say more about that in Chapter 10.

Any relationship involves two parties engaged in a process which affects them both. A positive relationship is one where each feels validated. A reciprocal relationship enables each to grow and develop. Engagement is about establishing such a relationship between yourself and your learners. It is an empowering experience for all involved. Engagement demands a level of commitment which many tutors may resist. It requires considerable investment and like all relationships, a willingness to share something of yourself.

Summary Points

☐ The reciprocal relationship depends on tutors' willingness to grow and develop with their learners and to see learning as ultimately unpredictable. We need to be confident enough to take risks and no longer view our credibility in terms of traditional ideas of authority.

☐ Learning today is less about telling learners how to do things and what to think, and much more about encouraging them to use their initiative and judgment. The role of tutor as pedagogue is inconsistent with encouraging greater learner responsibility.

☐ We need to view learners as collaborators and not see their more limited knowledge and understanding as a justification for monopolizing control. Rather than focusing entirely on learners' deficits, we need to develop a positive view of their strengths and reflect that back to them. We should also encourage the learners whose knowledge and experience may add to our own, rather than fear them as rivals.

☐ Tutors, as subject experts, are able to control the learning situation and influence learner willingness to question or disagree. They need to model an attitude where different ideas and opinions are open to discussion and individual learners feel respected and valued.

☐ Empowerment involves affirming people as they are, while also encouraging the potential they have still to realize. Tutors need to communicate their belief in their learners' ability to succeed, while at the same time giving reassurance that their respect and approval does not depend on that success.

☐ The duration of a learning program will affect the way the learning relationship is managed. The shorter the relationship, the more concentrated the effort will be to engage with your learners.

☐ Even though the reciprocal relationship requires us to move into a more shared space with our learners, we still need to maintain professional boundaries, in the sense that we ensure the same standard of service to all learners, irrespective of our personal feelings, likes or dislikes. We need to maintain our objective judgment while still committing to a relationship, in which we are prepared to invest a significant part of ourselves.

QUESTIONS FOR REFLECTION

1. *How far do you find that the process of helping others learn stimulates your own development? How comfortable are you with the prospect of unpredictable learning outcomes? Does that excite you or do feel that is the kind of excitement you could do without?*

It is sometimes difficult to maintain our own curiosity and enthusiasm when we feel we have settled into a familiar routine, covering the same ground, but maybe if we shift our focus from our prescribed material to the endlessly variable ways in which our learners exercise our skill and understanding, we might find the enterprise more interesting.

2. *How do you feel about the learner who appears to know more than you about a particular subject area? Do you immediately feel your own credibility and confidence undermined?*

It is very easy to feel that your authority as a tutor depends on your position as expert, which may seem more difficult to maintain if you fear learners being able to identify your limitations. But maybe we need to shift our focus and accept that not all the learning has to originate from ourselves and that no one can realistically claim completely comprehensive and exhaustive knowledge of a subject. You are still an important resource to your learners and even more so if you are secure enough in yourself to recognize the value of their contributions.

3. ***Do you feel that it is part of your responsibility to act as final arbiter of what is judged to be worthwhile and important in the learning situation? Do you find yourself doing this, sometimes unintentionally, simply because you assume your learners' judgment is deficient and unreliable?***

We may sometimes underestimate our learners and believe that, because they do not share our level of knowledge, we are blessed with a superior intelligence which renders our arguments more rational than theirs. We do not always question sufficiently the way our own routine ways of thinking may limit our ability to recognize the merit of seemingly naive, or perhaps more unorthodox ideas.

4. ***How far do you think your approval of your learners is dependent on their successful progress? Do learners who find such progress more difficult make you feel frustrated and inadequate as a tutor? Do we need our learners' success as reassurance of our own worth?***

We do not always recognize how our feelings of our own worth are inextricably tied up with our learners' achievements, which may in turn lead us to resent their failure to succeed. So, instead of clearly focusing on their performance, we confuse the message, appear personally rejecting and leave them feeling undeserving of our respect.

5. ***How comfortable do you feel with the time constraints on your relationship with your learners? Do you think that a short program makes it difficult to establish any very meaningful relationship with them?***

Relationships are obviously affected by how much time you have together and it would be all too easy to debate the relative merits of quantity vs. quality. Essentially the extent to which we connect with another individual, depends on the effort we invest, during whatever time available, in proactively demonstrating positive regard and ensuring our own agendas do not become obstacles in the communication.

6. ***How comfortable do you feel in managing the tensions within the reciprocal relationship; being open and collaborative with your learners while still maintaining a sense of objective distance?***

These are not easy to reconcile at times and this is where the professional support discussed in Chapter 10 provides a vital opportunity to reflect on our relationships with our learners; whose needs are being addressed, and how difficult it is to always recognize when we have overstepped those professional boundaries.

9

The Dynamic Dialogue

Long ago, Socrates adopted a method that depended on learners learning by thinking through and analyzing the questions he put to them. The questions were not designed to just elicit a particular, or even a correct answer, but to help the learners consider all the implications, consequences, and logical connections and contradictions in their response to a given issue. The learning was essentially through discussion and argument, which is supposedly what happens in our centers of higher learning today. Feedback from such institutions suggests the cumulative influence of fourteen years of school education takes its toll, and that sadly many learners are reluctant to explore ideas in this way. It is something they have little practice in. Perhaps lecturers are also ambivalent about the style of learning they wish to foster among their learners. The experience of many young people through the formal education system has conditioned them to expect to be processed, to have something done to them, to receive knowledge and then simply reproduce it.

Is it really so radical to suggest that tutors should be demonstrating and positively encouraging a skeptical attitude, one that is wary of making assumptions, that carefully evaluates what passes as evidence, that will confidently question the contribution of established and eminent thinkers and experts, that is not impressed merely by reputation and fashionable theories, that is open to difficult and controversial ideas and is prepared to subject even personally cherished notions to the same rational and rigorous process?

Socrates was regarded as a subversive influence, and ultimately paid the price for his uncompromising insistence on questioning what most people would rather take for granted. There is undoubtedly something dangerous in adopting such an attitude. Conventional authority may be undermined if people become too independent in their thinking. And this is where we return once again to the purpose of learning. Is it to condition people to accept the way things have previously been thought about and done, to fill empty mugs from our impressively full pitchers or is it to explore new options and possibilities? The Socratic legacy may still leave us uneasy. It challenges the status quo. Everything that is familiar must be viewed as potentially problematic. This is a stimulating, but also a very demanding way of approaching learning.

The value of the dialogue depends on the merit of the ideas and the quality of the discussion. These may be quite independent of the status and reputation of those engaged in the dialogue, although experience and expertise will obviously afford a considerable advantage. Those who readily make connections and recognize contradictions will feel well equipped. A naturally keen, agile and critical mind will relish this approach to learning. People who are less confident and unused to putting forward their views and ideas are more vulnerable. They need encouragement to make the effort. In many ways it is much easier to just follow the orthodox view, to accept other people's conclusions and not have to exercise you own mental faculties too strenuously.

Maybe many learners become worn down by the sheer volume of learning they are now expected to digest as they progress through the formal education system. Passing exams becomes the only objective, and they have little enthusiasm for anything not directly related to that end. So we churn out trained minds – but whatever curiosity, imagination, perceptiveness and discrimination they might have often only survives in spite of the process. It may well be difficult to persuade learners that engagement is a more rewarding way when it clearly calls for greater input and effort on their part. They have, after all, been conditioned by an educational system which has taught them to comply, and offered little incentive for more independent thinking. There is a legacy to be turned around.

Nevertheless there are learners who care and still have found it difficult to make themselves heard because we are worried they will make life difficult for us. We need to be ready to listen and to learn from them. Their more adventurous spirit should be welcomed. They can infuse the learning situation with real energy. Their enthusiasm may need to be subjected to more rational scrutiny, but that is all part of the dynamic dialogue.

If we truly want people to think more independently, and to be capable and confident in rational and reasoned thinking and discussion, then we need to actively promote this with our learners. Again I want to emphasize that this approach is not simply confined to certain subject areas, where intellectual rigor is more apparent. This applies to all learning disciplines. The dynamic dialogue is relevant to both food handling training and the study of law. Within all learning there is the potential to engage in this dialogue.

Speaking the same language

Any meaningful dialogue will be limited to the extent to which those involved share a common language. This would appear obvious, but how many learners have been frozen out of a learning situation by the failure of the tutor to communicate with them at their level. Language can be highly problematic in the learning relationship. We cannot assume our meaning will always be understood. Tutors will often express themselves in ways which learners find intimidating. What is the point of using words with which your learners are not familiar, obscuring your meaning with overly convoluted sentences or resorting to jargon and abbreviations they do not yet recognize? It is the tutors' responsibility to communicate effectively with their learners. They cannot possibly do this unless they employ language appropriate to the experience of their learners.

Language can be rich, colorful and an enormously potent cultural symbol, but its basic purpose is to enable people to understand one another. In a learning situation, the language should remain as simple and straightforward as possible. We should never be tempted as tutors to use language only to demonstrate our own verbal facility, when that may disadvantage our learners and leave them feeling ignorant and foolish.

If the dialogue is to be successfully engaged, it needs to happen quickly. There is little purpose in working on the principle that people cannot be involved until they are more informed. By then, the basis of interaction has been established. Learners have already received the message that their contributions are of only marginal value, for the most part no more than interesting diversions from the main business at hand. It is critical that they receive a far more positive message. Even when they are still simply enthusiastic amateurs, their opinions, thoughts and responses should be consistently encouraged. Returning to the example of language tuition, it is well understood that learners will only develop a confidence in speaking if they are prompted right from the beginning to engage in conversation, even when their vocabulary is limited and their mastery of grammar is practically non-existent. Despite the obvious lack of skill and knowledge, they need to feel they can perform at some level with what they are being taught, and their attempts, although faltering, deserve careful nurturing. The same applies to any area of learning. Learners respond far more positively if they derive a sense of achievement. So the dialogue must be one in which they are able to proactively engage, making their observations, expressing their doubts and clarifying their understanding.

While I am advocating that learners should be encouraged to engage in a dialogue, where the conclusions are not always predictable, and notions of absolute certainty and correctness are treated with some skepticism, I also acknowledge that many learning programs do demand an adherence to a more prescribed curriculum. To that extent, tutors are obliged to follow a more conventional line, although I think this can still be approached with a degree of pragmatism which does not compromise the principles of engagement. Learners are practical and realistic, and are quite capable of distinguishing between what they are obliged to do in order to satisfy certain evaluation criteria and what is intrinsically worthwhile. The first represents an instrumental approach to learning with which tutors can compromise, acknowledging what is necessary in order to play the game, but being quite explicit about the nature of the game. The second is concerned with a more authentic learning experience. Learners certainly want the bit of paper, but they are usually much happier obtaining it through a process in which they have also felt respected and involved.

'But you said ...'

Communication is one of the most complex and often frustrating areas of human activity. We are all familiar with the experience of discussing an issue among a group of people where everyone takes away a somewhat different interpretation of what they believe they have heard people say. I sometimes find myself doubting what I have actually said during a session when I hear a decidedly garbled version repeated back to me at some later point. It can be quite dispiriting to realize how difficult it is to ensure people understand what you *meant* to say.

One of the major problems lies in the fact that the way we hear any sort of message depends on our previous experience, our baggage. This baggage has accumulated into a certain way of understanding our world so that any new information will be processed in terms of our already established understandings. Our personalities, our expectations and aspirations, our anxieties and previous disappointments and set-backs will all contribute to the way we perceive and respond.

There is however, an additional factor to be appreciated. Along with our varying baggage, we also display real differences in the way we listen to one another. Failure to recognize these differences can result in all manner of confusion and unnecessary offense. We each have particular patterns of listening which affect the way we hear other people and the sense we make of what they are saying. A fairly simple distinction can be made between three broad categories of listener.

Firstly there are the 'literal listeners' who concentrate intently on what is actually being said, the precise words being used. They are less concerned with non-verbal cues and tend to see these as a distraction. They believe that people, on the whole, mean what they say, and so they are prepared to accept whatever is said at face value. These are very precise people who cannot cope with ambiguity and are unlikely to appreciate the subtleties of irony.

The second group, the 'feeling listeners' focus almost exclusively on the emotional aspect of someone's communication. They will hear the words, but they are much more concerned with how someone appears to be feeling. They will be acutely sensitive to non-verbal cues and set great store by the way someone is speaking, the tone and expression in their voice, the attitude they adopt. Such listeners key into emotional content and respond at a similar level. They are inevitably at risk of being all too easily manipulated.

The third group, the 'meaning listeners' start from the premise that few people really say what they mean and often will use displays of feeling for particular effect. They are reluctant to take anything at face value and will always look for the hidden meaning. They are keenly sensitive to any cue, no matter how seemingly insignificant. Indeed this highly tuned attitude can border on the paranoid at times. Nevertheless, these people will be very effective at looking beyond the obvious and being alert to what someone is trying to say even when they cannot find the words and are unable to show their feelings.

It does not take too much of a leap of the imagination to speculate on how problematic it may be for these different types of listeners to communicate with one another. They may all be listening to the same individual and each will come away with a contrary view of what was being said. The literal 'listener' will not look further than the actual words being spoken. The 'feeling' listener will focus on whether the speaker seemed happy, sad, angry, anxious or whatever. They will want to respond to those feelings and the words will be secondary to the emotion conveyed. The 'meaning' listener will concentrate on any inconsistencies in what is being communicated. They will be reading between the lines, wondering how genuine are the emotions on display, what is not being said and how to interpret what is being said. They will constantly be trying to establish the real meaning, unconvinced that words and gestures are anything more than a disguise for what we are actually thinking and feeling.

The 'literal' listener will dismiss the other two as making life unnecessarily complicated and become irritated when it is obvious they have not paid sufficiently close attention and so have missed important details. The 'feeling' listener will regard the other two as unsympathetic and unable to deal with emotions. The 'meaning' listener will become impatient with what they see as the 'literal' listener's lack of imagination and the 'feeling' listener's gullibility. Because these differences are rarely made explicit, people fail to recognize how their own assumptions are constantly influencing the way they interact with others.

We each of us have a capacity to switch into different modes, but most of us do have a more dominant style which characterizes our routine way of dealing with one another. The temptation is always to invalidate anything which does not readily fit with our own way of making sense of the world. But unless we can appreciate that there are various approaches which all have their own merits, we become stuck in a narrow and restricted perspective.

In attempting to establish a common language between yourself and your learners, it is worthwhile considering that all learners will have their own way of hearing what you say, depending on the type of listener they represent and the individual baggage they bring with them. This is why it is absolutely vital to view communication as inherently problematic. Never assume that because you mean something with a given word or phrase, everyone else will understand it in the same way. You need to be acutely alert to how your messages are being received. It is important to reassure your learners that you are aware of these stumbling blocks and they should not hesitate to ask for a point to be clarified if they are in any doubt.

Maps and codes

Another aspect to establishing a common language is in recognizing the extent to which we rely on the restricted code of our own topic or subject. It is incredibly difficult to think yourself back into the position of the novice for whom the territory is unfamiliar and daunting, to cast off all the short-hand terms, specialized language and the contextualized meanings which we routinely take for granted. It is the way we share our knowledge and expertise with others who have been similarly processed which characterizes our ease and familiarity with our area. Someone who has yet to be properly initiated will feel as though they are visiting a strange and alien territory, confronting the same awkwardness as those struggling to speak a foreign language in another country. It is vital to devise an intelligible map, which incorporates the learners' starting points. They can then locate themselves within this strange terrain. The signposts need to be clearly marked at the start of the journey as there are no established reference points at this stage and the whole experience may feel completely disorientating. The map should be to acknowledge where someone has come from and in what direction they are heading.

Learners come with a variety of experience which may be more or less relevant to the area of study at hand. All will have decided, for their own reasons, that this is an enterprise with which they wish to engage. It is a useful way of establishing the dialogue to look at their various motivations and expectations. This helps explore what assumptions they are making and the starting points they are all coming from. It then becomes a little easier for you as the tutor to begin to identify points of relevance and connection with previous experience which will enable the learners to acclimatize more comfortably. These are very preliminary attempts to involve your learners and it does not really matter at this stage whether they are being exposed to a somewhat generalized version of the topic and its key concepts; the important issue is to make them feel involved, to enable them to relate it to their own understanding.

When I introduce the main areas of psychological theory crucial for understanding the development of children, I provide a map in the form of an overview of each theory and relate it to how it would make sense to the rather more familiar and deceptively basic topic of potty training. Most people, whether parents or not, have some thoughts and feelings around the subject. It is from such a position that they are able to relate to the different ideas, give them meaning and start to engage in some degree of critical evaluation. So theorists such as Freud, Piaget and Skinner are introduced, albeit rather briefly. The mystique is dissolved and learners begin to see that these are ideas they can make sense of and talk about.

If there is any real art in the business of helping people learn, it is the ability to simplify complex information to a level which is valid and still accessible to the learner. This is one of the most demanding aspects of the tutor's role, to devise imaginative and stimulating strategies in order to explain the learning in terms relevant to the learner. While the many products on the market today considerably reduce the need to create your own material, you nevertheless have the ultimate responsibility for deciding which materials are most suitable and how they are best put together. Very rarely am I able to lift a package off the shelf and deliver it without any modifications. Mostly I am searching, like some greedy magpie, for good ideas which I can incorporate into my own strategy. The more you become tuned into your particular learners' needs, the more dissatisfied you become with material designed for only the most general audience.

It is part of your role to explore the learning objectives and to use your creative imagination to generate ideas for how to make the learning interesting, relevant, stimulating and satisfying – and arguably entertaining as well. All knowledge is accessible if we are committed to making it so. But if we believe only certain sorts of people are capable of understanding the intractable mysteries of our subject or topic, there is little chance of us making the necessary effort to decode it and present it in a more digestible form.

While it is imperative that you are confident in your learners' ability, you also need to be able to think yourself back into their position, to anticipate how they will approach a certain concept, how they will view a certain problem, and to consider how you can make it less baffling. What sort of things are they already familiar with? How can I utilize other areas of their experience to make the learning come alive? How can I best illustrate an abstract idea with a familiar example? How can I engage their imagination and curiosity as well as their retentive memories?

Mugs with attitude – encouraging questions

Achieving an ongoing and fruitful dialogue depends on your learners feeling sufficiently confident to question and challenge. They need to know we are comfortable enough with ourselves not to take this personally. Many tutors have developed such a personal investment in their area of expertise, they are reluctant to submit their cherished wisdom to more critical scrutiny. We may feel our learners have only such a rudimentary grasp of what we are trying to teach them, that there is little they can contribute to any meaningful discussion. If you adopt that sort of attitude, you will only make your learners feel unworthy and incapable of questioning anything or anyone – so awesomely clever. They need to believe they may have something valid to say. You may have heard the same facile points a hundred times before, but it does not matter. This is still an occasion when someone is daring to say something they fear might sound ridiculous but is important in their terms. It is up to you to respond thoughtfully and encouragingly.

Challenge should be seen as a positive opportunity to stimulate the dialogue, to break out of predictable exchanges. It is risky and can be uncomfortable. Learners may introduce issues and ideas which the tutor may not have considered or may feel ill-equipped to deal with but that is an inevitable consequence. Learners need to be encouraged to think critically about what they are learning, to care enough to ask questions, to point to inconsistencies and contradictions.

Asking questions should be a natural part of the dialogue and yet we often underestimate the skill involved in asking questions effectively. Perhaps we are not always sure why we are even asking the questions. Questions can be used to reinforce the authority of the tutor or they can provide a genuine opportunity to open up the dialogue. What are we trying to achieve with a question? Is it simply to prompt learners to provide the correct answer with the tutor as the only arbiter of what constitutes correctness? Or are we trying to encourage learners to think about an issue or a problem?

Questions can be used to ease learners into a session, to find out what they already know and to get them focused on the subject. This is not about giving learners the chance to show off to one another and to yourself, establishing themselves further up the pecking order by virtue of their clever erudition. This is simply a way of finding out where your learners already are in relation to a given subject area. What does it mean to them? Does it link with anything else they are already familiar with? So you clearly convey to your group that the purpose of your questions is to find out more about them, all of them, even the ones who appear to know very little about the topic in hand. Presumably there is some level of curiosity, some reason why they wish to learn more about this area and that is what you are interested to discover.

You may also wish to ask questions to invite opinion, to encourage participation and discussion, particularly if you want people to share experiences. This is inevitable if you are dealing with sensitive or controversial issues. At the beginning of a program, this strategy may well help to get learners involved, sharing their thoughts and feelings, and giving everyone the confidence to put forward their views. Again, to avoid the danger of one-upmanship games undermining the less articulate or the more timid, it is vital to respond just as positively to everyone's contribution. The manner in which people express themselves is far less important than their willingness to participate in the discussion. However, as learners become more comfortable with each other and with the process, you can then stretch them a little further, asking them to explain or substantiate a particular position, drawing on the learning and the requirement to form opinion on logical argument and empirical evidence. You gradually demonstrate to learners that mere personal opinion is insufficient without being based on a more objective foundation.

Questions can be asked to check understanding, to ensure that learners have absorbed and understood the learning, although this can feel very like school and so needs to be approached sensitively. I think we can all remember the awful sense of dread as we cowered in our seats, impending ignominy threatening to overwhelm us, as we waited for the teacher's eye to rest on us and ask the question we knew we could not answer. No adult learner should ever have to suffer that sort of anxiety – nor for that matter should any child. It is counter-productive. If you are going to ask questions for this purpose, then you need to give some very reassuring signals that all answers will be responded to respectfully. Incorrect answers can be acknowledged as incorrect, but maybe you can reduce your learner's unease by using their answer as an opportunity to look at how such errors can be made, highlighting common areas of misunderstanding and confusion. Even when individuals offer irrelevant or inappropriate answers, it is still necessary to preserve their dignity and avoid making them feel foolish. You try and extract something from what they have said which you can adapt and use to make a more general point. I myself never target individual learners with specific questions on what they have learned. Such questions are always addressed generally to the group. I rely on volunteers to offer an answer. There are other far more effective, and less publicly mortifying ways in which you can evaluate how much each individual has learned.

What about asking *for* questions? There is often a sense that we are somehow obliged to give our learners the opportunity, at some point in the proceedings, of asking the odd question. Too often this takes on an almost ritualized character, where learners feel uncomfortable if no one can actually think of anything to ask. Somehow questions have become equated with the level of interest generated and if there are no questions, then obviously no one is actually that interested.

This stage management approach to the asking for questions makes for an extremely stilted dialogue. Inevitably, if you do leave questions to the end of whatever you are talking about, and in effect deliver a presentation, learners will be very circumscribed in how far they can engage with you. They ask a question, you answer and if they are lucky they might get the chance to follow up with a further point, but it is unlikely they will be able to pursue the issue beyond that. Similarly, if you only ask for questions as a permission to continue, having finished one part of a topic you check with everyone before continuing with the next section, you are not really opening up any meaningful sort of dialogue. Too often this approach almost seems to be ensuring that the learners are still there in spirit as well as body, and not just merely going through the motions of attending. But their involvement is only partial. They are only invited to speak when the tutor decides it is appropriate.

The dynamic dialogue assumes that learners can ask questions as an ongoing part of the learning. It may seem as though you are giving them an unlimited license to interrupt which clearly has implications for the organization and timing of any learning sequence. However, it is still possible to maintain a purposeful focus and to ensure that questions are made relevant to the learning at hand. If learners raise questions which are not particularly germane, it will be necessary to explain why the question is not going to be very useful to explore at this present moment, although you might anticipate a point when it could be raised again. Maybe learners' questions reveal how disorientated they are with a topic and you have to spend some time resolving the confusion. Maybe some learners are clearly so determined to pursue an agenda regardless of how far it fits with the topic under discussion, you have to clarify the parameters of the learning and acknowledge that there are limits to what can be usefully debated, although you always need to be questioning your own judgment in these circumstances. Is it founded on a reasonable distinction between what is relevant and what is not, or is it motivated by a reluctance to engage in a dialogue which you find uncomfortably challenging?

Questions, asked by yourself or your learners, are a fundamental part of the dialogue. They should be encouraged as opportunities to explore ideas, rather than a tiresome routine one is expected to follow with one's learners, simply going through the motions without any real enthusiasm. Questions should form a quite natural and spontaneous part of the learning process. They should be asked and answered in a manner that promotes the dialogue. While questions form the most basic and essential elements of the dialogue, there are specific strategies which can be used to provoke the dialogue, which positively invite learners to respond to issues with their own thoughts and reactions.

Provoking the dialogue

You can kick start the whole process by a range of strategies. These are designed to deliberately invite a more skeptical and questioning attitude on the part of your learners. Their appropriateness depends on the nature of the learning content and the confidence of your learners. You can be selective and use the strategies in combination or one at a time, perhaps leaving some for a later stage when you and your learners are more at ease with each other.

First, you might present the learning as a series of options, all with their relative advantages and disadvantages, strengths and weaknesses, signaling that the list of points is not exhaustive and is still negotiable. Maybe your learners will feel something is not really a disadvantage after all, or the advantage is not that significant anyway. This very simple and undemanding way of looking at information not only emphasizes the idea that there is not always an obviously right way or right answer to resolving a problem, it also stimulates the learners to think for themselves about a number of issues, weighing up various factors to arrive at an overall conclusion. It discourages the view that only experts can have an opinion. You are responsible for presenting the options and may help to steer the points but you need to avoid being too explicitly directive, otherwise learners will simply feel they are being asked to jump through predictable hoops. The object is to attract their genuine interest and attention by helping them develop a point of view.

As an example from training skills programs, I might present the various audio-visual aids which trainers have at their disposal, and often feel obliged to use in order to guarantee the all-singing-all-dancing performance which they think is expected of them. As I present each one, I would draw out in discussion with the learners the particular strengths the different aids have to offer and the drawbacks they suffer from. Through the weighing up of the various points, we can begin to establish a criteria for selecting the most appropriate visual aid for a given type of learning – and to decide if we need to use a visual aid at all.

The second strategy relies on the question with which children continually torment their parents – why? The idea is to pursue a particular topic by teasing out the logical relationship between different points. So often those points are just stated and accepted as though there was no possible need to explain them, only the really naive and ignorant would be left wondering. Anyone who is capable of framing a question is someone who wants to learn, and deserves due respect because of that. We need to pre-empt the 'whys' and incorporate them into our own teaching.

Again using an example from the area of training skills, we might explore why experiential or active learning techniques are seen as so much more desirable than traditional 'chalk and talk' models. Lectures are often regarded as anathema to proponents of good training practice, but such assumptions are rarely examined. Why have lectures been judged so negatively? Why are they thought to be ineffective? Why are they still so widely employed in education? Why is it necessary to actively involve learners in the learning process? Why do they learn more by doing something with the learning? Why has experiential learning become so much more popular among tutors? Why do learners need to make the learning real through experience? These are only a few suggestions for how the issue might be addressed. The important aspect of this approach is to enable your learners to clarify the connections rather than simply taking things for granted in unquestioning agreement.

A third strategy involves developing a critique of the knowledge being presented. Learners very often feel it is quite beyond their capacity to find flaws in the work of some eminent individual, whose reputation is already well established. And yet it can be one of the most empowering of learning experiences for learners to critically evaluate the work of such an individual. They will need guidance and not a little support. Discrepancies with actual material evidence will be easier to appreciate. More difficult will be the logical inconsistencies.

Kolb's Learning Cycle is a traditional model for looking at what is involved in learning and how all of us demonstrate various styles of learning. As with most ideas, there are some valuable insights and understanding to be gained from this work, which I have already referred to in an earlier chapter. To recap on the general idea, Kolb argues there is a cycle of learning, beginning with experience, working through to reflecting on that experience, examining our feelings about it, giving it meaning. We then go on to generalize from those reflections. We construct concepts and devise principles which help us make sense of other similar situations, and which then provide guidance on how we might deal with such situations in the future. The final stage in the cycle, active experimentation, is when we try out those principles and see how effectively they work in practice. We then reflect on what happened and so go round the cycle again.

The other main idea of Kolb's is that we all have points on the learning cycle where we feel most at home and these will influence our preferred learning style. Some of us will like to reflect on individual experience, others will like to deal in general principles and abstract theories while others learn best by doing. The latter will always be the first to volunteer for role play. As I said, Kolb's ideas are very useful but they are not beyond criticism, and it certainly helps to sharpen learners' critical faculties to evaluate his ideas and identify their shortcomings. One obvious problem is that individuals inevitably adopt different learning styles in different learning situations. I am quite content to be a reflector looking at assertiveness, a natural conceptualizer when considering the medical and sociological models of mental illness, and an enthusiastic active experimenter when it comes to meeting-chairing skills. So, although Kolb has value, his ideas still have their limitations and it is important that learners feel sufficiently assured to identify them.

Earlier, I talked about the Socratic method of questioning as a general principle underpinning my idea of a reciprocal dialogue. However, the specific technique used by Socrates was to pursue arguments through to their logical consequences. Discussions were conducted on the basis of examining an idea and following it through to a point where its consequences became clear. If you think this and you think that, then this inevitably follows. How far had you anticipated this particular logical consequence? Maybe it does not accord with your understanding? Perhaps we need to go back and examine the logical progression of your ideas? We do not need to be discussing philosophy for this approach to have relevance. An obvious example for fledgling trainers might be to look at the assumptions they were making about their learners, how those assumptions would influence their behavior toward them, and how the learners would then in turn respond to them.

The final approach is one designed to be deliberately provocative. It is similar to playing devil's advocate. You quite consciously adopt a contentious and controversial line which you need not believe in or agree with. The purpose is to set up an opposing line to the one being assumed by your learners. This can be especially useful when there is an almost unthinking consensus around an issue – people taking a position because they have not really considered anything contrary. It may well be that everyone still holds on to their previous view, but they have been forced to examine why they think as they do. In most organizations, there is a widespread acceptance of the traditional 'happy sheet' as the conventional method of evaluating training. This is what everyone is used to. It provides immediate feedback on participants' impressions. Trainers, managers and participants all expect them, but what do they really measure? Because everyone's perspective on evaluation is so limited by the 'happy sheet', it is possible to throw a spanner in the works by even asking why we need them, and might there not be additional and more effective ways of evaluating a learning program.

With all these approaches, the idea is to engage your learners in a dialogue, in a debate where they can better understand the learning by actively thinking through the ideas. The tutor simply prods and prompts in the right places and at the right moments. Some tutors may object and say this is made almost impossible when you are trying to conduct such a debate with a normal sized group. I would agree that it can become very fraught with large numbers. As long as everyone is made aware that each person's point deserves to be listened to and there is no value in talking over one another, then such open discussion becomes a normal feature of the learning. The tutor obviously has to take some responsibility for ensuring the discussion is relevant, constructive and one where everyone is able to contribute their ideas. It is still necessary for you to keep the program to time and move things along so that the learning objectives are covered. It may well be that at times you have to curtail the discussion simply because of such time constraints, but these practicalities can be easily explained to your learners without jeopardizing the dialogue you have established.

Once the dialogue is ongoing, you can use it to obtain vital feedback from your learners. The dialogue ensures your learners will always be able to register a problem as it arises. It will be part of the natural way in which you communicate with them. Raising questions and openly admitting confusion is no longer an occasion where you risk losing face. It is simply something entirely normal and routine, evoking no more than a revised attempt by the tutor to explain something a little better, perhaps more imaginatively with more relevant examples.

Summary Points

☐ **The dynamic dialogue derives from the Socratic legacy. Learners are urged to question accepted ideas through rational discussion. Skepticism is encouraged. The objective is not simply concerned with reaching a correct answer, but rather with exploring and achieving a fuller understanding of the issues.**

- The dialogue depends on a common language, which does not disadvantage learners and enables them to contribute actively and confidently to the discussion.

- People will listen in different ways to what is being said. We should never assume that others hear in the same way as we do. Communication is inherently problematic. Tutors need to be constantly alert to potential misunderstandings and confusion.

- Learners may initially feel disorientated with a new and unfamiliar subject. They need to be provided with ways to make it meaningful in relation to their own experience and understanding. Tutors will need to develop a range of strategies for making their subject accessible to different learners.

- Tutors should positively encourage learners to challenge and ask awkward questions, even when they think their learners have insufficient understanding to ask anything very interesting, or when they so cherish a particular idea or approach, that it is very trying to have it scrutinized by those they feel are unworthy.

- Questions, whether asked by tutors or learners, provide vital opportunities to promote the dialogue. Too often they become part of a ritualized routine or they are viewed as a tiresome and time-consuming hindrance, their real potential never fully realized.

- The dialogue also depends on employing specific strategies to encourage a more skeptical attitude amongst your learners and invite them to engage in active and critical discussion.

QUESTIONS FOR REFLECTION

1. *How do you feel about encouraging your learners to value discussion for its own sake? Are you inclined to view this as just a bit indulgent, that it's all very well if you have time and your learners are sufficiently interested, but for most practical purposes you are just expected to get on and ensure everyone arrives at the appropriate answer, utilizing time and effort as efficiently as possible?*

There are indeed many pressures to deliver learning in this way and yet we have moved on from straightforward instruction to include a range of approaches that are more demanding in time and involvement. We have recognized the benefits of these developments. Perhaps we are using practical considerations to rationalize our unease with an approach which encourages a less conformist way of thinking and which positively promotes disagreement. The value of that approach lies in helping learners to engage in constructive and reasoned disagreement.

2. How do you think of language? Do you see it as essentially a means to express yourself or do you see it as a means to communicate with others? How do you feel about engaging in discussion with learners who still have only a very limited understanding of the concepts and issues?

Surely language is about both, you cannot communicate with others without expressing something of yourself. But it depends where you put the emphasis. You may decide that your priority is to maintain the integrity of your message and not risk compromising it for the sake of greater clarity. On the other hand you may decide that your priority is to make the message intelligible to your listeners and that may necessitate a degree of simplification. Similarly you may feel that there is little point in encouraging discussion until your learners have achieved some meaningful level of understanding. There is a danger here that you will always regard your learners' understanding as more limited than your own and so never value such discussion.

3. How do you respond to the idea that people listen in different ways? Do you find it intriguing, providing you with an insight into your own limitations or do you regard it as tiresome and just another indication of how difficult people can be?

Sometimes you may find it very hard to maintain this attitude of always striving to understand yourself and others and how you interact with each other. Sometimes it is easier to just fall back on simpler approaches and look for someone to blame, preferably not ourselves. But we know self-righteous indignation offers only temporary relief, and any problem in communication is more effectively resolved by understanding differences rather than invalidating them.

4. How far do you view your learners' initial disorientation with your subject as an inevitable part of the learning process which they will overcome without any special intervention on your part? How realistic do you think it is to expect you to devise different ways to make your subject accessible to a variety of learners?

Many learners will indeed settle down to a subject in much the same way workers settle down to a job, but just as a well planned induction will enable workers to be more effective more quickly, so learners will similarly benefit from a thoughtfully considered subject introduction. You may feel that as you work with many different learners, they will each have their own ways of making the learning meaningful, and that you can only address issues of accessibility in general terms. Nevertheless it is still your responsibility to make your subject accessible to all of your learners.

5. How do feel about encouraging learners, whose understanding may be rudimentary, to engage in critical evaluations of ideas and concepts, the sophistication of which they only partially grasp.

This may seem a particularly futile and frustrating exercise, but only from your vantage point. Your learners are not aware of what they do not know and so can quite readily engage in a debate that may not be very satisfying for you, but will help to develop their skills and understanding. If we adopt the view that learners are incapable of offering any critique until they have reached a certain level, we may so delay that opportunity, that when we finally judge them ready, they no longer have the inclination.

6. **How far do you view learner questions as a necessary evil, which constantly threaten to disrupt your carefully timed lesson plans, as an opportunity to catch you out on what you don't know, as evidence of respectful appreciation for your efforts, or as indications of learner curiosity and interest?**

We have probably experienced all of these reactions in different situations and still recognize the value of encouraging questions. Nevertheless, we often do not give very much thought to how we might systematically stimulate those questions. We simply assume they will emerge and if they do not, well, that's down to our learners and not really anything to do with us. But we need to take the initiative, perhaps by asking questions or speculating or devising means to generate questions.

7. **Do you feel there is a danger that in devising activities to promote a skeptical and critical attitude, we may still almost be encouraging learners to engage in a routinized process, where the same predictable points are always made?**

It is easy for even critiques to become just part of the learning routine, so that ideas seem stale and all too familiar. But this is where we need to view the learning through the eyes of our learners, for whom those same ideas will be new and challenging. We can all too easily inhibit their enthusiasm with our own jaded perspective. But we need to go further and encourage them to have more confidence in their own critical capacity and not just rely on rehashing the same old arguments.

10

There is No Such Thing as a Bad Group

This chapter title may well prove more irritating to fellow professionals than some of the other contentious issues I have so far discussed. I have certainly been aware through my career of just how easy it is to explain a less than satisfying session in terms of the negative characteristics of the group. We have all done it. 'They weren't interested.' 'They had their own agenda.' 'They just didn't want to know.' It is very difficult remaining dispassionate and objective when you are trying to analyze what happened and why things clearly did not go according to plan.

This is the true test of engagement – how you respond in this most personally demanding situation. You have probably, in your own terms, done a good job. You were properly prepared, or at least you thought you were. Your material was up to date, well organized, with a range of strategies you were able to draw upon. You thought you had understood the learning requirements and you assumed you were familiar with the sort of group you were going to encounter. Why then did it go wrong?

Our feelings in these situations are very mixed and often quite intense. There is usually a fair degree of resentment that our efforts have not been properly appreciated. And as with any role that demands a large personal investment, we experience some level of personal rejection. We feel unwanted and inadequate, that somehow we failed to win the group over. They didn't like us. All of us cope with those feelings in different ways.

Some suffer a crisis of confidence and indulge all their nagging self doubts. Others become angry and dismiss the group as unworthy and useless. Maybe quite a few of us struggle with these two reactions at the same time.

I think it is important to use these occasions as opportunities to further your own understanding of yourself in relation to your learners. Little will be gained by apportioning blame, merely condemning yourself or your group. It is easy to simply dismiss your group as just beyond the pale, so impossible not even the most inspired tutor would have made any positive impact. It is more painful directing the reproaches inwards, giving oneself up to a sense of self-recriminating failure. But both responses are self-defeating. They block us from looking any further and trying to work out why our learners behaved as they did, and why we reacted in the way we did. It is a complex process and involves a willingness to reflect at both an emotional and rational level.

Pressing buttons

We all need to recognize the way in which we most comfortably react to situations and experiences. Some find it very easy to connect with their feelings. Others prefer to rely on their analytical capacities to make sense of what happens to them. Some are uneasy with the process of reflection, and prefer to just get on with things and rely on a mixture of common sense and presumed goodwill to see them through. But even this seemingly straightforward identification of types is not sufficient. Some may very readily connect with their feelings and become overwhelmed by them, and then rely on an analytical approach to compensate for their discomfort. Some may connect with their own feelings, but find it difficult to connect with other people's feelings. We imagine their greater sensitivity would increase their empathic capacity, but it may well be that they find it difficult to break out of their own subjective view of the world.

Others may be so tuned in to the feelings of others, they find it hard to hold on to their own feelings and experience them as authentic. There are those who easily adopt the analytic attitude because they feel disconcerted by feelings. They see them as unreliable. They find it very difficult to get in touch with their own feelings and even more difficult to get in touch with the feelings of anyone else. Even those who appear less complex, not wanting to bother with the reflective process at all, may be avoiding uncomfortable issues, operating some degree of denial.

We need to be aware of what may be going on with our own buttons in order to better appreciate how we routinely try and understand and make sense of our world, and how our problematic or 'no go' areas may make it difficult to tune in to other people, particularly when their buttons conflict with our own. This may feel like negotiating with shadows or endlessly refracting mirrors, where our ability to really work out what is going on becomes compromised by our own blocks and confusion. Perhaps some of this almost suggests that a therapeutic intervention is necessary, that we all need to enlist professional help in exploring these elusive parts of ourselves. I am convinced there is immense benefit for anyone willing to embark on this road. However I think it is still possible to consider these issues in a less intense arena. Certainly talking with someone, a trusted friend or colleague, will enable you to check out your own perception with a more disinterested party.

I do not think you can avoid undergoing this self-questioning if you are to achieve any greater insight into yourself and how you relate to your learners, especially those you have found most difficult. As I have already indicated, this process of reflection should be both emotional and rational. We need to recognize what is our instinctive response and what requires a more self-conscious effort. I know my own particular response pattern with any troubling interaction is to want to rationally analyze on the basis of my presumed empathy, while often experiencing very strong emotional reactions which I tend to distrust, and again rely on my more rational self to make sense of. I am operating at both a feeling and thinking level, but it is often extremely hard to arrive at any clear and coherent resolution. It may be helpful to demonstrate this process even further by drawing more upon my own experience.

Some of my buttons are concerned with my feelings of insecurity, which I know are triggered by any dismissive or indifferent reactions on the part of my learners. I hate being ignored! I have always relished the directly challenging individual who argues. I can cope with someone who is openly rude and obnoxious. I don't even mind the moaners and complainers, but I know if I am confronted with someone who just appears contemptuously bored, and regards me with what feels like personal disdain, I find it difficult to overcome my own diffidence. I am reluctant to try and reach out and engage with the individual. Rarely will anything be said in these situations, it is all in the non-verbal expression, gestures and posture.

The verbal messages will be essentially ambivalent, nothing explicit, but an implied negative agenda. It is a strategy designed to undermine rather than confront and I find it very unsettling. I am convinced that if I try to approach them, even on an individual basis, I will only be acknowledging that they have indeed got to me and weaken my position still further. I have no expectation they will be willing to honestly discuss why they feel so hostile. That may be a correct or incorrect analysis depending on the individual and the situation, but I am aware that my own instinctive defenses make it more difficult for me to be objective and be both proactive and assertive in dealing with the problem.

Another sensitive button is one where I am confronted by behavior which I regard as unreasonable. This is a rather regrettable judgmental tendency on my part which I know can sometimes generate considerable antipathy in others. We all react somewhat differently to varying situations. Some of us will be able to be very tolerant and magnanimous in circumstances which others would find intolerable, while we become thoroughly exercised over something others would remain quite unfazed by. So the objective justification for our sense of what is right and reasonable can still land us in contested territory. I feel fairly certain about my perception and response when it comes to clear examples of hostile behavior which is obviously and deliberately meant to be hurtful and destructive. There are however, many ways in which we routinely engage with others, where different perceptions of what constitutes appropriate expressions of consideration for others and their feelings are constantly undermining our interactions with each other. We see slights where none are intended and feel aggrieved by an apparent unkindness to which the other party remains oblivious. These are the inevitable dilemmas of our complex social relations, where morality is a relative concept. We try to establish a more secure basis to these relations by behaving as if our own personal moral constructs should influence everyone else and then become angry and confused when they clearly do not.

This is an area where one can never expect to reach a satisfactory resolution. The main point is to be aware of how significantly it can lead to misunderstandings and create distrust and bad feeling. So I am aware that when I am confronted by behavior I consider unreasonable, this may be perceived very differently by the other party and that, furthermore, my reaction may be more intense because that behavior is pressing some of my less forgiving buttons.

I know I have a problem around behavior which I consider irresponsible, thoughtless and careless. This may be aggravated by associations with immaturity and self-centeredness. Possibly this has some connection with being quite a serious child who, through family circumstance, felt obliged to grow up fairly quickly. Whatever the dynamic behind the reaction, I know this is a problematic area for me and one where my normal capacity for empathy becomes decidedly limited. I can no longer rely on my intuition for understanding, because the judgmental attitude gets in the way and so I have to stand back and use my rational self to make sense of what is happening and help me devise a strategy for responding. I then risk going into school-marm mode. In trying to control my own negative feelings and the apparently irresponsible behavior in my learners, I simply present as emotionally cool and overly business-like. All my natural warmth and spontaneity evaporates. I may have some insight into what is happening, but I will admit to having a long way to go in dealing with this as well as I would like.

When I encounter any resistance, I have to try and figure out whether any of my own buttons are inadvertently triggering or exacerbating the situation. Where I feel completely comfortable empathizing with the learner, even though their behavior may be outrageous, I know there are no buttons involved. When I feel an almost instinctive resistance on my part rising in response to their resistance, I am certain my buttons are part of the problem. Our buttons may subtly communicate themselves to our learners and actually generate the resistance in the first place, or they may simply make it more difficult for us to constructively work with the resistance once it has presented itself.

Recognizing resistance

Resistance takes a variety of forms but falls into two broad categories, actively aggressive and passively aggressive. The first leaves you in no doubt as to how the learner is feeling – there is open hostility. The second is sometimes less obvious and can leave you feeling very confused as to what is actually going on. Many tutors find the prospect of overt aggression extremely threatening, whereas I, because of my own peculiar buttons find passive aggression far more worrying. But usually, all resistance is to some extent a defensive strategy and so needs to be viewed in the light of some of the issues we looked at in the section on learner anxieties.

Resistance is associated with resentment and a sense of inadequacy, and both can give rise to considerable levels of anxiety. Resentment is more likely to be encountered by trainers while a sense of inadequacy may be experienced in training and formal educational settings. The two underlying causes of resistance can often combine together to produce a potent cocktail.

Resentment arises because people feel compelled and constrained. They feel their autonomy and ability to decide for themselves have been eroded. This is a familiar problem in training where so many learners are conscripts. They are sent on a course which they believe they will find useless and irrelevant. Possibly the training is to support some organizational change or innovation in working practice to which they remain resolutely opposed. They are convinced the changes will only make a bad situation even worse. Possibly they perceive the training as more personally targeted, implicitly suggesting that they are not performing to expected standards. They may consider this a totally unfair evaluation, given resource levels and the generally impossible pressures with which they are constantly juggling. Perhaps they have a problem in their relationship with their line manager and dismiss every suggestion for further development as victimization.

The agendas can go on and on, but the essential point is that the learner or learners arrive in the learning situation with a deep-seated sense of grievance derived from their experience of work. Being sent on a course is just another manifestation of being treated as so many cogs in the machine.

The attitude adopted by the tutor can either reinforce this feeling of helpless and angry frustration, or it can try to restore some sense of self-determination. Learners may very well need the opportunity to express some of this anger. One should still avoid the dangers of the whole learning program being hijacked by negative agendas or appearing to encourage learners to bad-mouth their managers and employers. Neither will ultimately earn you very much respect in your learners' eyes. However, I do believe there should be some acknowledgement of your learners' resentment, otherwise the resistance will only become more stubborn.

All I am advocating is a standard assertive approach. Provide individuals with the chance to voice their concerns, demonstrate that you have both heard and understood what they are trying to say and then state what you want to achieve in the situation. It may be necessary to run through this sequence several times as you hopefully draw closer together to reach an accommodating outcome. We know from our own experience how effective it can be in defusing situations when someone shows that they understand the way we are feeling, even if they do not agree with us. We are more inclined to be reasonable. Apply this to the learning situation and you enable your recalcitrant individual to move forward. You cannot change the circumstances which have contributed to their vexation. You can however suggest there might still be something they can take from the learning which they could find useful, perhaps a greater insight into the factors influencing those circumstances, as well as a potentially more successful negotiating strategy.

Similarly, a learning program which encourages learners to be more actively involved, to use their initiative and to articulate their ideas, is more likely to overcome such resistance. What will almost certainly make their position even more intractable is an attitude from the tutor which invalidates their view of the situation, which is not interested in how they feel and is only concerned to proceed with the learning without any unnecessary hindrance. In trying to avoid the issue, the tutor only makes it more of an obstacle.

A sense of inadequacy may manifest itself in a range of aggressive postures, but the key to understanding lies in the very human tendency to avoid responsibility for ourselves and to blame others for making us feel uncomfortable. So the individual who is tormented by the fear he or she is not good enough, either in comparison with others or expectations, is unable to contemplate this view of self as sadly limited, and so instead concentrates on taking everyone else to task for making life so difficult. In the learning situation, such people are constantly critical of everything and everyone else. They will complain about the content of the program, the way it is being organized, the style of the tutor and the characteristics of the other learners. They present as very negative indeed. They feel far more secure playing the part of discriminating critic, attacking the efforts made by others, detaching themselves from any semblance of group identity and refusing to participate in anything which threatens their splendid isolation.

Such individuals have usually made a career of developing this particular role, and the original influences which gave rise to the feelings of inadequacy may be extremely complicated and long buried in personal history. As a tutor, one has to be realistic about how much progress you are likely to make with these learners. Perhaps all you might be able to achieve is simply to contain their negative impact and try to prevent them from contaminating the rest of the group. Acknowledging the criticisms and complaints may be counterproductive in this situation. This simply allows such individuals to continue diverting attention away from their own possible failings.

You therefore need to remove any possible platform which they might be able to use. Engaging in any sort of direct confrontation is unlikely to resolve the problem. They will feel more empowered even if you win the rational argument, and meanwhile the rest of the group become increasingly restless and uncomfortable as the struggle continues. Essentially, your objective is to reduce the learners' fear of threat which is feeding the sense of inadequacy. It is crucial to remain composed. This will not only make you feel more in control, it will also reassure your learners that you have no need to assert your authority through matching their aggression.

It is important to engage with the person rather than the behavior, again fairly standard advice when dealing with aggression. Such people are deeply insecure. They are determined to mask their anxiety and minimize the risk of exposure. A kindly and sympathetic response may just signal weakness. On the other hand, a firm and confident stance which says that you not only believe in yourself and the learning experience you have devised, but also in their ability to contribute something worthwhile. You do not want to silence them and believe their critical faculties can be put to good use. By demonstrating you are not trying to set yourself up as sole expert, or trying to manipulate your learners, you are more likely to reduce the resistance. I accept that every situation will be different, depending on the personalities involved and the chemistry they generate. However, I still maintain that a more effective strategy is one that actively addresses the underlying anxiety.

Active aggression is blatant and unambiguous. The behavior is concerned with dominance. The raised voice, the argument which cannot consider any other position than its own, the scornful criticism, the offensive remark, the dismissive put-down are all ways in which the protagonist attempts to gain the upper hand by attacking those they must subdue and control. People who engage in open aggression feel no need to apologize for their behavior. They believe they are totally justified and there is sometimes an almost self-righteous zeal in the way they launch themselves into the fray. Life is about survival of the fittest and they are determined to come out on top. People who they perceive as weak are fair game. This may sound rather extreme, but I would argue these basic assumptions underpin much of the behavior.

When you encounter this in a learning situation, it is all too easy for your respectful approach as a tutor to be construed as feebleness. The learner who expects to dominate will see most interactions in competitive terms, and will inevitably view the tutor's authority as a target. It is vitally important then, to maintain a basically assertive approach, one that is confident, but does not rely on putting other people down as a way of addressing conflict. Actively aggressive individuals must never feel they have the upper hand, but neither must they feel that you have accepted their rules of engagement. You are not trying to be more successfully dominant than they are. It is not about a win/lose situation. In classic assertiveness parlance it is about achieving a win/win outcome. You therefore have to refuse very firmly to be drawn into combat mode, defining your relationship with all your learners in respectful, but authoritative terms.

It is always difficult with someone who is adopting an actively aggressive attitude to decide at what point you need to address them directly.

It may be that by initially ignoring their behavior and proceeding resolutely with the rest of the group, you deny them the attention they expect and force them to develop a more acceptable strategy in order to be noticed or taken seriously. This is the standard tactic with a naughty child, and while it may work with those immature, egocentric individuals who are still struggling with the concept of personal responsibility, it will be less effective with more determined offenders. It is probably worth trying as a first resort, but if that clearly is not working you need to be prepared to switch to a more proactive strategy. You are then faced with having to acknowledge the behavior directly, either on a one-to-one basis or with the whole group.

Every person and every situation will be different and you have to use considerable judgment in deciding what course of action is likely to produce the most constructive result for everyone, yourself, the rest of the group and the individual or possibly individuals concerned. The advantage of the private word in the scheduled break or an unscheduled halt in proceedings, is that people are no longer having to maintain face in a public arena. The absence of an audience means you can establish a more open and meaningful exchange. You, as the tutor, can say you find the individual's behavior very negative and unhelpful within the context of the learning situation, accepting that you do not mind criticism and challenge, as long as the intention is constructive and not simply to be difficult for the sake of it. It is important to listen to what they have to say and demonstrate that you have heard and understood what you think they have said, but again make it clear that you have certain expectations of how people should behave in the learning scenario.

Suggest that you have no problem with them putting their point of view forwards as long as they are prepared to listen to other people and accept that a range of views can be considered. It is essential that you give no indication you find their behavior personally threatening, even if it that is precisely the effect they are having. Instead, you need to maintain a professional focus and concentrate on the resolution you are trying to achieve.

There may be reasons on particular occasions when you might decide that the issue is one which has wider repercussions for the whole group. You may deduce that the active aggressor is simply the most outspoken member of the group, and that they all in fact share the same view. In this situation, you make a clear distinction between the behavior and the substance of the challenge. The danger of confusing the two is that you appear to invalidate the basis of their grievance. You can point out that an aggressive attitude is unhelpful and simply risks getting in the way of a serious discussion.

It is important to engage with the whole group and listen to the reasons for their negative attitude. Again your objective is to move people on so they do not remain stuck, wallowing in their anger. Help them to understand their own responsibility for considering different options to find a solution, rather than just blaming everyone else for anything that goes wrong. These situations can provide invaluable learning opportunities for people, helping them to adopt a more assertive and positive approach to problems where they previously felt frustrated, helpless and destructively aggressive.

The other occasion when you might need to address the whole group is where the active aggressor has so disturbed the group dynamics that the issue is no longer one that can be simply sorted out on a one-to-one basis. Tensions have risen, positions have been taken, people have become upset, and it has now become something that affects everyone, even though they may each have their own very individual response. Arguably, if you had been monitoring the situation properly, it should not have been allowed to get so out of hand. Nevertheless, it is possible for seemingly manageable difficulties to suddenly and dramatically escalate, leaving you little opportunity to make a more timely intervention. The danger here is that everyone turns on the active aggressor, or they turn on you or they turn on one another. Again, it is important for everyone to be encouraged to step back, to look at their own reactions, to look at everyone else's reactions and decide what they want to happen. This is potentially very explosive.

You may need to take time out. You will, to some extent, be acting as an intermediary between the active aggressor and the rest of the group, discouraging any inappropriate scape-goating tendencies. It is all too easy for the active aggressor to become the displaced focus for all manner of unresolved agendas with different people which have nothing to do with the immediate situation. So you have the participant who starts seeing the active aggressor as the personification of their boss who they cannot get on with. Everyone needs air time, but they also need to be reminded that they are trying to work together to find a way forward.

You need to maintain a very firm control of this whole process or it can quickly degenerate into chaos. The easy and tempting solution is to simply put the lid on everything and impose your authority, ordering everyone to be quiet and get on with the learning program as planned. Not only would this leave the whole matter unresolved and be likely to sabotage any subsequent attempts to continue as normal, it is a denial of your whole attempt to engage, and misses a valuable opportunity to empower learners in resolving such problems. So I believe you have little choice but to try and work with your group in moving forward. The main challenge is to reintegrate the active aggressor with the rest of the group, and that may involve some very straight talking from people about how they feel. But again the emphasis must be on trying to maintain a respectful attitude so that even when criticisms are being made, they are being offered in an inclusive, constructive spirit.

You still have a responsibility to give a sense of direction, to reinforce positive assertive behaviors and discourage negative aggressive behaviors. You are not abandoning the group to find their own solution, you are guiding them through an experience from which hopefully they all can learn, even though it may at times feel rather uncomfortable. It may well be that you do have to impose some sort of time limit to this process. This might seem a contradiction in terms, but without some constraints, the process remains open-ended with no incentive to make progress, other than the discouraging ennui that settles on a group when they seem to be going round and round an issue without finding any apparent way forward. I think it is also part of your role to point out when groups are engaged in these self-defeating behaviors, and help them think a little more objectively about the process they need to be following.

Passive aggression is much less obvious, and often will have been going on for much longer before you either recognize it, or decide to do something about it. It can range from silent withdrawal from the group, the person who is physically sitting there but is emotionally and mentally absent, disinterested in anything that is going on, to the insidious saboteur, who never draws attention to himself directly, but is still quite systematically undermining any progress you or the group are trying to make. Passive aggressors are not motivated by the urge to dominate. They do not view social situations as opportunities for competitive one-upmanship.

Rather the dynamic for their behavior is based on a perception of the world as a threatening or constraining place, with which they constantly have to struggle in order to maintain their sense of autonomy and identity. They are disinclined to make their behavior very evident, because this would expose them to presumed attack. But they will nevertheless continue trying to weaken whatever opposition they have identified.

As I have suggested, the main problem in trying to deal with passive aggressors is first of all recognizing that it is actually going on. You may have your suspicions but you will probably be unsure and feel you need further evidence before you attempt to take any action, by which time the behavior may be very well established. You are then faced with a further obstacle in that as soon as you try to address it, you will encounter all manner of denials and evasiveness. It will seem like trying to grasp phantoms, as soon as you think you see them and reach out to grasp them, they slip from you and disappear into the shadows. You may start to doubt your own view of the situation and wonder if you are imagining things. Passive aggressors are notoriously difficult to deal with simply because they prove so elusive.

But once you are sure that you are dealing with passive aggressors, the most important objective is to address their perception of the world as a threatening and constraining place. An engaging approach is likely to be seen as less directly restricting, however it may be seen as potentially more manipulative and so the passive aggressors will still be wary. They need to be reassured that you are not trying to compromise or control them. Part of their pattern of behavior arises from their difficulty in expressing their aggression more openly. They resort to subversion because they fear the consequences of their anger. They again need to be encouraged to be more assertive, to learn that they can express their feelings of dissatisfaction more explicitly.

Again, there might be an argument for not addressing the passive aggressor directly and simply working with the individual, without referring to the behavior, hoping that with your positive attitude some of their resistance may diminish. However, you may find that the behavior is either too entrenched or too destructive, and you have no choice but to confront them directly. I would strongly urge that a one-to-one is always the first direct approach to a passive aggressor. They will be difficult enough to pin down anyway, without enabling them to use the rest of the group to confuse and distort what is going on. Another tactic is to concentrate on how their behavior is making you feel rather than trying to describe it in objective terms. This is quite different from the active aggressors to whom you did not want to reveal any small degree of vulnerability. Passive aggressors, on the other hand, will be so intent on denying your account of their behavior, they will argue over the objective details rather than consider the impact of what they are doing. Therefore you are more likely to make positive progress if you focus on your response, making it clear that you do not have a problem with people complaining as long as they are willing to engage with you. Passive aggressors are usually more intractable than active aggressors, and so you need to be realistic about how far you can turn someone around during the course of one learning program. Some passive aggressors cause little disruption and they are more likely to lose out through not taking full advantage of the learning available. In this sense, they can be all too easily ignored. The saboteurs will demand more attention. But all resistance is a challenge to our skills as a tutor and to our commitment to engage. I believe we have to take that commitment seriously and see resistance as an opportunity to develop the learning still further. It is when the going gets rough that we can demonstrate how far we are really prepared to engage in the reciprocal relationship. Otherwise we do not look very different from the autocratic pedagogue.

Pathological tendencies

There is a danger in the preceding discussion that in trying to explain the way in which different types of aggression may be motivated, I seem to be almost making problematic behavior sound pathological. It is all too easy to invalidate people by suggesting their actions are simply manifestations of some pathological process. We all seem to think we are amateur psychologists these days, and relish the way in which we can neatly and conveniently make sense of someone's difficult behavior by ascribing some clinical label. We then avoid the responsibility of trying to understand the behavior within a given social context and individual set of meanings. We just regard it as that person's problem, overlooking the complexity of social interactions and how we all influence one another's behavior. There is a constant process of action, interpretation and response going on between people, with much potential for crosswires and misunderstandings at the point of interpretation. Understanding psychological processes is immensely valuable in the added dimension they give to making sense of ourselves and one another. They can also make us very smug and arrogant.

As tutors, we are already in a privileged position, regarded as the expert, the wise one and it is very tempting to think of ourselves as blessed with some superior perception, where we can confidently assign all manner of motivations to our learners. So, in discussing resistance, we need to remember that although we may recognize certain features of active or passive aggression, and we may use a certain framework for analyzing the motivation for that resistance, we should still be trying to retain a humanistic approach. In other words, we should still be trying to understand someone in their own terms and then reconciling their view with whatever psychological insights we are able to make, rather than simply invalidating their view and imposing our own.

Bottom lines

Another note of caution needs to be raised in relation to resistance, and this is concerned with having a clear notion of what behavior is acceptable in the learning situation and what is not. This is about being able to identify your bottom line – the fundamental set of values which underpins a respectful and engaging approach with our learners.

If a learner is consistently, and despite all attempts on your part to deal with the resistance, offensively flouting those values, then you have to draw a line. There are behaviors which so abuse the rights and dignity of others they cannot be sanctioned. People who engage in insulting or discriminatory behavior must be left in no doubt that not only have they broken the ground-rules of the learning situation, but also the norms for socially acceptable conduct. Tutors have no choice but to take decisive action and condemn such behavior.

However, I am also aware that people can easily draw rather different bottom lines, and it may be useful to just examine some of the implications of this responsibility. Perhaps one of the areas which throws this into starkest relief is the whole question of discrimination and political correctness. I would like to share two experiences which highlight how difficult it can be to work appropriately as a tutor.

The first occasion was when I was still a relatively inexperienced training officer and we were running our regular induction program for newly appointed staff. As part of the program, we included an afternoon on anti-discriminatory practice in the social care situation. I was joined by two workers to present the session, one a Sikh woman working as an administrative assistant and the other a Black-Caribbean male social worker. The session had been designed to avoid the overly confrontational stance of much race awareness training at that time, and we had run many successful programs together. On this particular occasion, we soon became conscious of an exceedingly vocal member of the group. He had recently been recruited as a driver to work the last few years leading up to his retirement. He was voicing many very concerning opinions, especially for someone who was expected to follow an anti-discriminatory code of practice.

He took the view that English culture was being threatened by the requirement to accommodate to greater cultural diversity. Basically, anyone coming to Britain should be prepared to accept our way of life and not expect to have their cultural traditions maintained and respected. For sometime, we tried to engage with him, acknowledging that people may feel anxious, but that part of the English tradition had been its great capacity to adapt to many different immigrant communities and the tolerance that had encouraged. We tried to look at the ways in which cultural diversity had enriched our experience. Perhaps this was all a bit too rational, but tackling the issue in more personally directed terms felt very risky.

As it happened, despite our attempts to manage the situation, the man became more heated and frustrated. Many in the group were obviously feeling very hostile toward him and the last straw was his increasingly patronizing and insulting attitude toward the Sikh woman. There was no option but to draw a very definite line and point out that his intolerance was not compatible with the ethos of social care. He stormed out and resigned immediately. The incident soon assumed mythic status in the department. Most felt something along the lines of 'good riddance to bad rubbish'. And it was true that his attitudes were unacceptable and that his resignation was probably inevitable at some point. We had simply afforded him the opportunity to express those views sooner rather than later. And yet I was still left with a lingering sense of failure. I knew I had to draw the bottom line, and yet I still felt I should have been more effective in enabling the man to look again at his established attitudes.

Another incident involved a local college providing qualifying training for our staff. The first I knew about it was when the college informed me they had excluded one of our staff from a course he had been attending for several months. I soon heard from the man and his very concerned manager. The story that emerged illustrates how an overly dogmatic bottom line on the part of tutors can stifle all reasonable attempts to explore difficult issues. It seemed that the man had acknowledged in a group discussion his struggle with his own personal aversion to homosexuality. He maintained that he was able to make a clear distinction between his personal feelings and his working practice. He had worked very positively with many homosexual clients and this was endorsed by his manager. But he admitted that his background and family values had been difficult to overcome. He still found the idea of homosexual practices physically repellent, but that did not make him view homosexuals in a discriminatory way. He believed in their right to be respected and positively valued, but recognized the way the legacy from his own upbringing was constantly in tension with those principles. This was an individual process of development that this man was working through.

Staff at the college, on the other hand, were not interested to talk to his manager to find out about his actual working practice with clients. Instead they were only concerned with maintaining the party line of political correctness. He had admitted to feelings which they considered unacceptable, despite his own acknowledged struggle. Three tutors saw him on his own at the end of the college day, without speaking to me as training manager or to his own manager and, in what amounted to a kangaroo court situation, cross-examined him on what he had said earlier in the group. As a result, he was put off the course, with the suggestion he was not the right material for social care work. After futile protests to the college, I arranged for him to transfer to a more enlightened establishment, where he was able to gain a qualification and continue with his career.

The story still leaves me feeling angry at the intransigence and arrogance of the tutors involved. They did indeed draw their bottom line, but it arose, ironically from a basically intolerant position. They were not concerned to use the learning situation to explore difficult issues. Instead they expected learners to merely comply with their particular version of what they believed was right. They employed an almost religious zealotry in the advancement of their cause. Any view that did not quite fit had to be dismissed and denounced. As a consequence of this approach, any open and meaningful discussion of these issues is impossible. People will be wary of saying anything that does not conform to the established position. They will simply opt for the least risky tactic and avoid anything that might expose their doubtful ideas. The issues are driven underground and the opportunity is lost to really further people's understanding and actually encourage a more tolerant society.

I accept that these are very difficult areas to negotiate, and often people will disagree about where the bottom line should be drawn. However, I do believe that the values implicit in engagement do help to identify what actually constitutes a respectful attitude, both on the part of the tutor and on the part of the learners. Added to this a healthy dose of self-questioning will steer us away from the excesses of our own self righteousness.

Confidentiality clause

It seems appropriate to also mention the thorny issue of confidentiality in this chapter as it has repercussions for the options you might consider after encountering resistance. Many tutors include in their ground-rules some reference to confidentiality. Some still give the assurance that 'anything said within these four walls will remain between us.' I regard this as misleading. It suggests that confidentiality is about keeping secrets, whereas I prefer a definition emphasizing the need to share information appropriately. I believe all learners need to be made aware that there may be repercussions and consequences arising from the learning which make it necessary to take particular issues further.

Certainly organizations commissioning or organizing the learning will expect to be informed as to the outcomes. This is not purely concerned with the learning outcomes. There may be other issues which have been raised which need to be followed up. As a trainer, you may hear about instances of bad practice which are so serious you are obliged to bring the matter to management attention. I was involved in one such situation where workers described a regime which amounted to neglect and abuse of clients. The individuals who disclosed this information were extremely anxious, and greatly feared the personal consequences for their whistle-blowing. However there was a clear responsibility to share the information, and an investigation followed which resulted in a change of management at the establishment.

Similarly you may encounter such serious resistance, that the learning is compromised, and this obviously has to be brought to the attention of whatever organization is responsible for resourcing the program. They need to be made aware of all the relevant factors which have contributed to the resistance which may, on occasion, involve identifying individuals. This is another difficult issue to wrestle with as a tutor, and there is an obvious conflict between your encouragement of open communication within your group of learners and your subsequent responsibility to those who are paying for your expertise.

I have tried to resolve the tension by making it very clear that I do not give any undertaking to maintain confidentiality, and that issues may arise which I am obliged to take further. And while personal disclosures should, in the main, be respected, anyone sharing personally sensitive information should only do so in the knowledge that absolute confidentiality cannot be guaranteed. I think there is value in the group collectively agreeing to not take such information beyond the group, but the tutor remains in a different position. Learners have a right to expect that information will only be passed on appropriately and not simply be treated as irresponsible gossip. Likewise organizations are entitled to expect tutors to respect privileged information. But I think it is important that tutors make learners aware of what they can reasonably expect and not delude them into a false sense of security.

Supportive networks

Everything I have said in this chapter, and indeed throughout the book, points to how personally challenging an engaging approach can be. It is more stimulating, exciting and, I would argue, ultimately fulfilling, but it is still a demanding way of working with learners, where you are constantly having to scrutinize what you are doing and how you are approaching your learners. You are having to put aside many of the old certainties which made your role more predictable and secure. You are having to take risks and submit yourself to a degree of self-questioning which will at times feel acutely uncomfortable. It is essential therefore to have access to supportive networks of other tutors working with a similar approach.

I have found the support of colleagues enormously sustaining and realize the value of being able to talk over difficult sessions or potentially awkward programs with someone who is sympathetic to the principles underpinning my approach, and has enough insight to understand when some of my buttons are getting in the way of working positively with certain learners.

I realize how lonely it has sometimes been struggling with these issues. I also accept that my own approach was never a matter of choice. I never deliberately set out to work with an engaging approach. It was purely instinctive and so, even when I encountered situations which might have undermined my commitment, there was no real alternative. I only knew of one way of working with learners – anything else would have felt alien and a denial of myself.

I have become increasingly conscious since becoming involved with training skills programs, and more especially since embarking on this book, of how I need to articulate and explain what I have simply taken for granted. I have had to discuss my ideas more thoroughly and explore what I really mean. While I have tried to maintain an internal self-questioning dialogue with myself, there is no substitute for being able to discuss your ideas with someone else.

In social care, there is a system of professional support known as supervision. Usually this is provided by a line manager to their staff. It involves a regular one-to-one opportunity to sit down and discuss that individual's work and professional development. Supervision may also be provided by professional consultants or by colleagues. The main point is that individuals have a chance to review their practice, to look at what they have found challenging and why, and what strategies they might consider in the future. They are able to look at their own performance, valuing what they have done well and building on from that, as well as acknowledging where there is still room for improvement. Such a system clearly has a positive resonance for anyone committed to individual development.

I was curious that no such opportunity had ever been afforded me when I worked as a teacher, and even when I received supervision, while working with social services, I never had a manager with any experience of training. I saw the potential and felt frustrated that for me personally, it was never realized. What I am advocating now is that anyone involved in helping people learn should have access to the experience of supervision, even if it is with a fellow colleague; superior experience, expertise or authority is not a prerequisite for providing effective supervision. What is important is the chance to kick your ideas around creatively with someone who understands the situation in which you work. As tutors, we all need to be able to talk over our anxieties and self-doubts and to use them constructively in the way we work.

Engagement for many people will be a more deliberately selected strategy than it was for myself. As such it will be both more meaningful and more problematic. It will be one of a number of options which have been considered, and so there is likely to be a more explicit understanding of its defining characteristics, but perhaps a greater ambivalence when it starts to throw up its peculiar and complex problems. Ensuring support is vital in overcoming this ambivalence and learning to work through the problems. Being able to talk through experiences of resistance will be especially important, providing an additional perspective and further insight into the dynamics of the situation, and how your particular buttons are possibly being pressed without your always realizing it. Trying to reliably analyze such processes by yourself, when you are already so closely involved, is almost impossible. Recognizing the need for a more objective viewpoint is a sign of professional maturity.

Summary Points

- [ ] When we encounter problems with a group or individuals and we have checked out that we have discharged our professional responsibilities appropriately, we need to reflect on how the interpersonal dynamics of the interaction may have contributed to the problem, recognizing that our own particular way of reflecting may influence our perception. We need to be especially careful of how our own 'buttons' can make it difficult for us to deal with certain issues.

- [ ] Resistance may arise from a feeling of resentment, where learners have been coerced into the learning situation. Their anger is an attempt to regain control. Tutors can either exacerbate or defuse that anger. They need to acknowledge their learners' feelings and help them move forward.

- [ ] A sense of inadequacy may manifest itself in a tendency to blame and criticize others and so avoid looking at oneself. The tutor's objective should be to reduce the pressures in the learning situation which may be contributing to a feeling of insecurity which is in turn generating the overt behavior, rather than directly engaging with the behavior itself.

- [ ] Active aggression is an open and overt response which assumes that unless you dominate someone else they will try to dominate you. It may be expressed individually or by the group.

Either way, tutors need to demonstrate an alternative and more assertive way of dealing with disagreement and conflict.

☐ Passive aggressors try to avoid open confrontation. They use a more subtle and undermining strategy to deal with the potential threats they feel they are facing. Tutors need to offer a positive and reassuring response to enable the individual to express their feelings more openly and constructively.

☐ Tutors should try to avoid making learners sound pathological in their attempt to understand difficult or aggressive behavior. Such a tendency may reinforce our feelings as the superior wise one and invalidate our learners' interpretation of the situation. We then avoid the responsibility of looking at how we, ourselves, may have contributed to the problem.

☐ Tutors need to be clear about the standards of behavior they expect in the learning situation. Behavior which offensively abuses the rights and dignity of others must be dealt with decisively. We need to ensure, however, that our 'bottom lines' are not a manifestation of our own self-righteous intolerance.

☐ Tutors cannot guarantee confidentiality in the learning situation. Issues may arise which have to be taken further. The process of engagement need not be undermined as long as everyone understands how and why the information is to be shared.

☐ Engaging with learners is very demanding. Tutors are having to take risks and question their accepted ways of doing things. They are being asked to invest more of themselves in their role. Tutors will benefit from having access to the support system provided by supervision.

QUESTIONS FOR REFLECTION

1. *How comfortable do you feel with personal introspection? Do you feel it is unnecessary to delve into such subjective territory? Are you anxious about where it might lead you?*

It is understandable that you may feel very uncertain about examining yourself in this way. It is very challenging, but unless we are prepared to look at ourselves, recognize and try to come to terms with our 'buttons', we will remain oblivious to how we may be negatively influencing our learners, unwittingly triggering or intensifying reactions and making our relationships with them that much more frustrating. The positive pay-off for us is to feel better about ourselves and better about them.

2. *Do you feel that the anger and resentment demonstrated by conscripts is*

not really your problem, that someone else is responsible for ordering these learners to attend, and it is unreasonable that you should be taking the flak.

While it may be unreasonable at one level, nevertheless it is your problem in that, if you have an angry individual or group and you are the tutor, you have the option to ignore it, walk away or to try and deal with it, at least within the context of ensuring the program proceeds and that some effective learning is achieved. If failing to address the problem undermines that objective, then you have neglected your duty as a tutor.

3. **How do you feel about trying to understand someone who is complaining and criticizing everyone but themselves?**

It is very difficult to see beyond the disagreeable behavior, especially when we feel our efforts are not appreciated. Nevertheless if you suspect a sense of inadequacy is part of the problem, it makes sense to try to identify ways in which you might enable the individual to develop a more positive view of themselves.

4. **How do you feel about the tendency toward active aggression in yourself and in others? How comfortable are you with displays of strong emotion? How empathic are you able to be toward someone who is trying to dominate and intimidate others? Does your response depend on how confident you are feeling in the situation?**

These questions will stir up some very powerful emotions and moral judgments. Our own experience of dealing with aggression will have a profound impact on our answers. However we need to remember that aggression is often an understandable strategy in what are perceived as hostile circumstances. People will be unwilling to abandon a strategy that has served their interests, unless they are persuaded that the benefits of an alternative strategy are greater than those they already enjoy.

5. **How do you feel about the tendency toward passive aggression in yourself and others? Do you feel it is perhaps rather cowardly and underhand and does this make it more difficult to adopt a positive response?**

We need to focus on the difficulty that passive aggressors have with open confrontation, how they feel that by being more honest they will only make themselves more vulnerable. If we can gain some insight into their motivation, we will find it that much easier to demonstrate the positive regard which might encourage them to feel less defensive and more open.

6. **How far are you tempted to see the problems you encounter with other people as indicative of their dysfunction? Do you tend to try and understand someone in terms of how they might explain themselves or do you rely exclusively on what you regard as your own more informed judgment?**

It is very easy when you encounter problems with others to distrust their interpretation of the situation. We all have a vested interest in viewing ourselves in the most sympathetic light. With greater knowledge and insight, we may feel that our view is more valid, but we need to be careful that we are not just rationalizing an interpretation which affirms our power to define the situation and so discredit any alternative view.

7. Are you clear about your 'bottom-lines'? How can you ensure that they derive from a fair and reasonable standard of acceptable behavior and not reflect more personal beliefs and values?

We need to distinguish between our own individual values and those which are appropriate to uphold in our professional role. It will be important to keep these under review and discuss with colleagues in order to maintain an objective standard.

8. How comfortable are you negotiating the issue of confidentiality with your learners? How far do you think it may act as an uncomfortable reminder of your own limited independence?

Tutors and learners may feel that the learning situation exists in some sort of splendid isolation and there is little connection between what happens inside and outside of that situation. Tutors themselves may cherish the sense of autonomy they enjoy with their learners and be loath to acknowledge the accountability which constrains them all. But we delude ourselves and our learners if we lose sight of the way in which actions inside the learning situation may have consequences beyond it.

9. How do you feel about the prospect of being able to discuss the way you work on a regular basis with a manager or colleague? Are you concerned that it might leave you even more exposed without necessarily providing very much support?

Any system of supportive supervision, which is concerned with encouraging reflective practice, depends on the commitment of both parties involved. We need to accept that whatever the extent of our experience, there is still the opportunity for further development and that relying solely on ourselves not only imposes a lonely burden, but also reinforces the rather complacent attitude that while others may learn from us, we have little to learn from the support and resources provided by others.

11

That's All Very Well

Many tutors may feel that I am simply adding to the considerable pressure they are already experiencing. Higher and higher standards are expected with fewer and fewer resources. It can feel very like trying to pull rabbits out of hats, with not even a great deal of applause for your efforts. I accept that trainers, and especially teachers, are often already required to do the almost impossible, to devise more imaginative learning strategies, to be more sensitive to individual learner needs and yet also be more cost effective by accommodating even more bums on seats.

I agree that I am urging a more demanding approach. Some tutors may feel I am merely underlining what they would recognize as good practice, while others may think I am describing an idealized scenario, unlikely to be ever practically realized in most learning situations. But surely we have only to cast our minds back a little way to recall the elitist and authoritarian attitudes routinely adopted by the majority of tutors in the past, who never even paused to reflect on how they related to their learners. Such concerns would have been seen as unnecessary mollycoddling. Learner-centered approaches are now more predominant. In that respect, we are moving in the right direction, but, as I have argued, we still have some way to go and there are many obstacles to overcome and side-tracks to avoid.

There is always an inevitable resistance to the suggestion that you could be doing things differently and you could be doing them better. Anyone who takes it upon themselves to exhort their colleagues to improve their practice is likely to be seen as arrogant and interfering. The message will be especially hard to stomach if people are already feeling beleaguered and undervalued. Clearly, what I am proposing has very real implications for resourcing levels, both in terms of time and tutor/learner ratios. And yet I would argue that it is precisely at a time when tutors are under increasing pressure, that we need to explicitly state what we mean by effective learning and how that can be more readily achieved.

We are more clearly defining what we do in relation to organizing the learning. We are systematically identifying our inputs and outputs in terms of learning objectives, sometimes to the detriment of creative learning. And yet it is in the very area which is most challenging that we remain muted. We need to make a much stronger case for the importance of the learning relationship and how that requires the investment of time and effort in order to maximize its real potential. Unless we, ourselves, put a premium on this aspect of our role, how can we hope to persuade those resourcing learning to appreciate its value? We need to put the learning relationship on the agenda. We need to argue for its critical impact on the capacity of learners to adapt to the changing demands of life in the twenty first century.

Maybe tutors will feel they already have enough to contend with and do not need any further hassles to complicate their already overburdened workloads. They may just want to be left in peace to get on in the best way they know how. I do have sympathy with this weary reaction to the incessant calls for more and better. And yet I would suggest this essentially passive and reactive stance is self-defeating. One becomes more and more worn down and demoralized as one just tries to survive. A more radical approach can be invigorating. It can give you back a sense of shaping and influencing things, of making a difference.

Engaging learners may be challenging but it is also a far more intrinsically rewarding way of working. It generates energy and enthusiasm which is infectious. People who feel empowered will be capable of so much more. They will relish the joy and excitement of discovering latent talents and abilities. Inevitably there are risks with such a strategy, but I believe these are more than outweighed by the benefits of increased motivation and diligence on the part of both learners and tutors. Engaging learners is fun. It is satisfying. And it takes us away from the purely instrumental approach to learning which is in danger of corroding a genuine spirit of inquiry.

This will undoubtedly sound rather idealistic to a lot of people and yet I believe it is always important to have ideals to aim for, to have a vision of how things should be, even if present circumstances make it difficult to achieve. The idealized vision may seem irrelevant when one is struggling with day to day realities, but unless one retains a positive sense of where one is trying to go, the goals one is trying to reach, then we lose the incentive afforded by our notion of progress.

I realize I am advocating a radical strategy and one which many tutors might feel goes beyond their established remit. It is demanding in terms of time, energy and commitment and I accept these are precious resources in today's fast moving world. It is not easy. We have devoted much effort to improving techniques and yet we are still neglecting a vital part of our role.

Unless we are prepared to engage in the sort of relationship I have described, our learners are denied the opportunity to fully explore their potential in the learning situation. Whatever the learning subject, we can use the learning relationship as a powerful vehicle for encouraging learners to be more proactive and take responsibility for their own development. Most of us would welcome learners who are enthusiastic, keen to use their initiative, curious, resourceful and critical. And yet it is often our own attitudes and behavior toward them which discourage the very qualities we supposedly value. They will not change unless we are prepared to change and develop a very different kind of relationship with them.

Index

CPSIA information can be obtained at www.ICGtesting.com
Printed in the USA
BVOW080453290911

272157BV00005B/8/P